"These are the books, the arts,
the academes that show, contain
and nourish all the world."

—WILLIAM SHAKESPEARE

A Reader's COOKBOOK

✦ ✦ ✦

JUDITH CHOATE

Red Rock Press • New York

• •

"Tomatoes and oregano make it Italian;
wine and tarragon make it French.
Sour cream makes it Russian; lemon
and cinnamon make it Greek. Soy sauce
makes it Chinese; garlic makes it good."

—ALICE MAY BROCK

• •

A Reader's Cookbook
Copyright ©2010 Judith Choate
ISBN: 9781933176-34-5

Red Rock Press
New York, New York

www.redrockpress.com

Design by Lori S. Malkin
Index by Sayre Van Young

Additonal photo credits: p. 70 mojito in top row by Thomas Weiss; p. 75 pickles in top row by Michael Zacharzewski, kugel in middle row by Stuart Spivack; p. 77 olives in top row by Yucel Tellici, bottom row mamoul by fugzu.

Library of Congress Cataloging-in-Publication Data

Choate, Judith.
  A reader's cookbook / Judith Choate.
    p. cm.
  ISBN 978-1-933176-34-5
  1. Cookery, American. 2. Cookery, International. I. Title.
  TX715.C552 2010
  641.5973—dc22
                                    2010006044

Printed in China

Table of Contents

"The pages are still blank, but there is a miraculous feeling of the words being there, written in invisible ink and clamoring to become visible."

—VLADIMIR NABOKOV

Introduction

WHERE A DEDICATED READER MIGHT CURL UP IN SOLITUDE WITH A GOOD BOOK, a cup of tea and a cookie, I have found that book club readers often enjoy the camaraderie of a social gathering and the sharing of ideas and insights brought forth by reading a book together as much as they do the actual read.

Alone or together, many avid readers thirst for depth in their literary adventure, and love to delve into the history, culture and traditions of writers they appreciate. Among the many ways that exploration of the written word can be broadened is through exploring the culinary life of the region in which a writer places his or her adventure. In this cookbook, I offer readers a way to amplify their understandings through literal tastes from a particular culture in which a poem, novel, biography or reflection is set, or from the native land of the writer. For, as we know, some writers carry the imprint of "home" in all of their stories no matter where they take place, while others absorb and reflect on regions they have visited and/or settled. The recipes here are offered to all readers who enjoy following up a good book with related food.

The dishes I suggest are meant to be shared: I have formulated most of the recipes to serve eight to ten readers, and occasionally more. And, since book groups gather at various times of the day and evening—some at tea or cocktail hour, others over a meal, or afterwards—I have tried to offer ideas to meet every agenda. For the most part, these are recipes that don't demand a lot of time in the kitchen or well-honed culinary skills. Some foods might be considered finger foods, some good travelers, some stick-to-the-ribs.

I think that you will find a meal to fit your reading-club bill of fare here. A single host should be able to handle comfortably the making of an entire meal if that is how your group does things. However, just as a book club is a joint undertaking, I think that it is a wonderful idea for the suggested foods to come together as a collective menu.

The dishes contained in the following pages are just a few of the endless possibilities available to take the reader's table into a writer's territory.

And if you read without thought of an informal discussion to follow, I invite you to use these recipes to express the lingering impact of a literary work when you cook for family or friends, or just to make yourself a drink and quick something before you delve into your next chapter.

I should note, too, that many of the dishes that can be found under the heading of one region would also be welcome in others. It is the reader's pleasure to take what I have given and make it his or her own. Of course, it is not possible to offer a taste of every single cuisine, but I have attempted to provide a wide selection so that, for almost any book, readers should find something to deepen the tastes and satisfy that special hunger that a good read brings forth.

These recipes are, by no means, the only ones that could offer such reflection, but I hope that they will give the reader/cook the inspiration to find ways to partner a touch of native cuisine with the book she or he is reading.

"Food is our common ground, a universal experience." —JAMES BEARD

American
HORIZONS

Chapter 1

Heartland Writing and Dining

*U*NLIKE A GOOD BOOK WHOSE IMPRIMATUR COMES FROM THE HEART AND SOUL OF AN individual writer, a recipe has as its author many, many cooks—some skilled, some recalcitrant, some adventurous, some timid, and on and on as the recipe evolves. Some recipes can easily be traced back to immigrant origins while others are so distinctly American, their birthplace could only be on native soil. It took a very long time for culinary historians to admit that American cooking was nothing more than family recipes created through the use of native products and the cook's ethnicity combined with

necessity and ingenuity. Some foods have been eaten by people of the plains since Native Americans hunted with bow and arrow the buffalo that freely roamed there. Echoes of those times will be familiar to readers of Louise Erdich's novels.

Many recipes have evolved through the settlers who moved west from the eastern seaboard in the 1800s, or who tracked south from Canada. Most we easily call American, some we definitely place in the Midwest. In contrast, a recipe for Creole sauce could have no more evolved from Nebraska cooks than a recipe for dilly casserole bread could have been born in the kitchens of Louisiana.

Other dishes clearly are local adaptations of imports. Pizza, for example, may have originated in Italy, but its American form is so ubiquitous that even schoolchildren in the heartland are right to think of it as a sort of American pie.

A century ago it might have been fair to say that the families of most heartland inhabitants, authors included, originated in, if not England, then Scandinavia or Germany. A few, such as Willa Cather in *My Antonia*, chronicled the hard lives of farm families whose roots were in eastern Europe. Reading Willa Cather can take a reader back to the reality of farm life generations ago as well as bring forth thoughts about the difficulties faced by contemporary farmers and their families.

Of course, Cather also wrote of the Spanish who, hundreds of years earlier had founded missions in what is now New Mexico. Characterizing American authors by the settings of their books can be risky.

Today, it's hard to describe definitively the residents of Middle America, notwithstanding the upstanding citizens of Garrison Keillor's "Lake Woebegone." It would require an encyclopedic number of recipes to pay tribute to the varied backgrounds of Midwesterners. Still, the bounty of the region's rich soil and the struggle to bring forth that bounty has been the theme of several extraordinary writers. The recipes that I have chosen for this section are those that have long been a constant on the farm table.

✦ ✦ ✦

READS, DRINKS & NIBBLES
■ ■ ■

Watermelon Fizz

Pigs in a Blanket with Honey-Mustard Sauce

Deviled Eggs

STAR DISHES & DELICIOUS ASIDES
■ ■ ■

Plains Buffalo Burgers

Crispy Fried Chicken

Meatloaf

Three-Bean Salad

FOR A MOVEABLE FEAST
■ ■ ■

Four Cheese Macaroni and Cheese

Garden Salad

LITERARY TEA OR SWEET ENDING
■ ■ ■

Apple Pizza

Schaum Torte

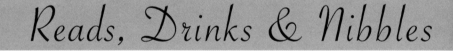

Reads, Drinks & Nibbles

Watermelon Fizz

Serves 8 to 10

Right after apples, is there anything more American than a big bright red slice of watermelon? Slices, however, are a bit oozy and drippy to eat. I think that this drink is the better alternative. Light, refreshing, and alcohol-free—unless, like me, you add a jigger of rum for a very refreshing cocktail!

10 cups seedless watermelon chunks

1 to 1½ cups sugar syrup (equal parts water and sugar, boiled and cooled)

¼ cup fresh lime juice

5 to 6 cups ice cold seltzer water

10 fresh mint sprigs, optional

A cup at a time, place the watermelon chunks and some of the sugar syrup in a blender and process to a smooth puree. When all of the watermelon has been pureed, stir in the lime juice. Taste and, if necessary, add more sugar syrup. Place in a container, cover, and refrigerate for at least 1 hour or up to 2 days.

When ready to serve, combine the chilled watermelon puree with the seltzer. Pour into tall glasses, add a sprig of mint, if desired, and serve ice cold.

Pigs in a Blanket with Honey-Mustard Sauce

Serves 8 to 10

No matter the time, place or occasion, when pigs in a blanket find a place on the buffet table or on a passed tray, you can bet that they will be gone in a flash. Even people who profess to not like them will be caught taking a surreptitious bite or two. An all-time American cocktail party favorite, they would make the perfect snack for a book club. Although they are easy to make using prepared roll dough, if you want to spend some extra time in the kitchen, by all means make your own pie pastry to wrap the little dogs in.

Honey-Mustard Sauce

1 cup German-style mustard
½ cup honey
1 teaspoon hot sauce

Combine the mustard, honey, and hot sauce in a small bowl, whisking to combine well. Use as directed or as a dipping sauce for grilled or fried chicken or pork. Store covered, and refrigerate for up to 1 month.

Pigs in a Blanket

Two 8-ounce cans refrigerated crescent roll dough
32 cocktail franks
1 large egg
1 tablespoon heavy cream

"Part of the secret in life is to eat what you like and let the food fight it out inside." —MARK TWAIN

Preheat the oven to 375°F.

Line two baking sheets with parchment paper or, alternately, use nonstick baking sheets.

Place about one-fourth of the Honey-Mustard Sauce into a bowl. Set aside.

Separate the dough from each can of rolls into 4 equal rectangles; then cut each rectangle into four 3-inch long strips.

Working with one piece at a time and using a pastry brush, lightly coat each dough strip with Honey-Mustard Sauce. Place a cocktail frank in the center of each piece and carefully roll the dough up and over the frank, leaving each end uncovered. Lightly push the ends of the dough together to seal it around the frank. As finished, place each pig in a blanket, seam side down, on the prepared baking sheets, leaving about 2 inches between each one.

Combine the egg and cream in a shallow bowl, whisking to combine. Using a clean pastry brush, lightly coat the top of each piece of pastry with the egg wash.

Place in the preheated oven and bake for about 12 minutes or until the pastry is slightly puffed and golden brown.

Remove from the oven and serve warm with the remaining Honey-Mustard Sauce as a dip. These may be reheated quickly in a microwave or served at room temperature; however, they are best when warm.

Deviled Eggs

Makes 24

I suggest that you double this recipe since I have found that, no matter how many eggs I stuff, they always immediately disappear from the buffet table or cocktail tray. Even those wary of cholesterol and fat can't seem to stay away from them.

12 hard boiled eggs, peeled
¼ cup mayonnaise
1 tablespoon Dijon mustard
Pinch cayenne pepper
Salt and pepper to taste
Paprika for garnish

Cut the eggs in half, lengthwise. Using a teaspoon, carefully remove the yolks, keeping each white half in one piece.

Place the yolks in a mixing bowl. Add the mayonnaise, mustard, and cayenne, mashing with a fork until very smooth. Taste and season with salt and pepper.

Scrape the mashed yolk mixture into a pastry bag fitted with a small star tip. Neatly pipe an equal portion of the mashed yolk into each white, mounding slightly.

Sprinkle with paprika and serve. If not serving immediately, cover lightly with plastic film and refrigerate.

NOTE: You can add any of the following to the mashed yolk mixture: ¼ cup minced ham, cooked shrimp, cooked chicken, or cooked crab or lobster meat OR 3 tablespoons minced cooked mushrooms OR 2 tablespoons anchovy paste, minced scallion, or minced red onion OR 1 tablespoon sun-dried tomato paste OR 1 tablespoon of any minced fresh herb, such as cilantro, parsley, chives, tarragon, or basil.

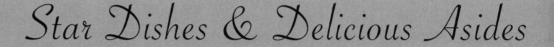

Star Dishes & Delicious Asides

Plains Buffalo Burgers

Serves 8

Although usually made on an outdoor grill, a great, juicy burger can also be grilled on a stovetop grill or fried in a big, seasoned cast iron skillet with spectacular results. Buffalo meat, that most American of protein, is low in fat, cholesterol and calories, and is very tasty. Its use also pays tribute to the Native American culinary heritage.

3 pounds ground buffalo meat
¾ cup minced red onion
1 teaspoon minced hot green chili or to taste
¼ cup ice water
Salt and pepper to taste
8 hamburger rolls, split and toasted

Preheat and oil an outdoor grill or preheat a stovetop grill pan or cast iron skillet.

Combine the buffalo with the onion and chili, and pour in the ice water. Season with salt and pepper to taste. Using your hands, mix together.

Form the meat mixture into 8 patties of equal size. Place the patties on the grill (or in the grill pan or skillet). Grill (or fry), turning once, for about 4 minutes per side for rare or 5 minutes per side for medium.

Place each burger on a toasted bun and serve with whatever condiments you prefer—ketchup, mustard, pickle relish, sliced onions, lettuce, tomatoes, and on and on go the desired toppings.

> "There was a chattering from the stall where Johanna Vavrika exhibited to the admiring women her platters heaped with fried chicken, her roasts of beef, boiled tongues and baked hams with cloves stuck in the crisp brown fat and garnished with tansy and parsley." —WILLA CATHER, The Bohemian Girl

Crispy Fried Chicken

Serves 8 to 10

All across America, fortunes have been made serving fried chicken. There isn't a part of the country that doesn't have a favorite recipe and ol' Colonel Sanders did a good job of creating an Everyman's version that has made the homemade version less than commonplace—and that's all the more reason to wow friends and fellow readers by doing it yourself. This recipe is the most basic—a mess of chicken, lots of salt and pepper, and plenty of grease—but I will offer you another that is a bit less "fried." Since it can be enjoyed at room temperature, fried chicken is a great make-ahead dish for any gathering. Needless to say, a classic home-made fried chicken dinner would also suit a Southern literary scene or a picnic dinner almost anywhere. Just remember to wipe your fingers clean before picking up your book.

Three 2½-pound frying chickens, cut into serving
*   pieces (or a selection of skin-on breast, leg, and*
*   thigh pieces to weigh about 7 or 8 pounds)*
4 cups buttermilk
4 cups all-purpose flour
Coarse salt and freshly ground black pepper
*   to taste*
Cayenne pepper to taste
Approximately 6 cups vegetable shortening or
*   vegetable oil*

Rinse the chicken under cold running water. Pat thoroughly dry.

Place the chicken in an extra large re-sealable plastic bag. Add the buttermilk, seal, and shake to coat. Place in the refrigerator and let marinate for at least 2 hours or up to 12 hours.

When ready to fry, combine the flour with the salt, pepper, and cayenne in an extra large re-sealable plastic bag. Seal and shake to combine.

Working with a few pieces at a time, shake the excess buttermilk from the chicken and drop the pieces into the seasoned flour. Shake to coat well. When coated, transfer the chicken to a platter or baking sheet. Do not crowd or layer, as the coating will stick and leave uncovered spots on the chicken.

Divide the shortening or oil into two large, deep frying pans. Place over medium-high heat. When almost sizzling, begin adding the coated chicken without crowding the pans. Cover and fry for about 15 minutes or until golden brown. Uncover, turn, and recover. Fry for an additional 15 or 20 minutes or until the chicken is crisp, golden brown all over, and cooked through.

Remove from the frying pans and place on a double layer of paper towels to drain.

Serve hot, warm or at room temperature.

NOTE: For less mess and somewhat less fat and calories, prepare the chicken as above, but instead of frying, bake the chicken as follows: Preheat the oven to 500°F. Place about ¼-inch of vegetable oil in two large rimmed baking pans. Place in the oven and when very hot, add the chicken without crowding the pans. (Bake in batches if necessary.) Bake for about 20 minutes or until golden. Turn, lower the oven temperature to 400°F, and bake for another 12 minutes or until the chicken is crisp, golden brown all over, and cooked through. Drain as directed.

Meatloaf

Serves 8 to 10

The wonderful thing about meatloaf is that it can be eaten hot, cold, or at room temperature, on a plate with the usual sides, or in a sandwich. This makes it perfect for gatherings, as the occasion dictates the style in which it is served.

3 pounds lean ground beef
1 pound ground veal
½ pound ground pork
1¼ cups minced onion
1 cup canned diced tomatoes, well-drained
1 tablespoon minced fresh parsley
2 teaspoons Worcestershire sauce
1 teaspoon minced garlic, optional
2 large eggs
½ cup milk
2 cups dry bread crumbs
Salt and pepper to taste
6 strips of bacon

Preheat the oven to 375°F.

Combine the beef, veal, and pork in a large mixing bowl. Add the onion, tomatoes, parsley, Worcestershire sauce, and garlic. Using your hands, mash the mixture together. Add the eggs and milk, and continue to mash the mixture.

When well-blended, add the bread crumbs and evenly mash them into the meat mixture. Season with salt and pepper.

Divide the mixture in half. Form each half into a loaf about 4 inches by 8 inches.

Place the loaves into a baking dish with sides, allowing about 2 inches between each one.

Place 3 strips of bacon on top of each loaf and then transfer the baking dish to the preheated oven. Bake for about 1 hour or until the tops are nicely browned and the loaves are cooked through.

Remove from the oven and let rest for about 15 minutes before cutting, crosswise, into slices.

Three-Bean Salad

Serves 10 to 12

This is a true salad of the heartland, perhaps because dried beans were always on hand, and green and wax beans were often canned in the summer to bring a bit of the garden to the table during the dark of winter. Since it tastes best after marinating for a day or two, it is a perfect salad to make when you want to spend time with your book, and still have a tasty dish at the ready for lunch or dinner or a late night buffet.

3 cups cooked kidney beans
3 cups cooked, sliced green beans
3 cups cooked, sliced wax beans or cooked
   garbanzo beans
1 cup finely diced red onion
¼ cup sweet pickle relish
3 tablespoons sweet mustard, such as
   German-style or honey
¾ cup cider vinegar
3 tablespoons canola oil
Salt and pepper to taste

Combine the beans in a mixing bowl. Add the onion, relish, and mustard, tossing to blend. Add the vinegar and oil and stir to blend. Taste and season with salt and pepper. Cover and let marinate for at least 1 hour before serving.

The salad will keep, covered and refrigerated, for about 1 week.

[Liberals think that] "unlike those from the East and Left coasts, the yokels from the heartland eat meatloaf and shop at Walmart. They even eat carbs!" —JANE SMILEY

Four-Cheese Macaroni

Serves 10 to 12

This is a luscious macaroni and cheese that bears no resemblance to the boxed variety. The addition of white wine and the mixture of cheeses give this make-ahead casserole a whole new range of delicious flavors. If you don't have the three cheeses that I suggest, substitute what's on hand—Gruyère, farmhouse cheddar, Caerphilly, Gouda and Brie are all good choices.

Macaroni and cheese is a great traveler and would make a wonderful addition to a potluck book group event. When reheating, cover the top with aluminum foil to keep it from drying out or taking on too much color. Reheat at the same temperature that the dish was baked.

¼ cup canola oil
½ cup minced shallots
¼ cup minced celery
¼ cup Wondra flour
3 cups hot half-and-half
1 cup dry white wine
1 cups mascarpone cheese
1½ cups grated sharp cheddar cheese
1 cup grated Fontina cheese
2 pounds elbow or tube macaroni, cooked and
*   well-drained*
Hot sauce to taste
Salt to taste
½ cup grated Parmesan cheese
1 cup bread crumbs

Preheat the oven to 350°F. Lightly butter the interior of a 13-inch by 9-inch baking pan.

Heat the oil in a large nonstick saucepan over medium heat. Add the shallots and celery and sauté for 5 minutes, or until the vegetables are very soft. Lower the heat and stir in the flour until well-incorporated. Whisk in the hot half-and-half, followed by the wine. Cook, stirring constantly, for about 4 minutes, or until the mixture has begun to thicken. Remove from the heat and, using a wooden spoon, beat in the mascarpone, cheddar and Fontina cheeses, stirring until they have melted into the sauce.

Stir in the cooked macaroni and season to taste with hot sauce and salt. When well-blended, pour the mixture into the prepared pan.

Combine the Parmesan cheese with the bread crumbs and then sprinkle the mixture over the top of the macaroni. Place in the preheated oven and bake for 20 minutes or until the edges are bubbling and the top is golden brown.

Remove from the oven and serve hot. (May be made in advance of use and stored, covered and refrigerated, for up to 2 days.) Bring to room temperature before reheating. This may also be made ahead of time and frozen.

Garden Salad

Serves 8 to 10

The perfect garden salad is much more than a toss of iceberg lettuce with a drizzle of bottled salad dressing. It should be a wonderful blend of soft and crisp and slightly sweet with a bit of bitter, highlighted with a tangy homemade dressing. It can also feature some cooked meat or fish to turn it into a complete meal. If transporting a salad, always keep it cold so that the ingredients hold their freshness, and add the dressing just before serving.

12 to 16 cups mixed salad greens (such as romaine, red and/or green leaf, Bibb, or Boston lettuces, chicory, spinach, endive, watercress, parsley, and so forth), trimmed, washed, and very well dried

½ cup fresh herb leaves or chopped pieces, such as chives, basil, mint

1 cup olive oil

¼ cup balsamic vinegar plus more to taste

½ teaspoon Dijon mustard

Salt and pepper to taste

Place the salad greens in a large bowl.

Place the olive oil in a container with a lid. Add the vinegar, mustard, and salt and pepper. Cover and shake vigorously until well-emulsified. Taste and, if necessary, add additional vinegar to taste.

When ready to serve, shake the dressing and pour just enough of it over the greens to lightly coat. Toss and serve.

NOTE: You can add tomatoes or any vegetable that you like to the greens for a more colorful presentation. However, remember that just as too many cooks spoil the broth, too many additions to a perfect green salad mask the crispness of the greens.

Literary Tea or Sweet Ending

Apple Pizza

Makes one 10-inch tart

Although the saying is "As American as apple pie," I think that the globalization of American cooking has allowed me to say "As American as apple pizza!" This is a most appealing dessert, and would certainly add some conversation points to an after-reading chat. It is particularly delicious served with a scoop of cinnamon, dulce de leche or vanilla ice cream.

4 medium Granny Smith (or heirloom tart) apples

Juice of 1 lemon

3 tablespoons apple cider

½ cup sugar

3 tablespoons Wondra flour

2 teaspoons ground cinnamon

3 tablespoons unsalted butter, melted

Flaky Pie Pastry (recipe follows)

2 tablespoons cinnamon-sugar

Peel and core the apples. Halve them lengthwise and then cut each half, lengthwise, into paper thin slices. Place the slices in a mixing bowl. Quickly sprinkle with lemon juice, add the cider, and toss to keep them from discoloring. Add the sugar, flour, and cinnamon, and toss to coat well.

Preheat the oven to 375°F.

Lightly flour a clean, flat work surface. Place the pastry in the center and, using a rolling pin, roll the dough, working from the center out, into a circle approximately 11 inches in diameter and about ¼-inch thick. Carefully transfer the dough circle to a pizza pan or pizza stone.

Fold about ½ inch of the edge under itself all around to give the pastry circle a double thickness around the rim. Using your fingertips, crimp a neat, fluted rim of dough.

Working from the outside edge toward the center, make concentric circles of slightly overlapping apple slices, with the outside edge of the slices toward the outside edge of the dough. When the center is reached, use a few apple slices to make a slightly raised rosette shape. Sprinkle the entire top with cinnamon-sugar.

Place in the preheated oven and bake for about 40 minutes, or until the apples are tender, caramelized, and beginning to brown around the edges and the crust is golden brown.

Remove from the oven and allow to cool for 15 minutes before cutting. May be served warm or at room temperature.

Flaky Pastry

Enough for two 9-inch pastry shells or one 9-inch 2-crust pie

2½ cups sifted all-purpose flour
1 tablespoon sugar
1 teaspoon salt
½ cup (1 stick) unsalted butter, chilled and cut into pieces
7 tablespoons chilled solid vegetable shortening
Approximately 6 tablespoons ice water

Combine the flour, sugar, and salt in the bowl of a food processor fitted with the metal blade and process to blend. Add the butter and shortening and process, using quick on-and-off turns, until the mixture is crumbly.

Add about ¼ cup of the water and process, using quick on-and-off turns. Continue adding water, processing as you go until the dough just barely comes together. Do not let the dough get too wet or it will be tough.

Remove the dough from the processor and form it into a flat disk.

Cover with plastic film and refrigerate for at least 15 minutes or up to 8 hours.

Use as directed in a specific recipe.

Schaum Torte

Serves 8 to 10

German in origin, this dessert is a long-time favorite in the heartland, often bearing different names in different states. It's easy to make and quite appealing at the table; since it is a refrigerated dessert, it can be made early in the day and served, with ease, later in the day.

6 large egg whites, at room temperature
2 cups superfine sugar
1 tablespoon white vinegar
1 teaspoon pure vanilla extract
¼ teaspoon salt
⅛ teaspoon baking powder
3 cups sliced fresh fruit (such as peaches, nectarines, plums, or apricots) or fresh berries
1 cup chilled heavy cream, whipped
Bittersweet chocolate, optional
Mint sprig, optional

Preheat the oven to 250°F.

Line a baking sheet with parchment paper. Set aside.

Place the egg whites in the bowl of a standing electric mixture fitted with the whip attachment. Beat on medium until frothy.

With the motor running, slowly add the sugar, beating until all of the sugar has been added and the whites are almost stiff.

Add the vinegar, vanilla, salt, and baking powder and continue to beat on high until the mixture is stiff and glossy.

Mound the meringue in the center of the prepared baking sheet and, using a spatula, spread it out to an even 9-inch round.

Place in the preheated oven and bake for 1 hour. Turn off the heat and allow the meringue to finish setting in the oven. Do not open the door.

When cool, remove the meringue from the oven and carefully transfer it to a serving platter.

Using a serrated knife, cut and reserve about ½ inch off of the top. Cover the lower portion with the fruit and then top the fruit with a generous layer of whipped cream.

Break the reserved top piece into chunks and nestle the pieces into the whipped cream. Lightly cover with plastic film and refrigerate for at least 1 hour.

If desired, just before serving, grate a bit of bittersweet chocolate over the top and garnish with a mint sprig.

Chapter 2

Prose and Plates of the Eastern Seaboard

*E*ACH OF THE FOUR SEASONS—FLEETING FOLIAGE, LONG, COLD WINTER, BLOSSOMING springtime and exhilarating summer—is intensely felt in the northeast, more so in the rural areas than in its cities, of course. Perhaps it is the combination of the breathtaking beauty of fall colors, the bone-chilling gray-white winter, the messiness of mud punctuated by pop-up crocus and the fabulous bursts of summer's soil that spur creativity while also pushing writers to look inward, examining human needs and cultural circumstance.

For the most part, the foods of New England and the mid-Atlantic states continue to access the bounty of the sea as well as the earth.

New York writers span the whole state, but somehow those who write about or in New York City especially pique the culinary imagination. Of course there are some who take us to the more rural parts of the state, where the big apples actually grow and where sugar maples may be as plentiful as they are in Vermont and New Hampshire. But somehow food is not quite as locale-defined in the farming areas or the suburbs as in the Big Apple.

Some urban writers sing of their ethnic or religious cultural roots, food included, while others are as urbane as they are urban. I tend to think of the latter as "martini writers"—their focus is as much on the partyscape of the city as it is on New York or Philadelphia food-scapes. While all of our treasured authors could be called sophisticated literary artists, these are the writers who make their mark depicting sophisticated (and sometimes dissolute) lives, or create personae of their own that turns them into very public figures leading sophisticated (and oftentimes dissolute) lives.

✦ ✦ ✦

READS, DRINKS & NIBBLES
■ ■ ■

Cape Codder
Manhattan
The Perfect New York Martini
Maine Lobster Rolls
Buffalo Chicken Wings with Blue Cheese Dip
Stuffed Mushrooms
Shrimp Cocktail

STAR DISHES & DELICIOUS ASIDES
■ ■ ■

New England Chicken Pot Pie
New York Strip Steak Sandwiches with
    Green Goddess Dressing
Connecticut Club Sandwich

Boston Baked Beans
Pennsylvania Dutch Corn Fritters with
    Maple-Mustard Sauce
Jersey Tomato Salad

FOR A MOVEABLE FEAST
■ ■ ■

Bagel Platter with the Works
Chocolate Truffles

LITERARY TEA OR SWEET ENDING
■ ■ ■

Cranberry Nut Bread
Individual New York Cheesecakes
Brooklyn Egg Cream
Hot Mulled Apple Cider

Reads, Drinks & Nibbles

Cape Codder

This is a light, refreshing drink that, with the antioxidants and vitamin content of the cranberry juice, can be considered almost good for you! Of course, you can eliminate the vodka for an alcohol-free drink. Or, if you want to fancy it up, freeze an individual cranberry in each piece of ice that you plan on adding to the finished drink. Whatever you choose, it will bring a whiff of Rhode Island or another northeast berry bog to your club chair!

FOR EACH DRINK:
½ cup cranberry juice
2 tablespoons fresh lime juice
1 tablespoon fresh orange juice
¼ cup vodka
Small lime wedge, optional

Combine the cranberry juice with the lime and orange juices. Add the vodka. Pour into a chilled glass and add ice. Serve garnished with a lime wedge, if desired.

Manhattan

Manhattans have been around almost as long as Wall Street has been the financial capital of the world. Much like the New York island, a good Manhattan is a bit sour, a bit sweet, a bit sneaky, and a whole lot delicious! It would be a perfect beginning (or ending) to an evening's reading of a great New York novel.

FOR EACH COCKTAIL:
¼ cup fine rye whiskey
2 tablespoons sweet (red) vermouth
A dash or 2 of bitters
Ice
1 maraschino cherry

Combine the whiskey, vermouth, and bitters in a cocktail shaker. Add about 1½ cups of ice, cover, and shake vigorously.

Strain through a cocktail strainer into a chilled martini-style glass. Garnish with a maraschino cherry and serve with a toast!

The Perfect New York Martini

Martinis seem to be the epitome of sophisticated drinking—unfortunately, I usually think of them matched with a cigarette in a 1950s setting. Each dry martini lover seems to have his or her own mix, but this one should please every one of them. It is important that the glass and the gin be ice cold so that, when mixed, the ice won't dilute the flavor. Some add a strip of lemon zest to the glass, but I think it unnecessary. A martini can also be made with vodka.

FOR EACH MARTINI:
1 ice-cold martini glass
Ice
¼ cup chilled gin
2 quick splashes dry vermouth
1 pitted green olive or cocktail onion*

Fill a cocktail shaker with ice. Add the gin and vermouth. Cover and quickly shake vigorously so that the ice doesn't melt and weaken the cocktail.

Place the olive or onion into the chilled glass. Strain gin and vermouth through a cocktail strainer into the glass, and serve immediately.

*Some call a martini splashed over a cocktail onion a "Gibson."

"First you take a drink, then the drink takes a drink, then the drink takes you." — F. SCOTT FITZGERALD

"Let's get out of these wet clothes and into a dry martini." —ROBERT BENCHLEY

"I'm still a martini man . . . sometimes you have to get a quick infusion of alcohol in order to face the night." —JAY MCINERNEY

Buffalo Chicken Wings with Blue Cheese Dip

Serves 8 to 10

Long, long ago, a bar in Buffalo, New York started serving deep-fried chicken wing pieces—the smaller flat part and the drummettes—with a spicy hot pepper sauce. This was probably done to encourage those extra glasses of beer needed to quell the heat. Although many variations of the sauce have been made, it really was nothing more than hot cayenne-based sauce and butter. The complete feast is usually combined with crisp, cool celery sticks and blue cheese dressing and would be great with one of New York State's terrific beers, such as Ommegang Abbey Ale from Cooperstown. This is a great way to cool out after an intense read of a novel by William Kennedy or another upstate New Yorker.

4 pounds chicken wings, tips removed
½ cup melted butter
6 tablespoons hot sauce
1 teaspoon hot paprika
½ teaspoon cayenne pepper
Salt and pepper to taste
Blue Cheese Dip (recipe follows)

Using a sharp knife, cut each wing into 2 pieces, the drummette and the second joint. Rinse under cold running water and pat dry. Place the wings in a large re-sealable plastic bag.

Combine the melted butter with the hot sauce, paprika, cayenne, salt and pepper. Reserving 2 tablespoons, pour the marinade into the plastic bag. Seal and push the wings around to ensure an even coating. Set aside to marinate for 30 minutes.

Preheat the oven to 375°F.

Remove the chicken wings from the plastic bag, discarding the marinade.

Place the wing pieces in a roasting pan in a single layer. Transfer to the preheated oven and roast, turning once or twice, for 25 minutes or until the chicken is thoroughly cooked and nicely charred. Watch carefully, as you don't want the wings to burn.

Remove the wings from the oven and place on a serving platter. Pour the reserved 2 tablespoons of marinade over the top and toss to coat.

Serve with Blue Cheese Dip along with carrot and celery sticks, if desired.

Blue Cheese Dip

6 ounces blue cheese, crumbled
½ cup whole milk
1 cup fine quality mayonnaise
1 cup sour cream
2 tablespoons fresh lemon juice
1 clove garlic, peeled and minced
Pepper to taste

Combine the cheese and milk in a small bowl. Using a fork, mash the mixture together until creamy with almost no lumps. Stir in the mayonnaise, sour cream, and lemon juice. When well blended, stir in the garlic and season with pepper to taste.

Cover and refrigerate for 30 minutes before serving to allow the flavors to blend.

Maine Lobster Rolls

Lobster rolls are the quintessential summer fare. You can find shacks all along the Maine coast bragging that "our lobster roll is the only roll." Truth to tell, the lobster roll has become a waterside offering as far south as Mystic or Montauk. There are also two Lobster Roll camps—the mayo or the butter—the cold or the hot. For either, an actual citizen of Maine will insist on big chunks of claw and knuckle lobster meat. I will offer both versions and let you choose the one you want to transform your den or library to a shack by the sea.

FOR EACH ROLL:
¼ *pound lobster meat*
1 to 2 tablespoons mayonnaise (homemade
  is best, see NOTE), optional
1 to 2 tablespoons melted salted butter
Salt and pepper to taste
1 lemon wedge
1 soft, buttery hot dog bun, split
1 tablespoon butter

Combine the lobster and mayonnaise, tossing to just lightly coat. Season with salt and pepper to taste.

Alternately, toss the lobster with the melted butter and season with salt and pepper to taste.

Preheat a nonstick skillet over medium heat.

Spread both of the cut sides of the bun with the tablespoon of butter. Place the bun, buttered side down, onto the hot skillet. Cook until just warm and lightly toasted.

Remove from the heat and mound the lobster into the opened, toasted bun. Sprinkle with lemon juice and serve.

The roll made with mayonnaise is served cold and that with butter is served warm.

NOTE: Homemade mayonnaise can quickly be made by combining 1 large egg yolk with 2 tablespoons fresh lemon juice, a pinch of dry mustard powder and a dash of hot pepper sauce in a blender. When blended and with the motor running, add 1 cup canola or peanut oil in a slow, steady stream. Season with salt and pepper to taste. If too thick, add a drop or two of hot water. Store, covered and refrigerated, for up to one week.

Stuffed Mushrooms

Makes 24

Stuffed mushrooms are perfect cocktail fare, a wonderful first course. You can make them as simple or as elegant as you wish and as large or as small as you like. Huge Portobello caps could even make a nice luncheon meal, particularly if the stuffing has the added protein. And they are just as delicious at room temperature as they are warm—plus, they can be made in advance and stored, covered and refrigerated, for up to 24 hours.

24 large stuffing mushrooms,
  well-cleaned
2 tablespoons butter or olive oil
¼ *cup minced onion*
1 cup dried bread crumbs
1 large egg
1 tablespoon dry sherry
2 tablespoons minced fresh parsley
1 teaspoon minced fresh thyme, chives
  or tarragon
Salt and pepper to taste
¼ *cup crab meat, chopped shrimp,*
  crumbled sausage, or minced
  chicken, optional
¼ *cup grated Parmesan cheese*

If cooking immediately, preheat the oven to 375°F.

Lightly oil a baking dish. Set aside.

Trim off and chop the stems from each mushroom.

Heat the butter in a medium frying pan over medium heat. Add the chopped mushroom stems and onion and sauté for about 3 minutes or until softened.

Place the bread crumbs in a mixing bowl. Scrape the mushroom-onion mixture into the crumbs. Add the egg, sherry, parsley, and thyme. Season with salt and pepper and stir to combine. If using any of the optional ingredients, stir them in to just combine.

Using a teaspoon, generously pack each cap full of the bread crumb mixture, mounding slightly in the center. As stuffed, place the stuffed mushrooms in the prepared baking dish. Sprinkle the top of each one with a light dusting of the cheese.

Place in the preheated oven and bake for about 15 minutes or until the mushrooms are just barely tender and the tops are nicely colored.

Serve warm or at room temperature.

Shrimp Cocktail

I know it is old-fashioned and kind of corny, but I swear a jumbo shrimp cocktail still says celebration and luxe to me. If you have bowls especially made for individual shrimp cocktails, use them tightly packed with shaved or chopped ice. If not, simply line a serving platter with shredded lettuce and garnish the platter with lemon wedges and celery leaves. It is another dish that conjures up sophisticated dining—think Scott Fitzgerald, John O'Hara, and on and on those evocative writers go.

The cocktail sauce can easily be made in large batches, as it keeps well. The following recipe makes enough for about 6 shrimp cocktails.

FOR EACH SERVING:
Shredded lettuce, optional
6 large or 5 jumbo cooked shrimp, peeled and
  deveined, tails intact
¼ cup Cocktail Sauce (recipe follows)
1 lemon wedge or slice

If desired, line each bowl with shredded or chopped lettuce—iceberg best holds the crisp crunch.

Lay the shrimp in an attractive pattern on top of the lettuce or hang them around the edge of the bowl. Top with cocktail sauce (alternately, place the cocktail sauce in a small container in the center of the shrimp) and garnish with a lemon wedge or slice.

Cocktail Sauce

1 cup commercial chili sauce
2 tablespoons well-drained commercial white
  horseradish
1 tablespoon fresh lemon juice
1 teaspoon hot sauce
½ teaspoon Worcestershire sauce

Combine the chili sauce with the horseradish, lemon juice, hot sauce, and Worcestershire sauce in a mixing bowl, stirring to blend well. Cover and refrigerate for at least 30 minutes or up to 1 week.

Star Dishes & Delicious Asides

New England Chicken Pot Pie

Serves 8 to 12

Pot pies have been a New England staple for generations. They evolved from the hearty meat pies of the early English settlers and have long been much loved during the long, bleak winters. Unfortunately, the modern cook tends to buy commercially-prepared pies, which is a shame because, with the availability of prepared frozen pastry, pies are very easy to make. To simplify the task even more, I have used boneless, skinless chicken breasts in place of cooking, deboning and skinning whole chickens.

3 pounds boneless, skinless chicken breast
4 cups low-sodium, fat-free chicken broth
    (homemade stock would be even better)
Salt and pepper to taste
5 carrots, peeled, trimmed, and diced
4 large potatoes, peeled, trimmed and diced
2 medium onions, peeled, trimmed and finely diced
1½ cups frozen petit peas, thawed
1½ tablespoons cornstarch dissolved in ¼ cup
    cold water
2 packages 9-inch double crust refrigerated
    pie pastry

Trim any excess fat or membrane from the chicken.

Place the broth in a large saucepan. Add the chicken and season with salt and pepper to taste. Place over medium heat and bring to a simmer. Lower the heat and cook at a bare simmer for about 12 minutes or just until the chicken is almost cooked.

Preheat the oven to 450°F.

Immediately remove the chicken from the broth and set it aside, but leave the broth on the stove.

Add the carrots, potatoes, and onions to the hot broth. Raise the heat and bring to a boil. Lower the heat and simmer for about 10 minutes or just until the vegetables are barely cooked.

While the vegetables are cooking, cut the chicken into bite-sized pieces.

When the vegetables are cooked, add the chicken and peas, stirring to blend. Stir in the cornstarch and bring to a simmer. Cook, stirring gently, for a minute just to thicken the broth slightly.

Immediately remove from the heat. Taste and, if necessary, season with additional salt and pepper. Let cool for about 15 minutes; if too hot, the mixture will soften the pastry.

Line two 9-inch pie pans with one of the refrigerated pastry crusts. Pour an equal portion of the chicken mixture into each pastry-lined pan. Working quickly so that the pastry stays firm, cover each pie with a top crust, then gently crimp the edges together to completely close.

Using a kitchen fork, randomly prick the top crust with air holes.

Place in the preheated oven and bake for 15 minutes. Lower the oven temperature to 375°F and continue to bake for an additional 20 minutes or until the interior is bubbling and the crust is golden brown.

Remove from the heat and let rest for about 10 minutes before cutting into wedges and serving.

The pies may be made in advance and reheated for about 15 minutes in a 400°F oven.

> **"As a rule, I'm no great fan of eating out in New York . . . SoHo is not a macaroni salad kind of place."**
>
> —DAVID SEDARIS

New York Strip Steak Sandwiches with Green Goddess Dressing

Serves 2

A New York strip steak is also known as hotel cut, shell, Kansas City or top loin steak among others. Although I give the recipe for preparing the steak, the sandwich can easily be made from leftover steak or deli roast beef—a perfect lunch for you and the person with whom you really want to discuss that New York novel you can't put down.

If, however, you're charged with nourishing a large group, the New York strip steak could prove an expensive choice unless you follow the lead of some of Manhattan's most fashionable hostesses: Serve a mini-sandwich and offer a ton of chips. Chic bakeries sell tiny rolls for the carb-conscious. Alternatively, you can use crusty baguettes, sliced lengthwise before ingredients are laid in, and eventually cut into small sandwiches. However many you make, it is the combination of flavors of the beef, dressing, peppers, and crisp romaine nestled into a toasted roll that you are looking for.

FOR 2 FULL-SIZE SANDWICHES:
One 12 to 14 ounce 1½-inch thick boneless
*   strip steak*
1 clove garlic, cut in half, lengthwise
Coarse salt and black pepper to taste
2 Kaiser rolls or other hard, crusty rolls, cut in
*   half, lengthwise*
Green Goddess Dressing (recipe follows)
½ cup chopped roasted red peppers in oil
¾ cup chopped romaine lettuce

Preheat the oven to 500°F.

Place a cast iron skillet over high heat and allow it to get very hot.

Season both sides of the steak with the cut garlic. Then, season with salt and pepper to taste.

When the skillet is very, very hot, add the seasoned steak. Fry for about 2 minutes or until a nice crust has formed. Turn and fry the remaining side for another 2 minutes or until crusty. Immediately transfer to the hot oven and cook for about 12 minutes for rare (14 minutes for medium and 16 to 18 minutes for well-done).

Remove from the oven and place on a cutting board to rest for a few minutes before cutting.

Place the two halves of each bread into the oven and toast for about 2 minutes or until just golden. Keep warm.

Using a sharp knife, cut the steak into thin slices, reserving any juices that flow.

Remove the rolls from the oven and generously coat each cut side with Green Goddess Dressing. Top one half of each roll with an equal portion of the sliced steak.

Cover the steak with a couple of spoonfuls of the roasted red peppers and a handful of chopped romaine. Top with the remaining half of roll, cut in half, and serve.

> **"The only time to eat diet food is while you're waiting for the steak to cook."**
> **—JULIA CHILD**

Green Goddess Dressing
(a.k.a. Statue of Liberty Sauce)

1 cup mayonnaise
½ cup sour cream
2 anchovy filets, finely chopped, optional
½ cup minced fresh greens, such as chives,
*   scallion greens, flat leaf parsley, and a little*
*   bit of mint*
1 tablespoon white vinegar
2 teaspoons fresh lemon juice
¼ teaspoon hot sauce
Salt and pepper to taste, optional

Combine the mayonnaise and sour cream in a mixing bowl. If using, whisk in the anchovies. Add the herbs, vinegar, lemon juice, and hot sauce, stirring to blend. Taste and, if necessary, stir in salt and pepper.

Cover and refrigerate until ready to use. May be stored covered and refrigerated, for up to 3 days.

Connecticut Club Sandwich

It is believed that the club sandwich was first served in Saratoga Springs, New York, in the late 1800s, probably a luncheon repast for attendees of the famed horse race. However, this tiered sandwich has been for so long a country-club favorite that some call it a Connecticut Club. This is the classic recipe—of course, prepared with house-made mayonnaise and freshly cooked chicken or turkey! But, a club can also be made with meat, poultry, or egg salads, fish, or lobster with the addition of avocado, and the lettuce can be any type you prefer. I can't think of a more inviting dish for an afternoon book club reading.

FOR EACH SANDWICH:
3 slices home-style white bread, toasted
About 2 tablespoons mayonnaise or to taste
3 slices cooked chicken or turkey breast
4 leaves Bibb lettuce
3 thin slices ripe tomato
4 strips cooked bacon

Place a slice of toast on a clean, flat work surface. Generously coat with mayonnaise. Layer the chicken or turkey on top of the mayonnaise-covered toast. Cover the meat with 2 lettuce leaves. Generously coat both sides of one of the remaining pieces of toast with mayonnaise and place it on top of the lettuce. Lay the tomato slices on top of the toast. Cover the tomatoes with the remaining 2 lettuce leaves and top the lettuce with the bacon strips. Coat one side of the remaining piece of toast with mayonnaise and place it, mayonnaise side down, on top of the bacon.

Using a sharp knife, cut the sandwich into 4 equal triangles. Place a frilled toothpick in each triangle to hold it together and serve. If the readers in your life are light eaters, you might figure on three triangles per person.

Boston Baked Beans

Serves 8 to 12

As soon as the first hint of chill is in the air, New England cooks bring out the bean pot and begin the winter's ritual of baked beans for supper (and for breakfast and lunch, hot or cold). Traditional baked beans don't have the addition of meat, but I think it adds the substance needed to turn the dish into a main course if that is what you seek. Sausage—all types—also make a nice addition. If using sausage, it should be added about an hour before the beans are done to allow the sausages to cook thoroughly.

4 cups dried navy beans
¾ cup pure maple syrup
½ cup molasses
1 tablespoon dry mustard powder
1 tablespoon tomato paste
Salt and pepper to taste
1 large onion, peeled and cut into wedges
½ pound salt pork, cut into cubes
1 pound smoked ham, cut into cubes

Rinse the beans under cold running water. Place in a large saucepan with cold water to cover by at least 2 inches. Set aside to soak for at least 8 hours or overnight.

Drain the beans well. Again cover with cold water to cover by 2 inches. Place over high heat and bring to a boil. Lower the heat and simmer, adding water as necessary to keep the beans well-hydrated, for about 90 minutes or until just tender.

Remove from the heat and drain well, reserving the cooking liquid.

Preheat the oven to 325°F.

Generously grease a large (about 4 quart) casserole.

Place the beans in the prepared casserole. Add the maple syrup, molasses, mustard, tomato paste, and salt and pepper to taste, stirring to combine. Add enough of the reserved cooking liquid to make a very soupy mixture. (The beans will absorb a lot of liquid as they bake.) Reserve any remaining liquid for later additions to the baking beans, if necessary. If you do not have sufficient cooking liquid left to make a soupy mixture, you can use boiling water or hot chicken broth.

Nestle the onion wedges and salt pork cubes into the beans. Cover and place in the preheated oven. Bake, uncovering and tasting, and adding liquid as necessary from time to time, for about 4 hours or until the beans are soft and the gravy is thick and rich.

About 30 minutes before the beans are ready, nestle the ham cubes into them. Recover and finish baking.

Serve hot or warm.

Pennsylvania Dutch Corn Fritters with Maple-Mustard Sauce

Serves 8 to 10

Late summer brings bushels of fresh corn. So much is harvested that seasoned cooks have found all kinds of ways to use corn. The ever thrifty Pennsylvania Dutch make these wonderful fritters that can be used as a snack, a side dish or, if you eliminate the scallions and cayenne, as breakfast pancakes served with warm maple syrup any time of day. Note, though, that the mustard-maple sauce I suggest is a tangy topping, better for spicy fritters than sweeter pancakes.

10 ears fresh corn, shucked (or 5 cups thawed
*   frozen corn kernels)*
4 large eggs, separated
½ cup finely chopped scallion greens
⅓ cup all-purpose flour
1 tablespoon sugar
Salt and cayenne pepper to taste
1 cup vegetable oil
Maple Mustard Sauce (recipe follows)

Using a serrated knife, carefully scrape the kernels from the ears of corn. Using the back of the knife, scrape any remaining pulp from each ear and combine it with the kernels.

Place the egg whites in a mixing bowl and, using an electric mixer, beat until stiff peaks form.

Stir the scallion greens, flour, sugar, salt, and cayenne into the corn mixture. When blended, stir in the egg yolks. When combined, fold in the beaten egg whites until just barely blended.

Heat the oil in a large skillet over medium-high heat. When very hot, but not smoking, drop the corn batter into the oil by the heaping tablespoon. Fry, turning once, for about 5 minutes or until the fritters are crisp and golden brown. Do not squish the batter down; you want the fritters to be light and airy.

Using a slotted spoon, lift the fritters from the hot oil and place on a double layer of paper towels to drain. Continue making fritters until all of the batter has been fried.

Serve warm or at room temperature with Maple-Mustard Sauce for dipping.

Maple-Mustard Sauce

1 cup Dijon mustard
½ cup pure maple syrup
1 teaspoon lemon juice

Combine the mustard, syrup, and lemon juice in a small bowl and whisk to blend well. Store covered and refrigerated, until ready to use or for up to 1 week. Bring to room temperature before serving.

Jersey Tomato Salad

Serves 8

8 very ripe farm-fresh New Jersey beefsteak tomatoes,
*   cored, peeled, and cut crosswise into thin slices*
3 cucumbers, well-washed, trimmed, and cut
*   crosswise into thin slices*
1 red onion, peeled and finely diced
About 3 tablespoons extra virgin olive oil
About 2 tablespoons balsamic vinegar
Salt and pepper to taste
Fresh basil leaves or sprigs

Place the tomato and cucumber slices in slightly overlapping concentric circles on a large round platter. Sprinkle with the diced red onion. Drizzle the top with olive oil and vinegar. Season with salt and pepper. Garnish with basil leaves or sprigs and serve immediately.

NOTE: This salad can also be made in individual servings, following the same directions. The olive oil and vinegar can also be replaced with your favorite low-fat or sugar-free salad dressing.

BAGELS with the WORKS

❖ ❖ ❖

For those non-New Yorkers—or for people outside the Tri-State area—lox is simply highly-salted, smoked salmon. Not-so-salty cured salmon is known in bagel country as Nova Scotia (where some but by no means all of it comes from). If you eat your cured salmon on thin-sliced buttered brown bread, chances are you call it something else altogether.

To complicated matters further, even Brooklynites or folks from the Bronx who regularly eat Nova Scotia on their bagels may call all smoked salmon lox, because "bagels and lox" long ago became a generic term in New York and its environs. The simplest bagel and lox is just that, a sliced bagel (an onion bagel is pre-

> **"Inside the house, people stood around a table piled with bagels, lox, and whitefish and talked about Isaac."**
> —NICOLE KRAUSS, The Last Words on Earth

ferred) stuffed with lox or smoked salmon. And, if you want to add that extra New York touch, a "shmeer" of cream cheese. However, for the full Jewish delicatessen experience, you will want to offer all of the trimmings: Sliced tomatoes, onions, and cucumbers, lemon wedges, capers, both whipped and plain cream cheese, cracked black pepper, chopped chives.

Traditionally, the reading matter of choice with a bagel platter has been the super-hefty Sunday-edition of the New York Times. For your purpose, it can be any book by a Jewish author from the Tri-State area. Consider Philip Roth, for example. He grew up in New Jersey and for most of his adult years has been a resident of Connecticut. I rest my geographical case.

FOR EACH SERVING:
1 bagel, cut in half, crosswise
¼ cup whipped cream cheese, either plain
*   or chive-flavored*
2 slices ripe, beefsteak tomato
2 slices red onion
2 ounces lox or smoked salmon
¼ teaspoon well-drained capers
Cracked black pepper to taste

Spread both sides of the bagel with cream cheese. Layer each half with a slice of tomato followed by a slice of onion. Lay about 2 slices of lox on top of the onion. Sprinkle with a few capers and grind black pepper over the top. Serve, open-faced, with 2 halves per serving.

NOTE: If you would rather make a platter for your group to put together their own repast, lightly toast the sliced bagels and put them in a basket lined with a clean kitchen towel to help keep them warm. Arrange the smoked salmon around the edges of a large platter and mound the various trimmings in the center. Place the cream cheese(s) in a bowl and lightly sprinkle the top with chopped chives.

A typical New York bagel was once just a plain round donut shaped dense roll that was boiled in water. Occasionally, it was topped with sesame or poppy seeds. Nowadays, bagels are made in a variety of ways with a variety of doughs, some with nuts, raisins, or other dried fruit or berries.

Chocolate Truffles

Makes approximately 1½ pounds

Truffles are very rich candies that should be enjoyed with a cup of coffee. Espresso is a particularly good match. They can replace dessert at the end of a meal or be offered as a satisfying tidbit at any point in the day or evening. They are a first-rate contribution to a potluck dinner for up to a dozen people, or a classy host/hostess gift.

1 pound fine-quality bittersweet chocolate,
*   cut into small bits*
1 cup heavy cream
2 tablespoons light corn syrup
1½ teaspoons pure vanilla extract OR
*   1 tablespoon amaretto, brandy, Grand Marnier*
*   or other liqueur*
1 cup sifted Dutch-processed cocoa powder

Place the chocolate in a heat-proof bowl. Set aside.

Combine the cream and corn syrup in a small heavy-bottom saucepan over low heat. Bring to just a bare simmer.

Immediately remove the cream mixture from the heat and pour it over the chocolate. Let rest for about 30 seconds.

Add the vanilla or other flavoring and, using a wooden spoon, slowly begin to beat the liquid into the melting chocolate. Continue beating until the mixture is completely smooth. Set aside to cool.

When cool, cover and refrigerate for about 2 hours or until firm.

Remove the truffle ganache from the refrigerator.

Place the cocoa powder on a large shallow plate.

Using a small melon-baller (or your hands), scoop up a bit of the ganache. Working quickly so as not to melt the chocolate, form the truffle into a small, even ball. Drop the ball into the cocoa and toss to lightly coat with powder.

When all of the truffles have been made, store in an airtight container, in layers separated by waxed paper, at room temperature.

Literary Tea or Sweet Ending

Cranberry Nut Bread

Makes one 9-inch loaf

This is a quick and easy treat that would be perfect served at a coffee-klatch book group gathering. It could even be made into little tea sandwiches: cut the loaf into thin slices and spread one piece with (see Note) whipped cream cheese, flavored with freshly grated orange zest, top with another slice, and cut sandwiches into triangles.

1 cup fresh cranberries
2 cups sifted all-purpose flour
1 cup sugar
1½ teaspoons baking powder
½ teaspoon baking soda
¼ teaspoon salt
¼ cup unsalted butter, softened
1 large egg
¾ cup orange juice
2 teaspoons freshly grated orange zest
1 cup chopped nuts

Preheat the oven to 375°F.

Generously butter the interior of a 9-inch x 5-inch x 3-inch loaf pan. Set aside.

Place the cranberries in the bowl of a food processor fitted with the metal blade.

Process using quick on-and-off turns to chop coarsely. Set aside.

Combine the flour, sugar, baking powder, baking soda, and salt in a mixing bowl.

Add the butter and, using your fingertips, work the butter into the dry ingredients until the mixture is crumbly.

Combine the egg with the orange juice and zest, stirring to blend. Add to the dry ingredients, stirring with a wooden spoon to just combine.

Stir in the reserved cranberries, along with the nuts. When blended, scrape the mixture into the prepared pan, smoothing the batter into the corners slightly. The top should be mounded slightly.

Place in the preheated oven and bake for about 1 hour or until golden brown and a cake tester inserted into the center comes out clean.

Remove from the oven and set on a wire rack to cool for at least 15 minutes before cutting and serving. The loaf may also be wrapped airtight and stored, refrigerated for up to 5 days or frozen for up to 3 months. Bring to room temperature before serving.

NOTE: Cream cheese, either plain or whipped, is often referred to as Philadelphia cream cheese, Philadelphia being the brand name given to the extremely popular Kraft Foods product. It is said that the brand name was bestowed on the cream cheese because, at the time of its introduction, Philadelphia was thought to be the home of fine foods.

Individual New York Cheesecakes

Makes 16

Many feel that a New York cheesecake is not complete without a cookie-type crust and a topping of slightly sweetened sour cream, but the

no-crust type was the first kind I experienced when I arrived in New York, so it remains my New York style. Obviously, it can be made into one large cake—you will need a 9-inch spring-form pan and a little extra baking time. If you want to fancy up the little cakes, place a piece of candied fruit, a whole berry, or a sprig of mint in the center. Whatever you choose, you can imagine yourself sitting in a New York Jewish deli listening to seasoned waiters barking orders to both the kitchen and their intimidated customers!

Butter and graham cracker crumbs for pans
2 pounds fine-quality cream cheese,
*   at room temperature*
1½ cups sugar
4 large eggs, at room temperature
¼ cup sour cream, at room temperature
¼ cup heavy cream, at room temperature
1 tablespoon pure vanilla extract
1 teaspoon lemon juice

Preheat the oven to 325°F.

Generously coat the interior cups of two 8-cup muffin tins (non-stick pans are

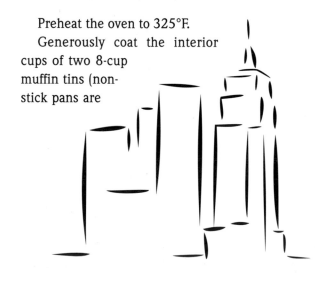

the best) with softened butter. Then, sprinkle each cup with graham cracker crumbs. Invert the pans to allow excess crumbs to drop out, noting that each cup should be generously coated with crumbs.

Place the cream cheese in the bowl of a standing electric mixer fitted with the paddle. Beat on slow to soften. Raise the speed to medium and continue to beat until the cheese is very creamy. Gradually add the sugar and continue to beat, scraping down the sides of the bowl with a rubber spatula, until light and smooth. Add the eggs, one at a time, beating well after each addition.

With the motor running, beat in the sour cream, heavy cream, vanilla and lemon juice.

When well-blended, using a ladle, spoon an equal portion of the batter into each of the prepared muffin cups.

Place about 1-inch of cold water into 2 baking pans large enough to hold a filled muffin tin. Carefully place the baking pans on each rack of the preheated oven. Then, carefully place a filled muffin tin into each pan. The water should come about three-quarters of the way up the sides of the muffin cups, but not spill over the top of the tins.

Bake for about 45 minutes or until the edge of each little cake is slightly colored, but the center is not quite set. Turn off the oven heat, prop the oven door open, and let the cakes finish baking and then cooling in the oven. This should take about an hour.

Remove from the oven, cover with plastic film, and refrigerate for at least 8 hours or up to 24 hours before unmolding and serving.

Brooklyn Egg Cream

You have to have grown up in New York City several decades ago to know what an egg cream is. Arguably, an egg cream from a particular corner candy store in Queens or Staten Island or the other two boroughs (as New York counties are called) was every bit as good or even better than those remembered by writers and readers of a certain age who grew up in Brooklyn. You had to have been there, and you can't go there now.

Given its name, you might think that an egg cream is something composed of eggs and cream, but it has nary a drop of either in it. An egg cream is a simple drink that is a perfect mixture of chocolate syrup, milk, and seltzer (preferably from a soda fountain or an old-fashioned pressurized seltzer bottle). When properly made, the pressure from the jet of seltzer should create a foamy topping. To be truly authentic, the chocolate syrup should be Fox's U-Bet Chocolate Syrup, which is now available nationwide.

Since this old-time candy shop and drugstore soda fountain favorite is now more elusive than a longtime out-of-print book, even New Yorkers have to be prepared to soda jerk at home to treat literate friends to egg creams. Combine the chocolate syrup and milk mixture ahead of time. When ready to serve, pour an equal amount of the chocolate mixture into each glass and have your guests give the seltzer squirt.

FOR EACH EGG CREAM:
Place about a ¼ inch of chocolate syrup in the bottom of a tall soda glass. Add about ½ cup of whole milk and stir to just combine. Then, squirt seltzer into the mixture to fizz and create a topping. Sip through a straw.

Hot Mulled Apple Cider

Serves a crowd

Mulled cider is a late autumn and wintertime favorite throughout the northeast and mid-Atlantic. It is a wonderful warm, relaxing drink to enjoy through an evening of sharing your thoughts. It can be made in even larger batches and stored, refrigerated. Just reheat as needed. For a bracing indulgence, some people add a bit of rum for extra warmth.

4 quarts apple cider
½ cup dark brown sugar
1 orange, organic and
*   well-scrubbed*
1 teaspoon whole cloves
3 cinnamon sticks
½ teaspoon black
*   peppercorns*

Place the cider in a large nonreactive saucepan. Stir in the brown sugar.

Stud the orange with the whole cloves and add it to the cider.

Combine the cinnamon sticks and peppercorns in a cheesecloth bag, tying to close securely. Add the bag to the cider.

Place the cider over high heat and bring to a boil. Immediately lower the heat and simmer for 15 minutes.

Remove from the heat and allow to sit for about 15 minutes to allow the spices to infuse into the cider.

Pour into warm mugs and serve. If desired, add a tablespoon or so of brandy into each mug just before serving.

Chapter 3

Southland Delights

I CAN THINK OF NO OTHER AREA OF THE COUNTRY that has produced as many delicious dishes or as many soulful writers as the South. The diversity of Southern cooking is as rich as the stories that Southern authors have given us. Hot and spicy, sharp and bitter, warm and comforting, sweet and sugary, smoky and savory— these describe the foods as well as the literature born in the American South.

The South is known for its soulful, long simmering stews and crispy chicken, as well as for its seafood, which includes Chesapeake crabs, river catfish and outsized Gulf shrimp.

✦ ✦ ✦

Reads, Drinks & Nibbles

Mint Julep

Most of us associate the Mint Julep with the Kentucky Derby, but one version or other is served all through the South. Some versions leave the mint whole, others add a piece of fruit, some add rum, and some decorate with a maraschino cherry or a sprig of mint, while the real heretics make their julep with brandy or rye whiskey in place of that smooth Kentucky bourbon.

> "Bourbon does for me what a piece of cake did for Proust."
>
> —WALKER PERCY

FOR EACH JULEP:
½ teaspoon super-fine sugar
About 8 leaves fresh mint
3 ounces fine quality Kentucky bourbon
Splash seltzer water
Cracked ice
1 tablespoon Southern Comfort

Place the sugar in a tall glass. Add the mint leaves and, using a muddler (see Note) or a wood spoon, mash the leaves into the sugar. Add a splash of seltzer, followed by the bourbon. Fill the glass with cracked ice and work an iced tea spoon up and down the edge of the glass to create a nice frosty look. Spoon the Southern Comfort on top and serve.

NOTE: A muddler, a bartender's implement, is a long rod with a flat end that is used to mash or "muddle" a mix—most often an herb and sugar—in the bottom of a glass, prior to filling it.

Mini Crab Cakes with Sour Cream-Mustard Sauce

Makes about 3 dozen

It seems as though every Maryland cook has his or her own method of making crab cakes. Some add breadcrumbs to the mix, some use mayonnaise as the binding agent, some put minced bell peppers, scallions, or onions, some use Old Bay seasoning, and so it goes. I prefer a simple mix that lets the sweetness of the crab remain. These would be perfect to serve after reading Anne Tyler or another Eastern Shore writer.

3 pounds lump crabmeat, picked clean of
*   all cartilage and shell*
2 large egg whites
3 tablespoons Dijon mustard
2 tablespoons minced flat leaf parsley
Salt and cayenne pepper to taste
2 cups unseasoned dry breadcrumbs
Butter or canola oil for frying

Place the crabmeat in a large mixing bowl.

Combine the egg whites, mustard, and parsley, whisking with a fork to combine. Add the egg white mixture to the crab along with salt and cayenne pepper to taste. Toss to blend, but do not smash the crab. You want to have whole lumps remaining.

Place the breadcrumbs on a large plate.

Use your hands to form the crab mixture into little cakes about 1 inch in diameter.

When all of the cakes have been formed, roll them in the breadcrumbs to coat lightly.

Heat enough butter or oil to cover the bottom of a large frying pan by about ⅛ inch over medium heat. When hot, but not smoking, add the crab cakes without crowding the pan. Fry, turn cake after about 2 minutes, and cook 2 minutes more until cakes are heated through and golden brown.

Place on a double layer of paper towels to drain. The crab cakes can be made in advance and reheated in a microwave or in a low oven.

Sour Cream-Mustard Sauce

1 cup sour cream
¼ cup Dijon mustard
2 tablespoons minced capers
1 tablespoon prepared white horseradish,
*   well-drained*
Hot sauce to taste

Combine the sour cream, mustard, capers and horseradish in a small bowl. Stir in hot sauce to taste. Use immediately or cover and refrigerate for up to 3 days.

Pickled Shrimp

Serves 8 to 10

Although pickled shrimp are terrific as hors d'oeuvres, they can also be used in a salad or as the base for a sandwich filling. A bit spicy and a lot citrusy, they are uniquely Southern. They're a perfect accompaniment for one of the great writers of the Southern Coast.

2 bay leaves
1 dried red chili pepper
1 orange, quartered
2 pounds medium shrimp, peeled and deveined
1 large red onion, peeled and finely diced
1 clove garlic, peeled and minced
1 jalapeño chili pepper, seeded and minced
  (or to taste)
1 tablespoon minced shallots
1 cup fresh orange juice
1 cup fresh lime juice
1 tablespoon extra virgin olive oil
Salt to taste

Place the bay leaves, dried chili and orange in a large pot of cold water over high heat. Bring to a boil and immediately add the shrimp. Return to the boil and cook for about 2 minutes or just until opaque.

Remove from the heat and drain well. Refresh shrimp under cold, running water. Pat dry.

Combine the shrimp with the red onion, garlic, jalapeño, and shallots in a nonreactive container or bowl. Add the orange and lime juices along with the olive oil. Season with salt to taste.

Cover and refrigerate for at least 1 hour or up to 8 hours before serving.

Shrimp *Rémoulade*

Serves 6 to 8

This is a shrimp appetizer that is made using a simple version of a classic French *rémoulade* sauce. The sauce is quite similar to tartar sauce and, like tartar sauce, is often used as a condiment for seafood. It can be seasoned with capers, anchovies, curry, horseradish or, in fact, almost anything you like. It can be made a day or so in advance of use

and then tossed with the shrimp about a couple of hours before serving. In New Orleans, *rémoulade* is the condiment of choice for oyster Po' Boys, the local fried-oyster sandwich favorite.

2 pounds cooked, cleaned large shrimp
Rémoulade *Sauce (recipe follows)*
Chopped lettuce, optional
2 tablespoons chopped fresh parsley or chives,
  optional

Place the shrimp in a medium mixing bowl. Add the sauce, tossing to coat.

If desired, line a platter with chopped lettuce. Mound the shrimp on top of the lettuce. Garnish with chopped parsley or chives and serve.

Rémoulade Sauce

2 large eggs, hard boiled, peeled and chopped
1½ cups fine quality mayonnaise
2 tablespoons minced fresh parsley
1 tablespoon minced garlic
1 tablespoon commercial white horseradish,
  well-drained
1 tablespoon white wine vinegar
2 teaspoons dry mustard powder
½ teaspoon paprika
Dash hot sauce
Salt and pepper to taste

Combine all of the ingredients in a food processor fitted with the metal blade. Process until smooth and creamy.

Scrape the mixture into a nonreactive container, cover and refrigerate until ready to use.

Carolina Pilau

Serves 10 to 12

Although called Carolina pilau, this savory rice and shrimp dish is commonly served not only in the Carolinas, but also throughout Georgia and along the mid and northern Florida coast. As pilau travels more inland, the shrimp is often replaced with chicken. And interestingly, perhaps the most famous of all simple pilaus is served at Mrs. Wilkes Boarding House in Savannah, Georgia. Since it can be made in advance and reheated just before serving, pilau also works for a potluck dinner in someone else's home.

½ pound slab bacon, cut into cubes
4 cups chopped sweet onions
4 cups uncooked long grain white rice
2 pounds tomatoes, peeled, cored, and chopped
4 cups low sodium, fat-free chicken broth
2 cups bottled clam broth
1 tablespoon Worcestershire sauce
3 bay leaves
Ground nutmeg to taste, but no more than
*   ¾ teaspoon*
Cayenne pepper to taste
Salt and pepper to taste
3 pounds large shrimp, peeled and deveined
2 tablespoons chopped flat leaf parsley

Place the bacon in a large deep pot over medium-low heat. Fry, stirring frequently, for about 10 minutes or until the bacon is crisp and brown. Using a slotted spoon, lift the bacon from the fat and place on a double layer of paper towel to drain.

Pour off all but about 3 tablespoons of the bacon fat. Return the pan to medium heat and add the onion. Cook, stirring frequently, for about 7 minutes or until the onions are quite soft, but not colored.

Stir in the rice and cook for about 3 minutes or until the rice is glistening. Stir in the tomatoes and, when blended, add the broths and Worcestershire sauce. Add the bay leaves and season with nutmeg, cayenne, and salt and pepper to taste. Bring to a gentle simmer. Cover and continue to cook at a bare simmer for about 30 minutes or until the rice is just cooked.

Add the shrimp along with the reserved bacon cubes, tossing to combine. Cover and continue to cook for about 15 minutes or until the shrimp is cooked and the moisture has been absorbed.

Fluff the rice and transfer the pilau to a serving bowl or platter. Garnish with parsley and serve.

The Original Hot Brown with Hot Cheese Sauce

Serves 8

The Original Hot Brown is the signature dish at Louisville, Kentucky's Brown Hotel. Created in the late 1920s, the Hot Brown was a favorite of late-night revelers enjoying a dance or two in the hotel ballroom. A classic open-face sandwich that I've turned into an almost-casserole, it can be put together early in the day and baked just before serving.

8 slices white toast, trimmed of crusts and
    cut into triangles
1 pound sliced turkey breast
Hot Cheese Sauce (recipe follows)
8 slices beefsteak tomato
8 slices cooked thickly sliced smoky bacon or ham
4 ounces grated Parmesan cheese
2 tablespoons chopped parsley, optional

Place the toast triangles in a single layer in a lightly greased 11-inch by 7-inch baking pan.

Arrange the turkey slices over the toast and cover with the cheese sauce. Then, layer with the tomatoes and bacon or ham. Sprinkle the top with Parmesan cheese.

When ready to serve, preheat the oven to 400°F.

Place the pan in the preheated oven and bake for about 15 minutes or until bubbly and lightly browned on top.

Remove from the oven and, if desired, sprinkle with parsley.

Cut into equal portions and serve hot.

Hot Cheese Sauce

2 tablespoons unsalted butter
¼ cup all-purpose flour
2 cups whole milk
¼ cup grated Parmesan cheese
¼ cup grated Swiss cheese
½ teaspoon Worcestershire sauce
Salt and pepper to taste

Place the butter in a medium saucepan over medium heat. When melted, stir in the flour. When blended, whisk in the milk. Whisking constantly, add the Parmesan and Swiss cheeses along with the Worcestershire sauce.

Cook, whisking constantly, for about 7 minutes or until the sauce has thickened and the flavors have blended. Season with salt and pepper to taste.

Remove from the heat and use as directed in the recipe. The sauce can also be made in advance and stored covered and refrigerated, for up to 3 days. Reheat before using.

Red Beans and Rice

Serves 8

Although few Creole cooks still do their wash only on Mondays, red beans and rice, a stew-like dish traditionally made on wash day using the leftover meat and bones from Sunday's dinner, is an embodiment of Creole cooking, embraced by chefs such as Emeril Lagasse. Red beans and rice is a staple of home cooking in Louisiana. It can be made with the addition of any type of meat, although Tasso ham and *andouille* sausage are most frequently used for their distinct seasonings.

1 pound dried red beans
1 pound Tasso ham, andouille *or other
    smoky sausage or smoked ham or smoked
    turkey wings or any type of smoky meat,
    optional*
3 tablespoons canola oil
1½ cups chopped onions
1 cup chopped green bell peppers
1 cup chopped celery
2 tablespoons minced garlic
1 cup chopped tomatoes
¼ cup white vinegar plus more
    for passing
3 bay leaves
1 teaspoon dried oregano
1 teaspoon paprika
½ teaspoon dried thyme
½ teaspoon cayenne pepper
½ teaspoon ground cumin
1 tablespoon hot sauce or to taste plus more
    for passing
Crushed red pepper flakes to taste
Salt and pepper to taste
1½ cups long grain rice
chopped parsley for garnish, optional

Rinse the beans under cold running water. Place in a large saucepan with cold water to cover by at least 2 inches. Set aside to soak for at least 8 hours or overnight.

Drain the beans well. Again cover with cold water to cover by 2 inches. Place over high heat and bring to a boil. Lower the heat and simmer, adding water as necessary to keep the beans well-hydrated, for about 90 minutes or until just tender. The beans should have a nice amount of "gravy." (If you wish to add meat to the dish, cook the beans for about 30 minutes and then add whatever meat you choose and continue to cook for another hour or until the beans are cooked and the meat has seasoned them nicely.)

Remove from the heat and set aside.

Heat the oil in a large heavy frying pan over medium heat. Add the onions, bell pepper, celery, and garlic, and fry, stirring frequently, for about 5 minutes or until the vegetables begin to soften. Stir in the tomatoes, vinegar, bay leaves, oregano, paprika, thyme, cayenne, and cumin. Bring to a simmer, lower the heat, and cook for about 15 minutes or until the vegetables are very tender and the flavors have blended. Scrape the mixture into the beans, stirring to blend.

Place the beans over medium heat. Add the hot sauce and red pepper flakes; then season with salt and pepper to taste. Bring to a simmer and simmer for 15 minutes.

While the beans are cooking, prepare the rice according to the package directions or to your taste.

Place the cooked rice in a large deep serving bowl. Spoon the beans over the top and sprinkle chopped parsley over all.

Serve with white vinegar and hot sauce passed on the side.

Okra and Tomatoes

Serves 8 to 10

Many people think that they don't like okra, but I can guarantee that, when mixed with tomatoes in this classic Low Country dish, you will be serving seconds. It is the perfect accompaniment to pork, poultry or shrimp and can be served room temperature, so it is a wonderful "take along" dish.

½ pound slab bacon, cut into cubes
1 cup diced onion
1 teaspoon minced garlic
1½ pounds fresh okra, well-washed, trimmed, and
    cut into bite-sized pieces
One 28-ounce can diced tomatoes with their juice
Cayenne pepper and salt to taste

Place the bacon in a large skillet over medium heat. Fry, tossing and turning for about 12 minutes or until the bacon cubes are very crisp. Using a slotted spoon, transfer the bacon to drain on a double layer of paper towels.

Lower the heat and add the onion and garlic to the bacon grease in the pan. Cook, stirring occasionally, for about 5 minutes or until softened.

Add the okra and cook, stirring occasionally, for about 4 minutes or until the okra just begins to shine with the grease. Stir in the tomatoes and season with cayenne and salt to taste. Raise the heat to medium and cook, stirring occasionally, for about 12 minutes or until the flavors have melded and the okra is tender, but not mushy.

Remove from the heat and serve hot or at room temperature.

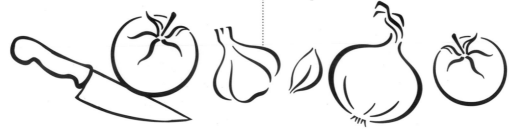

Spoon Bread

Serves 6 to 8

Spoon Bread is rather like a creamy pudding and requires a spoon to dish it up. It is a fancy, Sunday-go-to-meeting version of cornbread. It is sweetly delicious and is the perfect accompaniment for ribs or chicken. It would go well with the Crispy Fried Chicken (recipe page 14). Since Spoon Bread is at its best piping hot from the oven, you can prepare it in advance and bake just before serving.

3 large eggs, at room temperature
3 cups milk
1¼ cups yellow cornmeal
1¾ teaspoons baking powder
Salt and pepper to taste
¼ cup plus 2 tablespoons melted butter

Preheat the oven to 400°F.

Place the eggs in the bowl of a standing electric mixer fitted with the paddle. Beat on high until light and frothy.

Place the milk in a large saucepan over medium heat. Bring to a boil. Immediately begin slowly adding the cornmeal, whisking as you add. The mixture should thicken very quickly. As soon as it does, immediately remove it from the heat and, with the motor running, begin adding the cornmeal to the beaten eggs in small batches. When all of the cornmeal has been added to the eggs, beat in the baking powder along with salt and pepper to taste.

Add ¼ cup of the melted butter and beat, on medium, for 10 minutes, occasionally scraping down the sides of the bowl. The mixture should be very thick and creamy.

Place the remaining melted butter in a large cast iron skillet in the preheated oven. As soon as it is hot, scrape the cornmeal mixture into it. (Spoon Bread may be made up to this point, and then baked before serving. If holding for more than a couple of hours, refrigerate and then bring to room temperature before baking.)

Return to the hot oven and bake for about 25 minutes or until the top is golden and the sides have begun to pull slightly away from the edge.

Serve warm with melted butter drizzled over the top.

Macaroni Salad

Serves 8 to 10

There is no soul food get-together, from funeral gatherings to picnics, without some version of macaroni salad on the table. A book group featuring one of our great soulful African–American writers of the South or North cannot go wrong placing a great big bowl of macaroni salad in the center of the buffet or picnic table.

Macaroni salad has pride of place on the dining tables of many white Southerners, too. When planning to feed a crowd, you cannot ignore the possibilities of macaroni salad. You can add chopped red or yellow peppers or sprinkle with shrimp. You may embellish it in any way that pleases—this is a basic recipe that welcomes your touch.

1 pound elbow macaroni, cooked and drained
*   according to package directions*
1 cup diced green bell pepper
1 cup diced celery
1 cup diced sweet onion
½ cup sweet pickle relish
1¼ cups mayonnaise
Salt and pepper to taste

Place the cooked macaroni in a large mixing bowl. Add the bell pepper, celery, sweet onion, and relish, tossing to combine.

Stir in the mayonnaise and season with salt and pepper to taste.

Cover and refrigerate for at least 1 hour before serving.

Benne Wafers

Makes about 6 dozen

These savory wafers are baked throughout the South but are best known in the Carolinas. Sesame seeds are known as "benne" throughout West Africa, so it's reasonable to believe that the recipe and know-how for these crackers journeyed to America with African women, and were passed on here from mothers to daughters in slave households and eventually in free ones, black and white. Today, the wafers are usually served with cocktails.

2 cups all-purpose flour
1 tablespoon sugar
1 ½ teaspoons baking powder
¾ teaspoons baking soda
½ teaspoon salt
¼ teaspoon cayenne pepper or to taste
½ cup chilled vegetable shortening
¼ cup unsalted butter, chilled
⅔ cup toasted sesame seeds
1 large egg, at room temperature
½ cup milk

Preheat the oven to 350°F.

Sift the flour, sugar, baking powder, baking soda, salt, and cayenne together into a mixing bowl. Add the shortening and butter and, using a pastry cutter or fork, cut the fat into the dry ingredients until well-blended. Stir in the sesame seeds.

Combine the egg and milk, whisking to blend. Slowly add the liquid to the dry mixture, stirring to blend.

When well-blended, using your hands, form the dough into a flat disk.

Lightly flour a clean, flat work surface and place the dough in the center. Using a rolling pin, roll the dough out to a circle about ½-inch thick.

Using a 2-inch biscuit cutter, cut the dough into circles. Transfer the dough to ungreased nonstick baking sheets, leaving about 1-inch between each one.

When all of the wafers have been cut, place in the preheated oven and bake for about 20 minutes or until golden and crisp. Remove from the oven and allow to cool on the baking sheets.

Store tightly covered for up to 1 week. Serve alone or with cheese or deviled ham.

Deviled Ham

Makes about 1 pound

Deviled ham and pimento cheese have been constants on the Southern table for generations; they're also part of picnics. Although you can buy canned deviled ham, there is nothing quite as tasty as the homemade variety. The dish can be made a couple of days in advance of use.

1 pound smoky cooked ham, chopped
1 rib celery, trimmed and chopped
¼ cup chopped sweet onion
1 tablespoon chopped flat leaf parsley
½ cup mayonnaise
2 tablespoons Dijon or Creole mustard
1 teaspoon Worcestershire sauce
Salt and cayenne pepper to taste

Place the ham, celery, onion, and parsley in the bowl of a food processor fitted with the metal blade. Process, using quick on-and-off turns, until the ham is finely minced.

Scrape the ham into a mixing bowl. Add the mayonnaise, mustard, and Worcestershire sauce along with salt and cayenne pepper to taste. Stir to blend well.

Scrape into a serving bowl, cover, and refrigerate for at least 1 hour before serving on crackers or toast.

Cornbread Chicken

Serves 8

From Maryland through Mississippi, there are about as many ways of cooking up the "holy bird" as there are ways of setting up a bountiful table. (And I'm not counting the tasty tricks of Cajun cooks.)

The method I offer here yields crisp, golden pieces with just a hint of cornbread's sweetness. Because it can be served at room temperature, Cornbread Chicken is great as part of a traveling, theme meal, with each reader contributing a dish based on the book to be hashed and savored.

*5 pounds chicken pieces, well-washed
  and dried*
Seasoned salt and pepper to taste
3 large eggs
4 cups cornbread crumbs

Preheat the oven to 350°F.

Lightly coat a baking pan large enough to hold the chicken with nonstick vegetable spray. Set aside.

Place the chicken in a re-sealable plastic bag. Add the seasoned salt and pepper, seal, and shake to season all of the chicken.

Place the eggs in a small bowl and whisk to blend well.

Place the cornbread crumbs in a large shallow bowl.

Working with one piece at a time, dip the chicken into the eggs and then into the crumbs to cover evenly.

Place the coated chicken pieces in the prepared baking dish as they are coated.

When all of the chicken is coated, place the dish in the preheated

oven. Bake without turning for about 40 minutes or until crispy and cooked through.

Remove from the oven and serve hot or at room temperature.

Brownies

Makes about 18

Who doesn't love brownies? Nowadays, we make them with all kinds of additions, such as chocolate bits, butterscotch bits, coconut, and sometimes a mix of all kinds of things. I prefer

"Mrs. Reilly reached into her boxes and ate a brownie. 'Like one?' she asked the bartender. 'They nice. I got some nice wine cakes, too.' The bartender pretended to be looking for something on his shelves. 'I smell wine cakes,' Darlene cried, looking past Ignatius. 'Have one, honey,' Mrs. Reilly said. 'I think I shall have one, too,' Ignatius said. 'I imagine that they taste rather good with brandy.' Mrs. Reilly spread the box out on the bar. Even the man with the racing form agreed to take a macaroon."

—JOHN KENNEDY TOOLE,
A Confederacy of Dunces

the plain and simple chocolate and walnut combination, myself—as did the crew in *A Confederacy of Dunces*.

1 cup (2 sticks) unsalted butter, at room
   temperature
2 cups sugar
4 large eggs, at room temperature
1 teaspoon pure vanilla extract
1 cup sifted all-purpose flour
½ cup Dutch-processed cocoa powder, sifted
½ teaspoon salt
1 cup walnut or pecan pieces

Preheat the oven to 350°F.

Lightly coat the interior of an 8-inch square baking pan with nonstick vegetable spray. Set aside.

Place the butter in the bowl of a standing electric mixer fitted with the paddle. Beat on low to soften. Add the sugar, raise the speed to medium, and beat for about 4 minutes or until light and fluffy.

Adding one at a time, beat in the eggs followed by the vanilla.

Combine the flour, cocoa and salt, and slowly add the dry mix to the creamed mixture. When thoroughly combined, remove the bowl from the mixer and stir in the nuts.

Scrape the mixture into the prepared pan. Place in the preheated oven and bake for about 25 minutes or until a cake tester inserted into the center comes out clean.

Remove from the oven and place on a wire rack to cool slightly. Using a serrated knife, cut the brownies into squares while still warm. Let cool completely in the pan.

Store, airtight, at room temperature for up to 3 days.

Literary Tea or Sweet Ending

Ambrosia

Serves 12

Is this dessert? Or a sweet salad? Only a true Southerner knows for sure. The classic mix always uses sweetened coconut, but you could also use unsweetened or fresh. The liqueur adds a nice zing, but it is not at all necessary.

10 navel oranges
5 bananas
1 small whole pineapple, peeled, cored, and cubed
1 cup canned sweetened coconut, toasted
1 cup miniature marshmallows, optional
½ cup orange liqueur
Fresh mint leaves for garnish

Using a sharp knife, cut a thin slice off of the top and bottom of each orange. Continuing with the knife, remove the peel, including all of the white pith, from each orange. Working with one orange at a time and holding it over a bowl, carefully cut between the membranes separating the segments, to cut the orange into membrane-free segments. (These are called suprêmes.) Hold the remaining membranes over the bowl, and use your hand to squeeze out any remaining juice.

Peel the bananas and, using a small sharp knife, cut each one, crosswise, into ¼ inch thick slices. Add the slices to the orange segments.

Add the pineapple and coconut along with the marshmallows, if using. Add the liqueur and toss to combine.

Cover and refrigerate for at least 30 minutes or up to 4 hours.

Serve, garnished with fresh mint leaves.

Banana Pudding

Serves 10 to 12

Banana pudding reigns supreme as dessert in a great many Southern kitchens. It is simple to make nowadays with packaged vanilla pudding replacing the rich, homemade variety. I've kept to the old way, making the pudding from scratch. It makes the dessert very special. Just make sure that your bananas are quite ripe for the richest banana flavor.

6 medium bananas
About ½ box vanilla wafer cookies (not low-fat)
Vanilla Pudding (recipe follows)
4 large egg whites
2 tablespoons sugar

Preheat the oven to 350°F.

Lightly butter a 3-quart baking dish or casserole.

Peel and cut the bananas, crosswise, into medium slices.

Place a single layer of bananas on the bottom of the prepared baking dish.

Cover the bananas with half of the vanilla wafers. Then, cover the wafers with half of the pudding. Continue with another layer of bananas, wafers, and pudding.

Cover the top with aluminum foil and place the dish in the preheated oven. Bake for 20 minutes.

While the pudding is baking, combine the egg whites with the sugar in the bowl of a standing electric mixer fitted with the whisk. Beat on low until frothy. Raise the speed to high and beat until firm, but not dry peaks form.

Remove the pudding from the oven and raise the temperature to 400°F.

Uncover the pudding and using a spatula carefully mound the beaten egg whites over the top, making sure that the meringue comes to the edge of the dish.

Return the pudding to the oven and bake for an additional 7 minutes or until the meringue has colored nicely.

Remove from the oven and serve hot or at room temperature.

Vanilla Pudding

1 ¼ cups sugar
¼ cup cornstarch
3 cups whole milk
2 teaspoons pure vanilla extract
½ cup unsalted butter, at room temperature
4 large egg yolks, at room temperature

Combine the sugar and cornstarch in the top half of a double boiler. Whisk in the milk and vanilla and place over simmering water. Cook, stirring constantly, for about 10 minutes or until mixture begins to thicken. Beat in the butter and continue cooking until the butter is incorporated into the mixture.

While the pudding base is cooking, place the egg yolks in a small mixing bowl. Using a whisk, beat until frothy. Slowly whisk in about ¾ cup of the hot milk mixture to temper the egg yolks. Then, beat the egg mixture into the hot milk mixture in the double boiler. Cook, stirring constantly, for about 7 minutes or until the pudding has thickened and pools on the back of a spoon.

Remove from the heat and scrape into a clean bowl. Cover with plastic film and let cool before using.

True Southern Candies

These are three classic tea sweets. Serve with either hot or iced tea (sweet, of course, for the favored drink of the South).

Bourbon Balls

Makes about 6 dozen

2 ½ cups crushed vanilla wafer cookies
1 cup confectioners' sugar plus more
    for rolling
1 cup finely chopped walnuts
2 tablespoons Dutch-processed cocoa
    powder
⅓ cup bourbon (or rum)
3 tablespoons light corn syrup

Combine the crushed cookies with 1 cup of the confectioners' sugar, walnuts, and cocoa powder in a mixing bowl. Add the bourbon and corn syrup and, using your hands, knead the mixture together.

Place the confectioners' sugar for rolling on a plate.

Again, using your hands, form the mixture into 1-inch balls. Roll each ball in confectioners' sugar to coat well.

Place the coated sweets on a large platter and cover lightly. Refrigerate for 3 hours. Then store airtight for 24 hours before serving. They will keep, airtight, for up to 3 weeks.

Jumbles

Makes about 32

1 cup tightly packed light brown sugar
½ cup granulated sugar
¼ cup light corn syrup
½ cup evaporated milk
2 tablespoons unsalted butter, at room
    temperature
1 ¼ cups chopped nuts (any kind you like)
½ cup flaked coconut
1 ½ teaspoons pure vanilla extract or almond
    extract

Line a large baking sheet with waxed paper. Set aside.

Combine the sugars, corn syrup, and evaporated milk in a medium heavy saucepan over medium heat. Cook, stirring constantly with a wooden spoon, for about 20 minutes or until the mixture reaches 240°F (the soft ball stage) on a candy thermometer.

Remove from the heat and, using a wooden spoon, beat the butter into the mixture. When blended, beat in the nuts, coconut, and extract.

Working quickly, drop the mixture by the teaspoonful onto the prepared baking sheet. Set aside to cool for 2 hours.

Store airtight for up to 10 days.

Marvels

Makes about 6 dozen

4 cups all-purpose flour
1 ¾ cups sugar
4 teaspoons baking powder
1 teaspoon freshly grated orange zest
1 teaspoon ground cinnamon
¼ teaspoon ground nutmeg
¼ teaspoon salt
1 cup unsalted butter, at room temperature
Approximately 1 cup milk
One 10-ounce package currants

Combine the flour, sugar, baking powder, orange zest, cinnamon, nutmeg, and salt in a mixing bowl.

Using a pastry cutter or fork, cut the butter into the dry ingredients until well-blended.

Add the milk, a bit at a time, stirring until a firm dough is formed. Take care that you don't add too much milk or the dough will be sticky and unusable.

Using your hands, knead in the currants.

Lightly dust a clean, flat work surface with flour.

Place the dough in the center of the floured surface and, using a rolling pin, roll the dough out to about ¼-inch thickness.

Using a 2-inch round biscuit cutter, cut the dough into 2-inch circles.

Heat a nonstick griddle over medium-low heat. Add the cookies, a few at a time, and cook for about 4 minutes, turning once. The cookies should be light brown around the edges.

Transfer to wire racks to cool before serving.

May be stored airtight for up to one week.

Pralines

Makes about 2 dozen

Pray-leen or praw-leen: Whichever way you pronounce it, you are biting into a candy so rich and fudgy that it makes your teeth scream. Native to New Orleans (where it is pronounced praw-leen), praline candies are different than the classic French praline, which is a clear, brittle-like candy that is generally chopped or crushed for use in desserts.

2 cups granulated sugar
½ packed cup light brown sugar
1 cup half-and-half
1 teaspoon baking soda
Pinch salt
¼ cup unsalted butter, cut into pieces, at room temperature
2½ cups toasted pecan halves
1 teaspoon pure vanilla extract

> "I did get to interview a white woman and her [African-American] maid who were together in the 1960s . . . The white woman's strongest memory of her maid was of the delicious pralines she made. When I went to speak to the maid, she [remembered] working for this woman when [civil rights activist] Medgar Evers had just been assassinated. Her children were walking down the street in a protest and she was so afraid her employer would turn on the TV and see them and then she would lose her job."
> —KATHRYN STOCKETT, The Help

Line a baking sheet with parchment paper. Set aside.

Combine the granulated and light brown sugars with the half-and-half, baking soda, and salt in a heavy-bottomed saucepan over low heat. Cook, stirring constantly with a wooden spoon, for about 5 minutes or until the sugars have dissolved completely.

Add the butter, a bit at a time, stirring until melted into the sugar mixture.

Raise the heat to medium and cook, without stirring, for about 20 minutes or until the mixture reaches 236°F on a candy thermometer. Immediately remove from the heat and, beating constantly with the wooden spoon, stir in the nuts and vanilla. Continue beating for about 2 to 3 minutes, or until the mixture is almost opaque.

Drop by the tablespoonful onto the prepared baking sheet. You want to have fairly round patties about 2-inches in diameter.

Set aside to cool completely.

Store in layers, airtight, at room temperature.

Chapter 4

Westward Reading and Vittles

*T*HE PACIFIC, WESTERN PLAINS, ROCKY MOUNTAIN AND SOUTHWESTERN STATES cover such a vast area of the United States that no blanket statement about its cuisine could cover it—a boon to its residents and bookish visitors alike. The sea bounty of the Pacific is the gain of the West and beyond. Asian influence infuses the foods of Hawaii and California alike. Alaskans both savor summer seafood and send tons of the catch south. Long ago, indigenous fishermen of the Northwest made salmon a favorite, as Lewis and Clark, sent west by Thomas Jefferson, surely noticed.

Tuna—cooked or raw—is treasured even where every step kicks up dust. Wherever trout can be caught and eaten, it is. Buffalo no longer roam, but there's a season for hunting mountain elk; cattle are still driven, and sheep are raised in Nevada. Corn flourishes in southernmost New Mexico and on the mesas of Colorado. Mexican flavors fan beyond the border states of California, New Mexico, Arizona and Texas. Beans and more beans are enjoyed by Latinos, cowboys and everyone at backyard barbecues, from the borderlands through Oklahoma to Wyoming and Montana.

California is the vegetable and fruit basket—not to mention wine-maker—for much of America for most of the year, although Hawaii needs no fruit imports, and the same might be said of Oregon or Colorado in August. In fact, nearly every state in the union produces some wine, and some offer distinguished cheese.

Chances are that some of whatever you think of as honest grub reflects the American West, which should comfort the cook tasked with matching fare to a work

of the eastern visitor to the West, such as Jack Kerouac or John Steinbeck, or of such true Western writers (at least some of the time) as Jack London, Joan Didion, Larry McMurtry, Marilynne Robinson, Barbara Kingsolver and Rex Pickett. Matt Groening, who introduced the world to "The Simpsons," is only one of many influential contemporary Western artists who have created enthralling worlds. Tony Hillerman's

Navajo police tales and Cormac McCarthy's large-scale Western novels bring their respective territories alive. The list could go on and on, and so could the menu.

The recipes that I offer here are just hints of the deliciousness available out west. As you read an author whose work reflects a piece of the great American West, wild or tame, I would, at the same time, urge you to investigate the culinary history of the territory on the page. Go West, dear reader, and you will find such an array of interesting flavors, textures, and ingredients that you'll not regret the trip.

✦ ✦ ✦

READS, DRINKS & NIBBLES
■ ■ ■
Southwest Margarita
California Wine and Cheese Party

STAR DISHES & DELICIOUS ASIDES
■ ■ ■
Santa Fe Hot Supper
Tuna and Walla Walla Onion Sandwiches with Spicy Yogurt Sauce
Roast Salmon and New Idaho Potatoes

FOR A MOVEABLE FEAST
■ ■ ■
Texas Caviar

LITERARY TEA OR SWEET ENDING
■ ■ ■
Meyer Lemon Tart
Texas Sheet Cake

Reads, Drinks & Nibbles

Southwest Margarita

Serves 12

Margaritas reflect the warmth and relaxation of America's Southwest; easy to drink, refreshing, and yet conveying lots of energy. They can help make any conversation flow.

3 small cans frozen limeade
½ cup fresh lime juice
2 bottles light beer
2 cups tequila
Coarse salt, optional
12 lime wedges

Working with one can at a time, place the frozen limeade in a blender jar. Fill the jar with ice and process until almost smooth. Pour the mix into a large pitcher.

When the 3 cans of limeade have been processed, add the lime juice, beer and tequila, stirring to blend.

If desired, when ready to serve, wet the rims of each of 12 margarita glasses and then dip the rims into coarse salt to lightly coat.

Pour the margaritas into the salted glasses and serve with a wedge of lime, if desired.

CALIFORNIA WINE and CHEESE PARTY

◆ ◆ ◆

In a short number of years, California wines and cheeses have surpassed their classic French counterparts. If you and your friends are delving into the work of a contemporary California writer, I can't think of anything more appealing than a wine and cheese party featuring California goods.

You might also match this simple idea to a sophisticated novel rooted up the coast. There are also some award-winning wines from Washington and Oregon, and great cheeses, as well.

I will suggest some cheeses and wines, but both local and Internet specialty food stores will offer their own favorites. You can contact the California Artisan Cheese Guild or individual cheese makers. In California, Cowgirl

> "Pinot Noir country. My grape. The one varietal that truly enchants me, both stills and steals my heart with its elusive loveliness and false promises of transcendence." —REX PICKETT, Sideways

Creamery, Cypress Grove, Point Reyes and Laura Chenel are among my favorites—and I invariably enjoy a glass of pinot noir along with any of the cheeses I might choose. You'll also find several artisanal cheese-crafters in Washington, Oregon and Idaho.

A good cheese tray should feature at least 4 cheeses: A soft, fermented cheese, a fresh goat cheese, a veined cheese, and one hard or firm cheese. They should all be stored, lightly wrapped and refrigerated until about an hour or so before they're served. Room temperature is the ideal for cheese, so you'll want to shield them from a hot sun. They should be arranged on an attractive wooden board or platter with little tags naming them and individual knives to cut them. You can even purchase paper grape leaves to line a cheese board. If you have more than 10 people, you should prepare two boards.

The accompaniments can be commercially-produced crackers made especially for cheese, crisp toasts, thinly sliced country bread, an artisanal raisin-nut bread, or thinly sliced whole grain bread. Also try an assortment of fresh fruit such as apples, pears, grapes or figs, or dried fruits along with nuts, either in or out of their shells—depending on how much mess you can put up with! Many specialty food stores now feature jellies or fig cakes that have been created specifically to accompany cheeses. Whatever you choose, the fruits and nuts should also be attractively arranged.

Although red wine is the traditional wine served with a cheese course, this rule comes from classic dining and can easily be broken. Sweet wines and some white wines do just fine. These days, your taste—or inspiration from the book of the hour—can be the deciding factor.

Santa Fe Hot Supper

Serves 8

This is a great make-ahead casserole that can be baked while you are deep into a novel set in the Southwest. The flavors will immediately put you in the place. It is quite rich, so all you would need to make a wonderful meal would be a nice crisp salad and a basket of warm tortillas.

4 cups cooked white rice
3 cups cooked, drained pinto or other red beans
1 cup sour cream
¼ cup diced red bell pepper
¼ cup diced green bell pepper
¼ cup diced pickled jalapeño chilies
1 tablespoon pure chili powder
1 teaspoon ground cumin
¼ teaspoon dried oregano
Hot sauce to taste
Salt and pepper to taste
3 large eggs
2 cups milk
1 cup well-drained canned, sliced green chilies
1½ cups shredded Monterey jack cheese
½ cup shredded sharp cheddar cheese

Preheat the oven to 350ºF.

Generously coat the interior of a 3-quart casserole with nonstick vegetable spray. Set aside.

Combine the eggs and milk and, using a whisk, beat to blend well. Set aside.

Place the rice and beans in a large mixing bowl. Add the sour cream, red and green bell peppers, pickled jalapeños, chili powder, cumin, oregano, hot sauce and salt and pepper to taste, stirring to combine well.

Pour about one-third of the rice and bean mixture into the prepared casserole. Sprinkle with half of the sliced green chilies and then cover with a layer of half of the Monterey jack cheese. Pour 1 cup of the egg mixture over the top. Repeat with another layer of rice and beans, chilies, the rest of the Monterey jack cheese, and another cup of the egg mixture. Cover with a final layer of the rice and bean mixture and then pour the final cup of the egg mixture over the top. Let rest for about 10 minutes or until the egg mixture has completely soaked into the casserole. (The casserole can be made up to a day in advance and stored, covered and refrigerated. Since it will be chilled through, it will take slightly longer to bake.)

Place in the preheated oven and bake for about 35 minutes or until bubbly. About 5 minutes before the casserole is ready, sprinkle the cheddar cheese on top and bake to just melt.

Remove from the oven and serve hot.

> " Cooking is 80 percent confidence, a skill best acquired starting from when the apron strings wrap around you twice."
> —BARBARA KINGSOLVER,
> *Animal, Vegetable, Miracle: A Year of Food Life*

Tuna and Walla Walla Onion Sandwiches with Spicy Yogurt Sauce

There is nothing quite like a Walla Walla onion—huge and sweet, with no heat. Grown only in the Walla Walla valley of Washington state, it is the

> **"The shore of the stream that drained Far Lake was packed thick with salmon that had come up from the sea to spawn."**
> —JACK LONDON,
> Before Adam

perfect partner for a rich slice of quickly grilled tuna and a book set in the Northwest. And, since tuna is usually abundant in Pacific waters throughout the summer months, and the grill is easily lit, this is the best summer sandwich imaginable.

FOR EACH SANDWICH:
One ½-inch thick tuna steak
1 tablespoon olive oil
1 tablespoon lite soy sauce
Juice of ½ lime
1 large hard roll, cut in half
1 to 2 tablespoons Spicy Yogurt Sauce
  (recipe follows)
1 thick slice Walla Walla or other sweet onion
½ cup baby arugula leaves, well-washed
  and dried

Preheat and oil the grill.

Rub the tuna with the oil, soy sauce, and lime juice. Place on the preheated grill and grill, turning once, for about 4 minutes or until slightly charred and cooked to medium rare. Remove from the grill.

Slather both cut sides of the roll with the sauce. Place the tuna on top of one of the cut sides. Place a slice of onion on top followed with the arugula. Drizzle a bit of the sauce on the arugula, cover with the remaining half of roll, cut in half, and serve.

Spicy Yogurt Sauce

1 cup plain yogurt
¼ cup chopped arugula
¼ cup minced red onion
1 small green chili, stemmed and seeded,
  or to taste
2 tablespoons chopped cilantro
1 tablespoon chopped fresh mint
1 teaspoon minced garlic
Juice of 1 lime
Salt to taste

Combine the yogurt, arugula, and onion in a small mixing bowl.

Place the chili, cilantro, mint and garlic in the bowl of a food processor fitted with the metal blade. Process until smooth.

Scrape the chili mixture into the yogurt. Add the lime juice and stir to combine. Salt to taste.

Store covered and refrigerated, until ready to use or for up to 3 days.

NOTE: Walla Walla onions are generally available throughout the summer at specialty produce stores or through the Internet.

Roast Salmon and New Potatoes

Serves 8 to 10

In the Northwest, fishing is not only a major industry, but a passionate hobby for many. And we all know about the wonderful potatoes pulled from the rich earth of the state of Idaho. In this recipe, I bring them together for an elegant but casual buffet dish. Fresh salmon is often cooked over an open fire or cured for a winter's repast. Here, a whole salmon can feed a crowd of hungry readers without you having to spend a day on the river.

*2 pounds small new or fingerling potatoes,
    scrubbed*
*One large (about 8 pounds) fresh salmon,
    cleaned, head and tail left on*
1 tablespoon plus 1 teaspoon fresh rosemary
*1 lemon, washed and sliced crosswise, plus
    an additional lemon or two for garnish,
    if desired*
Salt and pepper to taste
¾ pounds slab bacon, cut into a small dice
*2 bunches watercress, washed, dried, and
    trimmed of large stems*

Preheat the oven to 375°F.

Place the potatoes in a large saucepan of cold, salted water over high heat. Bring to a boil. Lower the heat to a simmer and cook for about 10 minutes, or just until beginning to soften. Remove from the heat and drain well.

Rinse the salmon and pat it dry. Sprinkle 1 tablespoon of the rosemary in the cavity and then place the lemon slices on top of the rosemary. Season both the cavity and the exterior of the fish with salt and pepper to taste.

Combine the potatoes and bacon in a shallow roasting pan large enough to hold the salmon. Add the remaining teaspoon of rosemary and season with salt and pepper, noting that the bacon will add saltiness as it cooks. Toss to coat evenly.

Lay the salmon on top of the potatoes. Place in the preheated oven and roast for about 15 minutes, or until the potatoes are cooked through and an instant-read thermometer reads 135°F when inserted into the thickest part of the fish.

Remove the pan from the oven and let the salmon rest for at least 15 minutes before serving.

Lay the watercress over the bottom of a platter large enough to hold the fish. Sprinkle the potatoes and bacon over the watercress and lay the fish down the center of the platter. Garnish with lemon slices, if desired.

Serve slightly warm or at room temperature.

For a Moveable Feast

Texas Caviar

Serves 8 to 10

Texas caviar isn't caviar at all—just humble black-eyed peas all dressed up. It was invented by Helen Corbitt, who made her fame in the kitchens of the deluxe Dallas store, Neiman Marcus. It is said that once she found that Texans didn't much cotton to the real thing, but everyone seemed to love black-eyed peas, she invented this salad to be used as a dip with tortilla chips at cocktail parties. If you find yourself short of time, you can use well-drained canned black-eyed peas in place of the cooked dried ones.

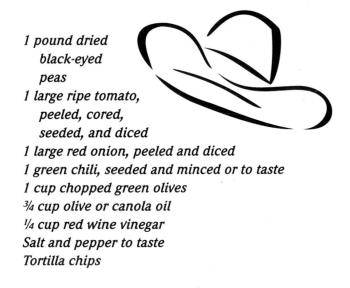

*1 pound dried
    black-eyed
    peas*
*1 large ripe tomato,
    peeled, cored,
    seeded, and diced*
1 large red onion, peeled and diced
1 green chili, seeded and minced or to taste
1 cup chopped green olives
¾ cup olive or canola oil
¼ cup red wine vinegar
Salt and pepper to taste
Tortilla chips

Rinse the black-eyed peas under cold running water. Place in a large saucepan with cold water to cover by at least 2 inches. Set aside to soak for at least 8 hours or overnight.

Drain the peas well. Again cover with cold water to cover by 2 inches. Place over high heat and bring to a boil. Lower the heat and simmer, adding water as necessary to keep the beans well-hydrated, for about 90 minutes or until just tender.

Remove the peas from the stove and drain well. Transfer the drained peas to a mixing bowl. Add the tomato, red onion, chili, and olives while still warm, stirring to combine. Stir in the oil and vinegar and season with salt and pepper to taste.

Cover and let marinate for at least one hour before serving with a basket of tortillas chips for dipping.

Literary Tea or Sweet Ending

Meyer Lemon Tart

Makes one 9-inch pie

Meyer lemons, uncommonly delicious and sweet, are just as commonly found in California backyards. But they have recently been commercialized and are available in many specialty produce markets throughout the country. Very thin-skinned, they make this wonderful tart based on a traditional lemon pie created by nineteenth-century Shaker cooks in the East. This recipe cannot be made with conventional lemons, as they are too thick-skinned and bitter.

3 whole Meyer lemons, preferably organic, cut, crosswise, into paper thin slices and seeded (see note)
2 cups superfine sugar
Flaky Pastry (see page 18)
6 large eggs, beaten

Place the lemon slices in a mixing bowl. Add the sugar, tossing to coat well. Cover and place in the refrigerator for 12 hours.

When ready to bake, prepare the pastry and roll it out as directed on page 18 into two circles about 10-inches in diameter. Fit one circle into a 9-inch pie pan,

leaving the edges hanging over the sides; reserve the remaining circle for the top.

Preheat the oven to 450°F.

Remove the lemons from the refrigerator. Uncover and add the beaten eggs, stirring to just combine. Pour the mixture into the pastry shell, smoothing it out into an even layer.

With a pastry wheel, cut the reserved pastry circle into strips about ¼- to ½-inch wide. Using the longest strips for the center of the pie and working from the center out, begin weaving the strips into a lattice pattern across the top of the pie. Trim off any extreme excess pastry, and then turn the edge of the bottom pastry up and over the strip ends and press firmly together to seal, crimping the edges together.

Place in the preheated oven and bake for 10 minutes. Lower the oven temperature to 350°F and continue to bake for an additional 30 minutes or until golden brown.

Remove from the oven and place on a wire rack to cool before cutting into wedges and serving.

NOTE: An inexpensive Japanese vegetable slicer known as a benriner is an excellent tool to cut the lemons into paper-thin slices.

In the window I smelled all the food of San Francisco. There were seafood places out there where the buns were hot, and the baskets were good enough to eat too; where the menus themselves were soft with foody esculence as those dipped in hot broths and roasted dry and good enough to eat too."

— JACK KEROUAC, On the Road

Texas Sheet Cake

Makes one 15½- by 10½-inch cake

I don't really know why this is called a Texas sheet cake, but some say that it was invented by Lady Bird Johnson, while others say that it got its name 'cause it is as big as Texas. Wherever it came from, the cake is very easy to make, but just know that it is as sweet as a Texas debutante and just as rich.

2 large eggs, at room temperature
½ cup buttermilk
2 teaspoons pure vanilla extract
1 teaspoon baking soda
2 cups sifted all-purpose flour
2 cups sugar
½ cup (1 stick) unsalted butter
½ cup pure vegetable shortening
¼ cup Dutch-processed cocoa powder
1 cup water

FOR THE FROSTING:
½ cup (1 stick) unsalted butter, at
*   room temperature*
¼ cup Dutch-processed cocoa powder
⅓ cup whole milk
One 1 pound box confectioners' sugar, sifted
2 teaspoons pure vanilla extract
2 cups chopped toasted pecans

Preheat the oven to 400°F.

Generously coat the interior of a 15½- by 10½-inch jelly roll pan with nonstick vegetable spray. Set aside.

Combine the eggs, buttermilk, vanilla, and baking soda in a mixing bowl. Using a whisk, beat until very smooth. Set aside.

Sift the flour and sugar together into a large mixing bowl. Set aside.

Combine the butter, shortening, and cocoa powder with the water in a medium heavy-bottomed saucepan over medium heat. Bring to a boil, stirring occasionally. Pour the hot mixture over the flour/sugar mixture and, using a wooden spoon, beat to blend. When blended, add the egg mixture and beat to blend.

Pour the mixture into the prepared pan. Place in the preheated oven and bake for about 20 minutes, or until a cake tester inserted into the center comes out clean.

About 5 minutes before the cake is ready, prepare the frosting.

Combine the butter, cocoa powder, and milk in a medium heavy bottomed saucepan over medium heat. Bring to a boil, stirring constantly. When the mixture comes to a boil, remove it from the heat.

Using a hand-held electric mixer, beat in the confectioners' sugar and vanilla until very light and smooth. Stir in the pecans.

Remove the cake from the oven, place on a wire rack and immediately pour the hot frosting over the cake. If necessary, use a spatula to spread it out to the edges.

Set aside to cool before cutting into squares.

"I must be getting old . . . I find I'm more interested in the food I eat than the girl who serves it."

—JOHN STEINBECK

Chapter 5

Under a Maple Sky—O Canada!

OFTEN, WHEN WE THINK OF CANADA, the immediate image is of snow, the Mounties, and Canada's native peoples rather than its sophisticated cities. Canadian literature is much the same—the early writers focused on subjects of regional and national import, while contemporary writers have brought a much more urbane viewpoint and, with that, have garnered

READS, DRINKS & NIBBLES
■ ■ ■
Deviled Nuts
Bloody Caesar

STAR DISHES & DELICIOUS ASIDES
■ ■ ■
Tourtière
Thai-Flavored Prince Edward Island Mussels

FOR A MOVEABLE FEAST
■ ■ ■
Maple-Walnut Bread with Maple Butter

LITERARY TEA OR SWEET ENDING
■ ■ ■
Sucre à la Crème
Rice Pudding

international recognition. Canadian foods not only represent these two conflicting views, but also bring to the fore the influence of French cuisine and the influx of Asian and Eastern European immigrants of recent years.

✦ ✦ ✦

Bloody Caesar

S aid to be Canada's national drink, a Bloody Caesar is much like a Bloody Mary. However, the original, created by bartender Walter Chell for the opening of an Italian restaurant in Calgary, had chopped clams added to the mix. This certainly makes for conversation, but the readily available Clamato Juice will work just fine.

FOR EACH COCKTAIL:
½ cup Clamato Juice
3 tablespoons citrus-flavored vodka
¼ teaspoon Worcestershire sauce
Dash hot pepper sauce or to taste
Celery salt to taste
1 raw clam, optional
1 small celery stick, preferably with
leaves

Combine the juice, vodka, Worcestershire sauce, hot pepper sauce, and celery salt in a large glass, stirring to blend well.

Fill the glass with ice. Float a raw clam on top and garnish with a celery stick.

Deviled Nuts

Makes 1 pound

T hese are terrific cocktail nibbles: Seasoned with a hint of East Indian spices, they are redolent of Canada's welcome to immigrants.

The recipe can be doubled, tripled, or whatever amount you need to keep a treat on hand when enjoying solitary reading or welcoming a group discussion.

1½ teaspoons salt
¼ teaspoon cayenne pepper
¼ teaspoon ground cumin
¼ teaspoon chili powder
⅛ teaspoon paprika
3 tablespoons unsalted butter
1 tablespoon olive oil
1 pound cashews (or any nut or combination
of nuts you prefer)
Dash Worcestershire sauce

Combine the salt with the cayenne, cumin, chili powder, and paprika in a re-sealable plastic bag. Set aside.

Combine the butter and oil in a large frying pan over medium heat. When the butter has melted, add the cashews and fry, stirring constantly, for about 4 minutes or until the nuts are golden. Stir in the Worcestershire sauce.

Remove from the heat and, using a slotted spoon, transfer the nuts to a double layer of paper towel to drain slightly.

Transfer the nuts to the spice mixture in the plastic bag. Seal and shake to cover the nuts with the spice mix. Allow to cool in the bag.

When cool, transfer to a clean re-sealable plastic bag and store, airtight, at room temperature.

Tourtière

Makes 1 Pie

A tourtière is a traditional Quebecoise meat pie, usually homemade during the Christmas season and store-bought during the rest of the year. French-Canadian in origin, tourtière can be found throughout the provinces. Its name comes from its original main ingredient, the passenger pigeon or "tourte" in French, but today's pies are usually made with pork. It is a hearty dish that would be welcome on a cold winter's night. Although delicious hot from the oven, it can be eaten at room temperature. A tossed green salad, perhaps with some orange segments, would complete the meal.

Flaky Pastry (see page 18)
1½ pounds lean ground pork
2 cups finely chopped cooked chicken or turkey
    meat
½ cup minced Canadian bacon
2 ribs celery, trimmed, well-washed, and chopped
1 medium onion, peeled and chopped
¼ teaspoon ground cloves
¼ teaspoon ground cinnamon
¼ teaspoon dried marjoram
1 large egg
½ cup breadcrumbs
Salt and pepper to taste

Preheat the oven to 500°F.

Prepare the pastry and roll it out as directed on page 18 into two circles about 10-inches in diameter. Fit one circle into a 9-inch pie pan, leaving the edges hanging over the sides and reserve the remaining circle for the top.

Combine the pork, poultry, and bacon in a large mixing bowl. Use your hands to mix in the celery, onion, cloves, cinnamon, and marjoram. When well-blended, add the egg and breadcrumbs and again mix to blend. Season to your taste with salt and pepper.

Scrape the mixture into the pastry-lined pie pan, smoothing down the top with a spatula.

With a pastry wheel, cut the reserved pastry circle into strips about ¼- to ½-inch wide. Using the longest strips for the center of the pie and working from the center out, begin weaving the strips into a lattice pattern across the top of the pie. Trim off any extreme excess pastry and then turn the edge of the bottom pastry up and over the strip ends; press firmly together to seal, crimping the edges together.

Place in the preheated oven and bake for 15 minutes. Lower the temperature to 375°F and continue to bake for an additional 25 minutes or until bubbly and golden brown.

Remove from the oven and allow to rest for 15 minutes before cutting into wedges and serving.

Thai-Flavored Prince Edward Island Mussels

Serves 8

Mussels from Prince Edward Island, a spectacularly beautiful Canadian province, are the perfect host for the slightly sweet-spicy flavors so much a part of southeast Asian cooking. This is a great dish for entertaining as the broth can be made in advance. The broth can be reheated and the mussels can be added while you make sure the table is ready and waiting.

2½ cups unsweetened coconut milk
1 cup dry white wine
½ cup fresh orange juice
⅓ cup fresh lime juice
3 tablespoons minced garlic
2 tablespoons minced fresh ginger
2 tablespoons Thai red curry paste (see Note)
1½ tablespoons Asian fish sauce (see Note)
1 tablespoon light brown sugar
8 pounds fresh Prince Edward Island (or other)
    mussels
1 cup minced fresh cilantro leaves
½ cup minced fresh mint leaves

Combine the coconut milk, wine, orange juice, lime juice, garlic, ginger, curry paste, fish sauce, and sugar in a large stock pot over medium heat. Bring to a simmer and simmer for 5 minutes.

Add the mussels, cover, and raise the heat. Bring to a boil and boil for about 8 minutes or until the mussels have opened.

Uncover and add the cilantro and mint, tossing to blend.

Serve hot with lots of crusty bread for dipping into the broth.

NOTE: Thai red curry paste and Asian fish sauce are both available at Asian markets, specialty food stores and many supermarkets.

For a Moveable Feast

Maple-Walnut Bread
with Maple Butter

Makes one 9-inch loaf

This is a lovely tea bread that can be served at an afternoon book gathering with a nice cup of tea, or it can be thinly sliced, covered with plain or flavored cream cheese, and made into tea sandwiches for a more elaborate tea service. Either way, the maple flavor sings of the Canadian table.

1 large egg, at room temperature
¾ cup milk
2 tablespoons canola oil
2 cups sifted all-purpose flour
½ cup maple sugar
¼ cup granulated sugar
1½ teaspoons baking powder
½ teaspoon baking soda
¼ teaspoon salt
1 cup coarsely chopped cranberries
1 cup chopped walnuts
1 teaspoon grated orange zest
Maple butter, optional (see Note)

Preheat the oven to 350°F.

Lightly coat the interior of a 9-inch loaf pan with nonstick vegetable spray. Set aside.

Whisk the egg, milk, and oil together in a small bowl. Set aside.

> **"Houses turn black, maple syrup has a taste no maple syrup produced elsewhere can equal, bears amble within sight of farmhouses."**
>
> **—ALICE MUNRO, Friend of My Youth**

Sift the flour, maple and granulated sugars, baking powder, baking soda, and salt into a mixing bowl. Stir in the cranberries, walnuts, and orange zest. Beat in the reserved egg mixture, stirring to just combine.

Pour the mixture into the prepared pan. Place in the preheated oven and bake for about 50 minutes or until a cake tester inserted into the center comes out clean and the top is golden brown.

Remove from the oven and place on a wire rack to cool. Serve with maple butter, if desired.

NOTE: Maple butter (also known as maple cream) is available from specialty food stores or via the Internet.

Literary Tea or Sweet Ending

Sucre à la Crème

Makes about 1 pound

Rather like American fudge, *Sucre à la Crème* is a very rich, fudgy candy from Quebec. It is very, very easy to prepare and makes a wonderful treat with a steaming cup of dark coffee. The fact that it can be made in a microwave assures that you can always have a special nibble on hand.

1 packed cup light brown sugar
1 cup granulated sugar
1 cup heavy cream

Lightly coat the interior of an 8-inch square baking pan with nonstick vegetable spray. Set aside.

Combine the sugars with the cream in a microwave-safe bowl. Place in the microwave and cook at full power for 3 minutes. Stir and continue to cook on full power for 4 minutes. Again, stir and continue to cook on full power for 3 more minutes.

Remove from the microwave and, using a hand-held electric mixer, beat on high for about 5 minutes or until thick and creamy.

Pour into the prepared pan and refrigerate for 1 hour or until set.

When set, use a serrated knife to cut into small squares.

Store, airtight, in layers separated by wax or parchment paper.

Rice Pudding

Serves 6 to 8

In Canada, rice pudding is often made with wild rice, but I prefer white rice pudding. It is another great dessert to make for guests, as it can be served hot or cold. Spooned into individual serving dishes and topped with whipped cream, it is as elegant as a fancy pastry.

1 cup white rice
4 cups whole milk
¾ cup sugar
2 teaspoons pure vanilla extract
1 teaspoon lemon zest
¼ teaspoon ground nutmeg
Pinch salt
2 large egg yolks
½ cup heavy cream
Whipped cream, optional

Preheat the oven to 325°F.

Generously coat the interior of a 2-quart casserole with unsalted butter. Set aside.

Wash and drain the rice well.

Combine the rice with the milk, sugar, vanilla, lemon zest, nutmeg, and salt in a mixing bowl. When well-blended, pour into the prepared casserole.

Place the casserole in a baking pan large enough to hold it with at least 2-inches all around. Fill with enough cold water to come 1 inch up the sides of the casserole.

Place the baking pan in the preheated oven and bake, stirring occasionally, for 90 minutes.

Whisk the egg yolks and heavy cream together in a small mixing bowl.

Quickly stir the egg mixture into the baking rice pudding. Continue to bake for an additional 30 minutes, or until the top is golden brown and the pudding is set.

Remove from the oven and serve hot, or place on a wire rack to cool. When cool, cover and refrigerate for at least an hour or until nicely chilled.

Serve with whipped cream, if desired.

NOTE: Rice pudding also lends itself to all sorts of flavors and additions to reflect the cuisine you are featuring. Feel free to add about ½ teaspoon ground sweet spices like cinnamon, ½ teaspoon of extracts like almond or waters like rose or orange, 1 cup of any chopped dried fruit or raisins, or ¾ cup unsweetened coconut to the egg mixture before adding it to the baking rice.

"When Joe had finally finished cooking the dinner we went into the house and ate it, seated around the heavy table in the dining-room. The baby had been fed and exiled to the carriage on the front porch, but Arthur sat in a high-chair, where he evaded with spastic contortions of his body the spoonfuls of food Clara poked in the direction of his mouth. Dinner was wizened meat balls and noodles from a noodle mix with lettuce. For dessert we had something I recognized.

"'This is that new canned rice pudding; it saves a lot of time,' Clara said defensively. 'It's not too bad with cream, and Arthur loves it.'

"'Yes,' I said. 'Pretty soon they'll be having Orange and Caramel too.'"

— MARGARET ATWOOD,
The Edible Woman

Chapter 6

Latin American Lovers of the Word

*T*HE MAGICAL REALISM ASSOCIATED WITH CERTAIN Latino authors might also be used to describe a few marvelously seductive dishes. Just as the literary history of the diverse continent-plus is exuberant and complex, so are its best food offerings.

In the mid-20th century, Latin American writers of towering talent—such as Gabriel Garcia Márquez, Mario Vargas Llosa, Octavio Paz, Pablo Neruda, and Jorge Luis Borges—came to international prominence, and have since been joined by several lively, moving writers from Central America and the Caribbean, such as Edwidge Danticat, to name only one.

During those same decades, more Europeans and Americans—north of Miami—began to take an interest in Caribbean and Latin American dishes and drinks.

READS, DRINKS & NIBBLES
■ ■ ■
Mojito
Daiquiri
Garlic Almonds
Jerk Chicken Bites

STAR DISHES & DELICIOUS ASIDES
■ ■ ■
Feijoada with Spicy Lime Sauce
Cuban Sandwich
Mixed South American Grill
   with Chimichurri
Pollo Barracho

FOR A MOVEABLE FEAST
■ ■ ■
Banana Bread with Citrus Cream Cheese

LITERARY TEA OR SWEET ENDING
■ ■ ■
Mexican Hot Chocolate
Tres Leches Cake

Mojito

It is believed that the ingredients for this potent but delicious cocktail came together as a way to disguise the harshness of the early Caribbean rums. It has become one of the most refreshing and easily drinkable summertime spirits. Ernest Hemingway discovered the mojito in a Cuban bar, La Bodeguita del Medio, and he popularized the cocktail throughout the Northern Hemisphere. Hemingway's graffiti script, *"Mi mojito en la Bodeguita"* (My mojito at the Bodeguita) remains readable on the wall of the bar.

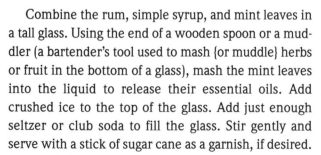

PER DRINK:
2 ounces Myers rum
2 tablespoons simple syrup
*   (see Note)*
4 fresh mint leaves,
*   torn apart*
Crushed ice
Seltzer water or club soda
Stick of sugar cane for garnish,
*   optional*

Combine the rum, simple syrup, and mint leaves in a tall glass. Using the end of a wooden spoon or a muddler (a bartender's tool used to mash {or muddle} herbs or fruit in the bottom of a glass), mash the mint leaves into the liquid to release their essential oils. Add crushed ice to the top of the glass. Add just enough seltzer or club soda to fill the glass. Stir gently and serve with a stick of sugar cane as a garnish, if desired.

NOTE: Simple syrup is equal parts granulated sugar and water that has been brought to a boil and then cooled. It can be made in advance and stored, tightly covered and refrigerated, for long periods of time. It is great to keep on hand to sweeten all types of drinks.

Daiquiri

According to Dale DeGroff in his seminal cocktail book, *The Craft of the Cocktail**, this marvelous cocktail was created for Ernest Hemingway by the Cuban bartender Constantino Ribailagua at the El Floridita Bar in Havana in 1921. It is now a favorite summer drink in our house. You must use the prescribed maraschino liqueur to achieve the perfect flavor, and you will need a whiskey jigger to measure.

FOR EACH DRINK:
1½ ounces white rum
¾ ounce Simple Syrup (see Note on left)
¾ ounce fresh lime juice
½ ounce fresh grapefruit juice
¼ ounce maraschino liqueur

Combine the rum, syrup, lime and grapefruit juices, and maraschino liqueur in a cocktail shaker. Add ice, cover, and shake vigorously. Pour into a martini-style glass and serve, ice cold.

*Dale DeGroff: The Craft of the Cocktail: Everything You Need to Know to Be a Master Bartender, with 500 Recipes; Random House

> **"I cannot separate eroticism from food and see no reason to do so."**
> —ISABEL ALLENDE

> **"The myths eat with us at our table."**
> —NÉLIDA PIÑON

Garlic Almonds

Almonds are favored throughout Central and South America, and when you flavor the sweet nuts with garlic they are wonderfully warm, aromatic, and slightly zesty, just like the people of these Latin countries.

¼ cup unsalted butter
¼ cup olive oil
1 tablespoon garlic salt
½ teaspoon garlic powder
4 cups raw almonds

Preheat the oven to 325°F.

Combine the butter and oil in a large baking sheet with sides. Place the pan in the oven and bake for about 3 minutes or until the butter has melted.

Remove the pan from the oven and stir in the garlic salt and powder. Add the almonds, stirring to coat.

Return the pan to the oven and bake, stirring frequently, for about 20 minutes or until golden and aromatic.

Remove the pan from the oven. Using a slotted spoon, transfer the nuts to a double layer of paper towels to drain.

Store, airtight, in a cool, dark spot, for up to 6 weeks.

Jerk Chicken Bites

Serves 8 to 10

Jerk seasoning is the seasoning for all types of meat and fish in Jamaica. Once used in hot-climate places as a preservative, the seasoning can be found all through the Caribbean islands. Although you can buy commercially prepared jerk seasoning, it is easy to make to have on hand, so you can often put a little of the Caribbean on your table. The seasoning will keep, covered and refrigerated, for up to 1 month. I have reduced the heat, as Jamaicans use too many blisteringly hot habanero chilies for my taste.

½ cup fresh lime juice
¼ cup fresh orange juice
2 tablespoons white vinegar
1 tablespoon hot sauce or to taste
2 tablespoons mustard seeds
1 tablespoon dried thyme
1 tablespoon ground allspice
1 teaspoon ground cloves
½ teaspoon ground nutmeg
Salt and pepper to taste
2 pounds boneless skinless chicken breast or
    chicken tenders

> "Salt and the center of the world have to be there, in that spot on the tablecloth."
> —JULIO CORTÁZAR

Combine the lime juice, orange juice, vinegar, and hot sauce in the bowl of a food processor fitted with the metal blade. Add the mustard seeds, thyme, allspice, cloves, and nutmeg. Process to a thick sauce-like consistency. If too thick, add additional citrus juice or vinegar.

Using a sharp knife, cut the chicken into bite-size pieces. Place the pieces in a re-sealable plastic bag and add just enough of the marinade to lightly coat all of the chicken. Seal and refrigerate for 30 minutes.

When ready to cook, preheat the oven to 400°F.

Lightly spray the interior of two large baking pans with nonstick vegetable spray.

Remove the chicken from the refrigerator and place the pieces in a single layer in the prepared baking pans. Do not crowd the pan.

Place in the preheated oven and bake, turning occasionally, for about 12 minutes or until lightly charred and cooked through.

Remove from the oven and place on a platter with toothpicks and wedges of lime, if desired.

◆◆◆ LATIN AMERICAN LOVERS ◆◆◆
OF THE WORD

◆◆◆ LITERATURE AFLOAT ◆◆◆

◆◆◆ THE BEST AND WORST OF PLACES ◆◆◆

Feijoada with Spicy Lime Sauce

Serves 8 to 12

*F*eijoada is the national dish of Brazil, although it can be found in almost all of the countries that were once part of the Portuguese empire. It is based on a bean stew from traditional regional Portuguese cuisine and is a very hearty, filling extravaganza. Like all stews it can be made in advance and reheated when ready to serve which, of course, makes it a great dish to feature when deeply involved in Brazilian literature.

2 cups dried black beans

4 cups chicken or beef broth

One 3 pound smoked beef tongue, skinned and well-trimmed

2 pound chorizo or kielbasa

2 pounds beef brisket, trimmed of all fat

2 pig's feet, cleaned and halved

1 pound salt pork, diced

3 tablespoons canola oil

2 jalapeño chilies, trimmed, seeded, and minced (or to taste)

2 cups chopped onions

2 tablespoons minced garlic

4 cups canned chopped Italian plum tomatoes with their juice

2 bay leaves

Peel of 1 orange

Salt and pepper to taste

10 to 14 cups hot, cooked white rice

4 seedless oranges, peeled and cut, crosswise, into thin slices

Spicy Lime Sauce (See page 82)

Rinse the beans under cold running water. Place in a large saucepan with cold water to cover by at least 2 inches. Set aside to soak for at least 8 hours or overnight. Drain well and set aside.

Combine the broth with 8 cups of water in a large stockpot over high heat. Bring to a boil and immediately add the drained beans. Then, add the beef tongue, chorizo, brisket, pig's feet, and salt pork. Again, bring to a boil. Lower the heat and simmer for 45 minutes.

While the bean mixture is cooking, heat the oil in a large heavy frying pan over medium-high heat. Add the chilies, onions, and garlic, and sauté for 5 minutes. Then, add the tomatoes along with the bay leaves and orange peel. Season with salt and pepper. Bring to a simmer, then lower the heat and cook at a gentle simmer for 20 minutes.

When the beans have cooked for 45 minutes, remove about 2 cups along with some broth. Using a fork, mash the beans and then stir them into the tomato mixture. When well-blended, stir the entire tomato mixture into the pot of cooking beans and meat. Bring to a simmer and continue to simmer for at least 1 hour, or until the meats are very tender. The mixture should be quite soupy. If the broth gets too thick, add additional broth.

Remove the pot from the stove and carefully remove the bay leaves and orange peel. Remove the large pieces of meat and cut them into bite-size pieces.

Mound the rice in the center of a large platter. Place the meat around the edges of the rice. Garnish the platter with sliced oranges. Pour the soupy beans into a large bowl or soup tureen. Serve immediately with Spicy Lime Sauce on the side.

Spicy Lime Sauce

1½ pounds fresh plum tomatoes, peeled, cored,
* and seeded*
1 jalapeño chili, trimmed and seeded
* (or to taste)*
1 cup chopped red onions
1 tablespoon minced garlic
2 teaspoons chopped fresh cilantro
½ cup fresh orange juice
¼ cup fresh lime juice
½ cup olive oil

Combine the tomatoes, chili, onions, garlic, and cilantro in the bowl of a food processor fitted with the metal blade. Process, using quick on-and-off turns, until the mixture is almost smooth.

Scrape the tomato mixture into a serving bowl. Stir in the orange and lime juices. Add the olive oil, whisking to blend. Season with salt and pepper and serve.

The sauce may also be stored, tightly covered and refrigerated, for up to 1 week.

Cuban Sandwich

Serves 8 to 10

A classic Cuban sandwich is made in an old-fashioned sandwich iron or press. The currently popular panini press does an excellent job of toasting and melting this heavenly sandwich. You can cut it into small pieces, as it is very filling.

Two loaves French baguette or Cuban bread
½ cup salted butter, at room temperature
½ cup honey mustard
1 pound thinly sliced baked ham
1 pound thinly sliced Muenster cheese
1 cup sliced sandwich pickles plus more
* for serving*
1 pound thinly sliced roast pork

Cut each loaf, lengthwise, into halves.

Generously coat one cut side with butter, and the other with mustard.

Layer half of the ham down the buttered side of each loaf. Top each one with half of the cheese and then with an equal amount of pickle. Top each with an equal portion of the roast pork. Place the remaining half of the bread, mustard side down, on top of the pork.

If you have a panini press, cut the sandwiches into four equal pieces and toast them in the press, following manufacturer's directions.

If you don't have a panini press, preheat the oven to 400°F. Cut the loaves in half, crosswise. Place them on a lightly oiled baking sheet and cover with aluminum foil. Place another baking sheet on top and then place a heavy pot or frying pan on top to press the sandwiches down. Bake for about 25 minutes or until the sandwiches are golden brown and the cheese has melted.

Serve hot with more pickles on the side.

Mixed South American Grill
with *Chimichurri*

Serves 8 to 10

A lthough many traditional meat dishes in South and Central America are stews, certain countries, particularly Argentina, Uruguay and Brazil, are known for both their fine-quality beef and outdoor cooking, called "*asado*" in Spanish; "churrasco" in Portuguese. The representative grill recipe that follows can only be done on an outdoor grill. However, the *Chimichurri* Sauce is one that can be used for all types of meat (even a hamburger), poultry and fish, even if cooked indoors. You can also use any red or green salsa that you prefer.

½ cup coarse salt
¼ cup minced garlic
Two 6-pound boneless sirloin steaks, about
    2 inches thick
Olive oil for rubbing
Cracked black pepper to taste
Chimichurri Sauce (recipe follows)

Preheat and oil the grill.

Combine the salt and garlic with 2 cups of cold water, stirring to dissolve the salt. Set aside.

Generously coat both sides of the steaks with olive oil. When the grill is very hot, place the steaks on it, cover, and grill for 12 minutes, basting every couple of minutes with the salt/garlic water. Turn, recover, and continue grilling and basting for an additional 12 minutes for medium-rare, or until the meat reaches the desired degree of doneness.

Remove from the grill and season both sides with pepper. Let stand for about 4 minutes before cutting and serving with *Chimichurri* Sauce.

Chimichurri Sauce

4 cups chopped Italian parsley
1 cup chopped scallions, including some
    green part
¼ cup chopped fresh oregano
¼ cup chopped fresh cilantro
2 tablespoons chopped garlic
Juice and zest of 1 lemon
2 cups olive oil
⅔ cup white wine vinegar
Salt to taste

Combine the parsley, scallions, oregano, cilantro, and garlic in the bowl of a food processor fitted with the metal blade. Add the lemon juice and zest and pulse, using quick on-and-off turns, to just mince. Do not over-process or purée.

Scrape the mixture into a bowl. Add the olive oil and vinegar, and season with salt to taste. Stir to blend well.

Cover and refrigerate until ready to use, or for up to 4 days.

"The colonel: 'He [the rooster] is worth his weight in gold . . . He'll feed us for three years.'

"Woman: 'You can't eat hope.'

"The colonel: 'You can't eat it but it sustains you.'"

—conversation in No One Writes to the Colonel by GABRIEL GARCÍA MÁRQUEZ

NOTE: You can also grill lamb chops or racks in this same fashion. And, if you have adventuresome eaters, you can add some veal kidneys, sliced beef heart, and/or beef or veal liver to the grill.

Pollo Barracho

Serves 8

This dish is a very simple one that can be found, in one form or another, throughout all of Latin America. The seasonings may vary from country to country, but the basic formula remains. It can be made in advance and reheated when needed.

¼ cup olive oil
1 pound sliced ham, cut into 2-inch wide strips
¼ cup minced garlic
1 teaspoon ground cumin
¼ teaspoon dried oregano
7 pounds chicken pieces with skin
Salt and pepper to taste
3 cups dry white wine
½ cup white wine vinegar
3 cups low-fat, low-sodium chicken broth
1 cup pimento-stuffed olives
½ cup capers, well-drained

Preheat the oven to 350°F.

Heat the oil in a large Dutch oven over medium heat.

Remove the pan from the heat and place about one-third of the ham strips over the bottom.

Combine the garlic with the cumin and oregano.

Generously season the chicken with salt and pepper and then rub the garlic mixture over the skin on all pieces.

Place the legs and thighs over the layer of ham in the Dutch oven and cover them with another third of the ham. Top the ham with the breast and wing pieces. Finish with the final third of ham to cover the top.

Pour the wine and vinegar into the pan. Add enough chicken broth to cover all of the meat.

Cover the pan and place in the preheated oven. Simmer for about 1 hour or until the chicken is almost falling off the bone.

Remove from the oven and uncover. Using a slotted spoon, transfer the chicken pieces to a warm platter. Tent lightly with aluminum foil to keep warm.

Return the pan to the stove top over high heat. Bring to a boil and boil for about 10 minutes or until slightly thickened. (To speed this process, you can, if desired, dissolve 2 teaspoons of cornstarch in about 2 tablespoons of water and whisk it into the boiling broth.)

When reduced, untent the chicken and drizzle with the sauce. Garnish the platter with olives and capers and serve the remaining sauce on the side.

For a Moveable Feast

Banana Bread with Citrus Cream Cheese

Makes one 9-inch loaf

This is a great way to use over-ripe bananas, which give a rich, deep banana flavor to the bread. To serve, the bread can be sliced with the cream cheese on the side or the combination can be made into delicate little tea sandwiches. Either way, the flavors absolutely sing South of the Border.

1¾ cups sifted all-purpose flour
2 teaspoons baking powder
¼ teaspoon baking soda
¼ teaspoon salt
¼ cup unsalted butter, at room temperature
⅔ cup sugar
2 large eggs, at room temperature
3 very ripe bananas, peeled and mashed
1 teaspoon pure vanilla extract
1 cup chopped nuts
½ cup toasted coconut flakes

Preheat the oven to 350°F.

Lightly coat the interior of a 9-inch loaf pan with nonstick vegetable spray. Set aside.

Sift the flour, baking powder, baking soda, and salt together. Set aside.

Combine the butter and sugar in the bowl of a standing electric mixer fitted with the paddle. Beat on medium until light and fluffy. Add eggs, one at a time, and beat until well-incorporated. Add the bananas and vanilla and beat to combine.

Add the flour mixture and beat until well-incorporated.

Remove the bowl from the mixer and stir in the nuts and coconut. Scrape the batter into the prepared pan. Place in the preheated oven and bake for about 1 hour or until the top is golden and a cake tester inserted into the center comes out clean.

Remove from the oven and invert the pan onto a wire rack. Turn the bread right side up and let cool.

When cool, slice and serve with Citrus Cream Cheese.

Citrus Cream Cheese

1 pound cream cheese, at room temperature
¼ cup fresh orange juice
2 tablespoons confectioners' sugar
1 teaspoon lime juice
1 teaspoon orange zest
¼ teaspoon lime zest

Combine the cream cheese, orange and lime juice, and sugar in the bowl of a standing electric mixer fitted with the paddle. Beat on medium for about 5 minutes or until light and fluffy.

Remove the bowl from the mixer and fold in the orange and lime zest. Serve immediately or store, covered and refrigerated, for up to 3 days.

Literary Tea or Sweet Ending

Mexican Hot Chocolate

Serves 12

With the exception of some Caribbean islands where British influence lingers—and also Argentina—most Latinos eschew tea in favor of the local treasures of hot chocolate or coffee. Argentines all day tote tall covered maté cups, equipped with a special straw, periodically adding hot water to soak the maté leaves resting in the cup's bottom. If one is not a born Argentine, this tea is an acquired taste. Hot chocolate, however, is almost universally enjoyed. This Mexican version is a rich and delicious brew that is reminiscent of the one written about in *Like Water for Chocolate*. To be completely authentic, the hot chocolate must be mixed with a "*molinillo*," a primitive-looking wooden stirrer used specifically for this purpose.

12 cups whole milk
1 cup light brown sugar
7 ounces Mexican chocolate, chopped
1½ teaspoons ground cinnamon
¼ teaspoon salt
1 tablespoon pure vanilla extract
12 cinnamon sticks

Combine the milk with the sugar, cinnamon, and salt in a large saucepan over low heat. Cook, stirring, for about 5 minutes or until the sugar has dissolved. Add the chocolate and continue to cook, stirring, for about 12 minutes or until the chocolate has melted. Add the vanilla and, using a *molinillo* or whisk, vigorously beat until very frothy.

Pour an equal portion into each of 12 warm mugs, garnish with a cinnamon stick, and serve.

> "She felt so lost and lonely. One chili in walnut sauce left on the platter after a fancy dinner couldn't feel any worse than she did."
>
> —LAURA ESQUIVEL, Like Water for Chocolate

Tres Leches Cake

Serves 16 to 20

Throughout Latin American cultures, you will find some version of this incredibly sweet cake. So exceedingly rich, it absolutely demands a cup of strong black coffee as an accompaniment. It is an ideal get-together dessert, as it is best eaten a

"Around two in the morning, the bar ran out of mojito mix and the guests ate the last morsel of the wedding-size *tres leches* cakes from my aunt's famous La Deliciosa Bakery."

—LISA ALVARADO, Sister Chicas

day or two after it has been put together. Its dense richness is equal to the most demanding Marquez novel. *"Tres Leches"* translates as "Three Milks," identifiable in the ingredients for the filling.

9 large eggs, separated, at room temperature
2 cups sugar
2 teaspoons pure vanilla extract
1 tablespoon baking powder
½ cup whole milk
2 cups cake flour, sifted
Tres Leches *Cake Filling (recipe follows)*
Tres Leches *Cake Frosting (recipe follows)*
1 cup unsweetened coconut flakes, toasted

Preheat the oven to 350°F.

Lightly coat the interior of a 13- by 9- by 2-inch glass baking dish with nonstick vegetable spray. Set aside.

Combine the egg yolks with the sugar in the bowl of a standing electric mixer fitted with the paddle. Beat on low to blend and then raise the speed to medium and beat for about 5 minutes or until pale and thick. Beat in the vanilla.

Dissolve the baking powder in the milk. With the motor running, add half of the milk to the beaten eggs, followed by 1 cup of the flour, beating well to incorporate. Repeat the process, beating until a smooth batter forms. Remove the bowl from the mixer and set aside.

Using a hand-held mixer, beat the egg whites until stiff peaks form. Using a spatula, carefully fold half of the egg whites into the batter, folding just until the batter has stiffened slightly. Then fold in the remaining egg whites until blended. Do not over-mix or beat the batter, or the cake will be tough.

Pour the batter into the prepared dish. Place in the preheated oven and bake for about 30 minutes or until a cake tester inserted into the center comes out clean.

Remove from the oven and place on a wire rack to cool.

When cool, invert the cake onto a serving platter. Using the end of a wooden spoon, poke holes in neat rows down the cake. Slowly pour the chilled filling over the cake, allowing the filling to soak into the holes as you pour so that the cake can absorb all of the filling.

Using a spatula, swirl the frosting over the top and sides of the cake to completely cover. Sprinkle the coconut over the top, pressing down slightly so that it adheres to the frosting. Cover lightly with plastic film and refrigerate for at least 3 hours or up to 24 hours before serving.

Serve well-chilled, cut into squares.

If I could again live my life,
In the next . . .
I'll climb more mountains,
I'll swim more rivers,
I'll go more places . . .
I'll eat more ice creams and fewer
     (lima) beans

—JORGE LUIS BORGES, Instants

Tres Leches Cake Filling

1½ cups heavy cream
3 large egg yolks
2 ripe bananas, peeled and chopped
1 cup unsweetened coconut milk
1 cup sweetened condensed milk
One 5-ounce can evaporated milk
2 tablespoons dark rum
1 teaspoon pure vanilla extract

Place the heavy cream in a small heavy-bottomed saucepan over medium heat. Bring to a boil and immediately lower the heat to a simmer. Simmer, watching carefully so that it doesn't boil over, for about 8 minutes, or until reduced to 1 cup. Remove from the heat.

Place the egg yolks in the bowl of a standing electric mixture fitted with the paddle. Beat until light and fluffy.

Slowly add the reduced cream, beating for about 5 minutes or until cool and foamy. Add the bananas, beating to just blend. Add the coconut milk followed by the sweetened condensed milk and evaporated milk, beating well after each addition. Beat in the rum and vanilla.

Cover lightly with plastic film and refrigerate for at least 2 hours or until very well chilled. (The filling may be made up to 1 day in advance of use.) Use as directed in the recipe.

Tres Leches Cake Frosting

1½ cups sugar
1 cup light corn syrup
½ cup water
3 large egg whites

Combine the sugar, corn syrup, and water in a medium heavy-bottomed saucepan over medium heat. Bring to a boil, stirring frequently. Lower the heat and simmer, stirring occasionally, for about 15 minutes or until a clear syrup forms and the liquid reaches 234°F on a candy thermometer. Take care that the syrup does not begin to color and caramelize. Remove from the heat and set aside.

Place the egg whites in the bowl of a standing electric mixture fitted with the whisk. Beat until stiff peaks form. With the motor running, begin slowly adding the hot syrup down the sides of the bowl (so that it doesn't splatter and burn your hands or arms). Beat for about 10 minutes or until the frosting is shiny, fluffy, almost cool, and stiff peaks are held when lifted.

Use as directed within 1 hour of being made.

"There was now employment for the whole party; for though they could not all talk, they could all eat; and the beautiful pyramids of grapes, nectarines and peaches, soon collected them round the table." —JANE AUSTEN, Pride and Prejudice

European
TASTES

Chapter 7

Pages and Platters of the Anglo/Irish Isles

NOT ONLY IS THE ENGLISH-LANGUAGE LITERARY CANON ROOTED IN THE LITERARY genius of Chaucer, Shakespeare and Austen, writers of Britain and Ireland continue to inform, provoke and entertain readers wherever English is spoken, and in translation where it is not. Poets, playwrights and prose stylists of English and Irish isles ask us to look into the deepest recesses of human frailty; they lead us to hope and laughter, too.

The sun has not set on the talent of the varied writers who today call England home. The artful works of such authors as Doris Lessing, Martin Amis, Michael Ondaatje, Kazuo Ishiguro and Zadie Smith travel beyond the once vast British Empire. Yet, is there a writer more interested in traditional English morés than Ishiguro, or better able to read the minds of many Londoners than Smith? Not that either residence or citizenship is a prerequisite for setting indelible English scenes, as fans of Mary Ann Shaffer and Annie Barrows may attest.

Those writing of Ireland, such as William Trevor, Sebastian Barry or Maeve Binchy, do not lack sophistication even if the palates of many of their creations are plain. Whole new worlds—new ways of thinking—flowed from the pens of James Joyce and Samuel Beckett. Their characters, however, often stayed close enough to home—think of Leopold and Molly Bloom of Dublin—for readers to guess what they ate. Today, it is the rare Trevor character who is worldly enough to stray from a rasher of bacon.

The traditional foods of the United Kingdom and Ireland are as simple as the literature is varied. The damp, temperate climate encourages hardy grains, root vegetables, rich pies and fatty roasts, strong beverages and straightforward sweets. Tea time can be near sacred with the experience ranging from a "cuppa" and a hand-held meat pie to an elaborate high tea.

❖ ❖ ❖

READS, DRINKS & NIBBLES
■ ■ ■

Gimlet
Mulled Wine
Smoked Irish or Scotch Salmon with
    Chives, Black Bread, and Sweet Butter

STAR DISHES & DELICIOUS ASIDES
■ ■ ■

Shepherd's Pie
Guernsey Potato Pie
Sautéed Creamed Cabbage
Irish Soda Bread with Homemade Whipped Butter

FOR A MOVEABLE FEAST
■ ■ ■

Ploughman's Lunch
Scotch Shortbread
Irish Oatmeal Cookies

LITERARY TEA OR SWEET ENDING
■ ■ ■

High Tea with Scones
Cranachan
Irish Coffee

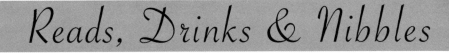

Reads, Drinks & Nibbles

Gimlet

Rose's Lime Juice was created in the 1800s when the Royal Navy and Royal Merchant Navy were required to provide seamen with a daily ration of citrus juice to prevent scurvy. It was the first product that preserved citrus juice without alcohol, and it quickly became popular. Now, it is most known for the distinct flavor it gives gin in the refreshing gimlet.

FOR EACH COCKTAIL:
3 tablespoons gin
2 tablespoons Rose's Lime
    Juice
Sliver of lime zest,
    optional

Combine the gin and lime juice in a cocktail shaker filled with ice. Shake vigorously to blend.

Pour the liquid into a martini-style glass. Garnish with a sliver of lime zest and serve.

Mulled Wine

Serves a crowd

Mulled wine is a traditional holiday drink throughout the British Isles. This sweetly spiced, heated drink warms the spirits and the tips of the toes. It is a powerful blend that will certainly encourage conversation and reflection.

Three 750 ml. bottles red wine
1 cup brandy
12 cinnamon sticks
3 oranges, well-washed and cut, crosswise, into thin slices
One 1-inch knob fresh ginger
¼ cup whole cloves
1 tablespoon allspice berries
2 cups light brown sugar
Orange slices for garnish, optional

Combine the wine and brandy in a large, nonreactive saucepan. Add the cinnamon sticks, orange slices, ginger, cloves, and allspice berries. Place over medium heat. Stir in the sugar and bring to a simmer, stirring occasionally. Simmer for about 7 minutes or until the sugar has dissolved.

Remove from the heat and let stand for about 2 hours or until the flavors have blended. Once cool, the wine may be stored, covered and refrigerated.

When ready to serve, reheat. When hot, pour into mugs and serve garnished with a fresh orange slice, if desired.

Smoked Irish or Scotch Salmon with Chives, Black Bread, and Sweet Butter

Serves 10 to 14

These little open-faced sandwiches work as an hors d'oeuvre with a glass of champagne, a tumbler of scotch or a mug of ale.

Or each slice can be topped with another slice of bread and the resulting sandwich served at a book group luncheon. Open-faced or closed, and kept small, they also make splendid tea sandwiches.

12 ounces cream cheese, at room temperature
¼ cup chopped fresh chives
1 teaspoon fresh lemon juice
16 thin slices dark bread, such as cocktail pumpernickel, crusts removed
¼ cup unsalted butter, at room temperature
16 thin slices smoked salmon
Cracked black pepper to taste
Lemon wedges for garnish

Combine the cream cheese with the chives and lemon juice in a small mixing bowl.

Lightly coat one side of each piece of bread with butter. Then, generously coat with the seasoned cream cheese. Lay a piece of salmon on top of the cream cheese, taking care that the entire top is covered, but not hanging over the edges.

Sprinkle a bit of cracked pepper over the salmon. Cut each piece into four equal triangles. Serve with lemon wedges on the side.

Shepherd's Pie

Serves 8 to 12

Traditionally, a shepherd's pie was made from leftover cooked meat. Today, we so seldom use large cuts of meat that most cooks rarely have enough leftovers to make this substantial pie, but it may be even better with fresh ground meat. The pie can be made in advance and easily reheated before serving. There is no better entrée to finish off a meeting sharing the work of one of the Brontë sisters, a Hardy or Lawrence novel, or any number of Irish, Scotch or English writers who look to the countryside in their work.

½ cup butter
2 tablespoons canola oil
3 pounds ground veal (or beef, lamb, pork,
    or poultry)
1 large onion, peeled and minced
1 teaspoon dried thyme
½ teaspoon dried dill
2 cups chopped, cooked spinach, thoroughly
    drained
Salt and pepper to taste
6 cups mashed potatoes
Two 9-inch unbaked pie shells (see Flaky Pie
    Pastry recipe, page 18)
2 tablespoons melted butter
¼ cup dried breadcrumbs

> "Some hae meat and cannae eat.
> Some nae meat but want it. We hae
> meat and we can eat and sae the
> Lord be thankit." —SCOTTISH BLESSING

Preheat the oven to 500°F.

Combine the butter and canola oil in a large deep frying pan over medium heat. Add the ground meat, onion, thyme, and dill and cook, stirring constantly, for about 8 minutes or until the meat begins to lose its color. Add the spinach and 2 cups of the mashed potatoes. Season with salt and pepper to taste and continue to cook, stirring constantly, for an additional 5 minutes.

Place an equal portion of the meat mixture into each of the pastry shells, mounding slightly in the center.

Using a spatula, generously cover the top of each filled pie shell with mashed potatoes, taking care that the potatoes come to the edge all around.

Using a pastry brush, lightly coat the potatoes with melted butter and then sprinkle with breadcrumbs.

Place in the preheated oven and bake for 15 minutes. Lower the heat to 350°F and continue to bake for 30 minutes or until hot in the center and golden brown on top.

Remove from the oven and let rest for about 5 minutes before cutting into wedges and serving.

Guernsey Potato Pie

Serves 10 to 12

In honor of *The Guernsey Literary and Potato Peel Pie Society*, a most deserving book-group favorite, I have changed the name of my own family-favorite potato dish. Although originally made as a side-dish, it is so rich that I often use it as a main course served with a salad and, of course, a lovely glass of white wine. However, one could toast the World War II valor of Channel Island residents with a pint of ale or any pub drink.

1 cup heavy cream
½ cup warm clarified butter (see Note)
¼ cup nonfat, low-sodium chicken broth
1½ cups finely shredded Gruyère cheese
¾ cup finely chopped leeks
¼ cup finely chopped celery
6 very large baking potatoes
Salt and white pepper to taste

Preheat the oven to 375°F.

Generously coat the interior of a 9-inch by 12-inch baking pan with butter. Set aside.

Pour half of the cream along with the clarified butter and broth into the prepared pan. Sprinkle half of the cheese along with the leeks and celery over the liquid. Season with salt and pepper to taste. Set aside.

Peel the potatoes and cut them in half, lengthwise. Working with one piece at a time, cut each potato half, crosswise, into slices about ¼-inch thick, keeping the entire half together. As cut, carefully place the sliced potato half into the pan, keeping it in one piece.

When all of the potato halves are nestled into the pan, pour the remaining cream over the top. Season with salt and pepper to taste and then sprinkle the remaining cheese on the surface.

Cover the entire pan with aluminum foil. Place in the preheated oven and bake for about 45 minutes or until the potatoes are tender and the liquid has been almost absorbed into them.

Remove from the oven, uncover, and let rest for about 5 minutes before serving.

Serve one potato half per person, with the slices gently fanned out.

NOTE: Place the butter in a medium saucepan over low heat. Allow the butter to melt and then continue cooking until the foam disappears from the top and a light brown sediment forms on the bottom of the pan. The melted butter should now be a clear, golden yellow. This is called clarified butter.

Sautéed Creamed Cabbage

Serves 6 to 8

Cabbage has traditionally been a much used vegetable throughout the British Isles. It can be seen in classic dishes such as colcannon in Ireland and creamed cabbage in England. Along with marrows (squashes) and root vegetables, cabbage has a long storage life, so it can provide a vegetable for the table throughout the long, damp winter.

One 2-pound green cabbage
3 tablespoons unsalted butter
1 tablespoon light brown sugar
Salt and pepper to taste
¾ cup heavy cream, at room temperature

Core and wash the cabbage. Allow it to drain well.

Using a sharp chef's knife, cut the cabbage into long, thin shreds. Set aside.

Heat the butter in a large skillet over medium heat. When melted, begin adding the cabbage, a bit at a time so that it doesn't overflow the pan. As the cabbage wilts, continue adding additional cabbage until all has been added. Sprinkle with the sugar and toss. Cover and allow to cook for about 6 minutes or until the cabbage is just barely cooked. Add the cream, season with salt and pepper to taste, and cook for about 4 minutes or until slightly thickened.

Remove from the heat and serve hot.

Irish Soda Bread with Homemade Whipped Butter

Makes one loaf

There is nothing that speaks of the Irish country-side better than a freshly baked loaf of soda bread. It is even better served with homemade butter. Soda bread with butter is fit to accompany almost any meal.

With a sweet berry jam, the buttered bread is a lovely tea treat. Traditionally, thick slices of warm soda bread were slathered with home-churned butter and carried to the fields along with a jug of hot, sweet tea to warm the men working there.

2 cups whole-wheat flour, sifted
2 cups all-purpose flour, sifted
1 teaspoon baking soda
½ teaspoon salt
2 cups buttermilk
1 cup dried currants

Preheat the oven to 450°F.

Line a baking sheet with parchment paper. Set aside.

Combine the whole wheat and all-purpose flour in a large mixing bowl. Stir in the baking soda and salt. Add the buttermilk and, using your hands, pull the dry ingredients up and into the milk, mixing until well blended. Add the currants and continue mixing until they are well-distributed throughout the dough. The dough will be slightly sticky.

Generously flour a clean, flat work surface.

Scrape the dough out onto the floured surface and, using your hands, work the dough into a neat round shape. Turn it over and pat it out to about 2 inches in thickness.

Transfer the round to the prepared baking sheet. Using a serrated knife, make a cross in the center of the loaf.

Place the bread in the preheated oven and bake for 20 minutes. Lower the heat to 400°F and continue to bake for an additional 30 minutes or until the bread is nicely browned and sounds hollow when tapped on the top.

Remove from the oven and place on a wire rack to cool slightly before cutting.

Serve just barely warm with butter, and jam if you wish.

Homemade Whipped Butter

Makes about 1 cup

1 cup cold heavy cream, preferably organic
*   and unpasteurized*
½ cup ice water
2 large ice cubes
Salt to taste, optional

> "At a dinner party one should eat wisely but not too well, and talk well but not too wisely."
> —W. SOMERSET MAUGHAM

> "One cannot think well, love well, sleep well, if one has not dined well."
> — VIRGINIA WOOLF

> "People who were actually there (witnesses to history) rarely ever tell you anything of wider interest . . . I have a friend whose grandmother was born in 1902; she's a 98 year-old, intelligent Jewish lady who's lived this whole century. Ask her what the First World War was like, and she'll tell you the woman she lived next door to in 1916 really knew how to cook rabbit."
>
> —ZADIE SMITH

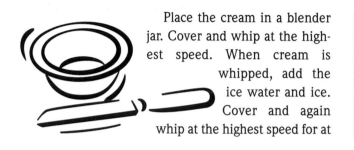

Place the cream in a blender jar. Cover and whip at the highest speed. When cream is whipped, add the ice water and ice. Cover and again whip at the highest speed for at least 2 minutes or until all of the cream has turned into butter particles.

Pour the contents of the blender jar into a fine mesh sieve to drain. When all of the liquid has drained off, transfer the butter to a small bowl. If using, add the salt and knead it in with a wooden spoon.

Cover and refrigerate until ready to use.

For a Moveable Feast

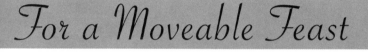

Ploughman's Lunch

Serves 1

Prior to World War II, most pubs were meeting places for drink rather than eats, so very little food was served except for that which would encourage the need for another drink to wet the whistle, such as pickled eggs, heavily salted "crisps" (potato chips) or chips (french fries), peanuts, or pork scratchings (fried pork rind). At some point in the 1950s or early '60s, a ploughboy lunch was introduced. Now known as a Ploughman's Lunch, it is a simple meal comprised of a hunk of cheese, a piece of coarse bread, butter, relish (usually a type called Branston pickle, as throughout the United Kingdom relishes are referred to as "pickle"), and, perhaps, an apple or other fruit.

One 3-ounce piece English cheddar or Stilton cheese
1 whole-grain roll, warmed and cut in half, crosswise
1 tablespoon unsalted butter or to taste
¼ cup sweet pickle relish or fruit chutney (see Note)
1 apple or other fruit

Place the cheese, roll, butter, relish, and fruit on a serving plate. That's it—unless you add a pint of ale to finish the meal.

NOTE: Branston pickle is a jarred relish that more resembles a chutney than the condiment that Americans know as relish. It is a combination of chopped vegetables, dried fruits, and spices seasoned with vinegar and sugar. A chutney, such as Major Grey's, would be a good substitute.

Scotch Shortbread

About 7 dozen cookies or 16 wedges

Traditionally, Scotch shortbread is made in cake pans and cut into small pie-shaped wedges. I prefer to make it using a cookie press, which yields far more cookies; when you use an assortment of templates and decorative sugars or sprinkles, one batch of dough will create a variety of cookies. However, you can cut or form the dough into any shape you desire. The baked cookies freeze very well and thaw very quickly, so they are terrific to always have on hand for a quick goodie.

2 cups unsalted butter, at room temperature
1 cup superfine sugar
4 cups sifted all-purpose flour
Preheat the oven to 300°F.

Place the butter in the bowl of a standing electric mixer fitted with the paddle. Beat on low speed to soften. Add the sugar, raise the speed, and beat for about 5 minutes or until very light and fluffy.

Add the flour and beat until very well blended.

If the dough is very warm, refrigerate for about 10 minutes to firm slightly. Do not let it get hard.

If using a cookie press, fit the press with the desired template and fill the hopper with dough. Press the cookies out onto ungreased, nonstick cookie sheets, leaving about an inch between each one. If desired, decorate the tops with colored sugar or sprinkles. (Alternately, fit an equal portion of the dough into each of two 9-inch cake pans. Press the edges with the tines of a kitchen fork and prick the entire top with the fork.)

Place in the preheated oven and bake for about 15 minutes or just until the edges are light gold. Do not over-bake or the butter will taste burned.

Remove from the oven and transfer to wire racks to cool. (If baked in cake pans, immediately upon removing the dough from the oven, cut it into small wedges. Cool as for cookies.)

Irish Oatmeal Cookies

Makes about 3½ dozen

Who doesn't like oatmeal cookies? They always seem to be a welcome treat with or without a cup of tea or a glass of milk.

1 cups all-purpose flour
1 teaspoon baking soda
1 teaspoon ground cinnamon
¼ teaspoon ground nutmeg
¼ teaspoon salt
1¼ cups unsalted butter, at room temperature
¼ cup granulated sugar
¼ cup packed light brown sugar
1 large egg, at room temperature
1 teaspoon pure vanilla extract
3 cups rolled oats
1 cup golden raisins
1 cup chopped walnuts

Preheat the oven to 375°F.

Line 2 cookie sheets with parchment paper. Set aside.

Sift the flour, baking soda, cinnamon, nutmeg, and salt together. Set aside.

Place the butter in the bowl of a standing electric mixer fitted with the paddle. Beat on low to just soften. Add the sugars, raise the speed to medium, and beat until light and airy. Beat in the egg and vanilla.

Add the reserved flour mixture and beat to blend. Add the oats and continue to beat until well-incorporated.

Remove the bowl from the mixer and, using a wooden spoon, beat in the raisins and walnuts.

Drop the dough by the teaspoonful onto the prepared baking sheets, leaving about 2 inches between each one.

Place in the preheated oven and bake for about 12 minutes or until golden brown and cooked through.

Remove from the oven and transfer to wire racks to cool.

Store, covered, at room temperature for up to 3 days.

HIGH TEA with SCONES

◆ ◆ ◆

In England, high tea is served between 5:00 and 7:00 pm.

During the Victorian era, the meal known as tea was generally consumed by the working class as the last meal of the day. It was, therefore, quite substantial with meats and cheeses and salads, often the leftovers of the noontime meal, as the featured items. Bread, jam, and butter and sweets were also part of the repast. Tea is still the last meal of the day for some, especially children.

Nowadays, a high tea is almost the same as afternoon tea (enjoyed in the late afternoon from 3:00 to 5:00 p.m.), with dainty finger sandwiches followed by scones and clotted cream and finally tiny cakes and cookies to finish the light meal. Many of these items can be easily purchased, particularly the sweets. The sandwiches are easy to make early in the day and they'll stay fresh if covered with a slightly damp kitchen towel.

> **"You can never get a cup of tea large enough or a book long enough to suit me."**–C. S. LEWIS

The Perfect Pot of Tea

You should have a teapot of ceramic, silver, porcelain or any nonreactive-material, china cups and loose tea. Connoisseurs believe that a proper cup of tea cannot be brewed using a tea bag.

There are many, many types of teas used in a British high tea. Many of the favorites date from the height of the Empire: Darjeeling, Ceylon, Earl Grey, Lapsang Souchong, and Keemun. You can, of course, also serve an herbal tea, but this would not be traditional.

The most particular might start with spring water, but cold tap water will do. Bring a pot of cold water to just a boil and immediately remove it from the heat.

While the water is coming to a boil, fill a teapot with hot water to warm it. It is a nice idea to warm the cups, also.

When the teapot is warm, pour off the water. Add 1 teaspoon of loose tea for each cup of tea to be made, plus 1 teaspoon for the pot. Pour the just-boiled water over the tea, cover, and allow the tea to brew for 5 minutes.

Uncover the tea and give it a quick stir. Let the tea leaves drop to the bottom and then strain the tea into the warm cups. Serve immediately with lemon slices, sugar, and warm milk on the side.

Wrap the tea pot in a tea cozy or a warm towel to keep the tea warm. Have another pot of hot water handy, so that the continuing-to-brew tea can be diluted with hot water should your guests require a second cup.

Tea Sandwiches

Tea sandwiches are always very light, with thinly sliced sandwich-type white or whole wheat bread filled with thinly sliced meats and cheeses or a light coating of salad greens or vegetables. Some suggested fillings for tea sandwiches:

Egg salad
Cucumber and/or radishes and sweet butter
Watercress and sweet butter
Thinly sliced chicken or turkey breast
Cheddar cheese and tomato
Smoked salmon
Baked ham

Scones

Makes 1 dozen

Scones (properly pronounced to rhyme with John) are now ubiquitous in coffee bars and bakeries throughout the United States, but they were once only known in the United Kingdom. My Scots grandmother made them on a griddle and they had no resemblance to the now familiar fluffy, sweet treats. This recipe is just a little bit sweet and a little bit fluffy—somewhere in between the original and the muffin-like scone.

2 cups all-purpose flour
¼ cup sugar
1 tablespoon baking powder
Pinch salt
½ cup (1 stick) cold unsalted butter, cut into pieces
1 large egg, at room temperature, beaten
A little milk
½ cup heavy cream
¾ cup dried currants
Heavy cream for glazing

Preheat the oven to 450°F.

Combine the flour, sugar, baking powder, and salt in the bowl of a food processor fitted with the metal blade. Process, using quick on-and-off turns, to blend. Add the butter and continue to process, using quick on-and-off turns, until the mixture resembles coarse meal.

Place the beaten egg in a glass measuring cup. Add just enough milk to come to ½ cup. With the motor running, pour the cream and egg mixture into the dry ingredients and process to just blend.

Lightly flour a clean, flat work surface.

Scrape the dough onto the floured surface and, using your hands, knead the currants into it.

> "Tell the cook of this restaurant with my compliments that these are the very worst sandwiches in the whole world, and that when I ask for a watercress sandwich I do not mean a loaf with a field in the middle of it."—OSCAR WILDE

Carefully pat the dough into a circle about ½ inch thick. Using a 2-inch round biscuit cutter, cut the dough out into circles. Place the circles on a nonstick baking sheet as they are cut. Pull any scraps of dough together and then cut into circles, using all of the dough.

When all of the scones have been cut, using a pastry brush, lightly coat each one with heavy cream.

Transfer to the preheated oven and bake for about 15 minutes or until golden brown and cooked through.

Remove from the oven and place on wire racks to cool slightly before serving with clotted cream or sweet butter and jam.

vidual dessert dishes. Cover with plastic film and refrigerate for 6 hours.

When ready to serve, remove the pudding(s) from the refrigerator. Uncover and decorate the top with individual berries and a mint sprig.

Cranachan

Serves 12

This is a quintessential Scottish dessert that uses the wonderfully fragrant local liqueur, Drambuie, to bring everyday oats to new heights. It is easy to make and, since it requires a period of refrigeration to set properly, it would be the perfect ending to an evening spent deep in a tale of the Empire.

1 cup rolled oats
4 cups cold heavy cream
½ cup superfine sugar or to taste
2 tablespoons Drambuie liqueur
2 cups raspberries, blackberries, blueberries, or
    sliced strawberries plus more for garnishing
Mint sprigs for garnish

Preheat the oven to 350°F.

Place the oats in a baking pan, pushing them out to a single layer. Place in the preheated oven and bake, tossing and turning occasionally, for about 15 minutes or until nicely toasted. Remove from the oven and set aside to cool.

Place the cream in the bowl of a standing electric mixer fitted with the whisk. Beat on low until just frothy. Add the sugar and liqueur, raise the speed, and continue to beat until stiff peaks form.

Remove the bowl from the mixer and, using a spatula, fold in the berries along with the reserved oats.

Either scrape the pudding into a decorative serving bowl or place an equal portion into each of 12 indi-

Irish Coffee

Makes As Many Glasses As You Like

Irish coffee is usually served in a tall glass mug as a late evening warmer-upper. If you have the hot coffee on hand, it is quite simple to make individual servings. This slightly sweet libation would be the perfect ending to an evening of immersion in an Irish novel or play.

FOR EACH MUG:
6 ounces hot, strong coffee
1 ounce Irish whiskey
1 teaspoon sugar
3 tablespoons whipped cream
Ground cinnamon for sprinkling, optional

Place the hot coffee in an Irish coffee mug. Stir in the whiskey along with the sugar. Spoon the whipped cream over the top and serve, sprinkled with cinnamon, if desired.

Chapter 8

French Tastes

𝒯HE WORK OF WRITERS SUCH AS BALZAC and Proust and the experimental art of Camus, Ionesco, Genet and Sartre have had a profound effect on contemporary writers of many places.

Although many realize or might guess how devotedly the French extol their culinary heritage, it surprises outsiders to discover how large a place literary and aesthetic debate have

READS, DRINKS & NIBBLES
■ ■ ■
Pissaladière

STAR DISHES & DELICIOUS ASIDES
■ ■ ■
Croque Monsieur
Frisée Salad with A Perfect French Vinaigrette
Poulet Chasseur

FOR A MOVEABLE FEAST
■ ■ ■
Provençal Picnic with *Anchoiade, Rouille* and Marinated Cheese

LITERARY TEA OR SWEET ENDING
■ ■ ■
Madeleines

in the national discourse conducted by the French media. One of the most popular contemporary television shows has been "Apostrophes," a talk show focused on the world of art and literature.

Whether you are a devotee of a classical or a modern French author or philosopher, a rediscovered one such as Irène Némirovsky or a new talent like Muriel Barbery, you'll be chewing over ideas as well as character between sips of your apéritif or wine and, I hope, bites of something deliciously French.

✦ ✦ ✦

The French like nothing more than enjoying an apéritif, a light alcoholic drink meant to encourage digestion, before a meal. Even the smallest café—particularly in the south of France—will have a pre-dinner (or pre-lunch) special house apéritif. Although champagne, Dubonnet, Lillet or other commercially manufactured apéritifs can be served, it is with great pride that the host will have devised his own house-made drink. Most often it is a glass of white or sparkling wine flavored with a home-made fruit syrup, purée, or juice or herb-scented syrup. There are now many syrups and fruit purées made for this purpose to be found in specialty food stores.

Pissaladière

Makes one large pie

This traditional pizza-style tart from the south of France is usually made with oil-cured anchovies as part of the topping. You can use sun-dried tomatoes to approximate the briny saltiness of the traditional fish for a vegetarian version. You can also eliminate the tomatoes and use extra onions that, when combined with the roasted garlic, will make a rich, almost-sweet topping. The pie may be made in advance and reheated just before serving so that the warm *Provençal* sun will embrace your guests. And if you bring chilled bottles of rosé wine to the table, your meal will be complete.

PIZZA DOUGH (enough for 1 large pizza)
1½ teaspoons yeast granules
¾ cup warm (105°F to 115°F) water
2 cups all-purpose flour plus more for finishing
½ cup whole-wheat flour
½ teaspoon salt
¼ cup extra virgin olive oil

Combine the yeast with the water in a small bowl. Stir to combine.

Combine the flours and salt in the bowl of a heavy-duty mixer fitted with the dough hook. With the mixer running at low speed, pour in the yeast-water mixture followed by the olive oil. Continue mixing, raising the speed to medium, for about 12 minutes or until the dough is smooth and elastic (or follow manufacturer's instructions for bread-making with your mixer, or knead by hand).

When the dough is smooth and elastic, remove it from the mixer bowl and form it into a slightly raised circle or oblong, spreading it out and tucking the raw edges under. Place the dough on a floured baking sheet, cover and place in a warm, draft-free spot for about 2 hours or until the dough has tripled in volume.

Lightly flour the top of the risen dough as well as your hands. Lift the dough circle by placing your fists underneath it. Begin stretching the dough by simultaneously turning the circle and pulling your fists away from the center, re-flouring your hands as necessary. You will need to stretch the dough out to a ¼-inch thick rectangle large enough to fit an 11-inch by 17-inch jelly roll pan. (If this seems too difficult, sprinkle equal portions of flour and cornmeal onto a cool, smooth surface. Turn the dough circle onto the floured surface and toss to coat. Gently push the circle some-what flat using the palms of your hands and then use a rolling pin to flatten the dough to the appropriate size. When doing this, roll lightly or the dough will compress and toughen.)

Fill and bake as directed in the recipe below or use as a base for any pizza.

Pissaladière Topping

3 pounds sweet white onions, peeled
1 tablespoon herbes de Provence
    (see Note)
¼ teaspoon ground cloves
¼ cup extra virgin olive oil
Coarse salt and freshly ground pepper
    to taste
¼ cup finely ground yellow cornmeal or
    semolina flour
12 cloves roasted garlic, peeled
1 cup sliced, pitted Niçoise olives
1 cup anchovies packed in oil or sun-dried
    tomatoes packed in oil, well-drained and
    cut into thin strips

Preheat the oven to 350°F.

Using a chef's knife, cut the onions, crosswise, into paper-thin slices. Pull the slices apart and place the rings in a mixing bowl.

Sprinkle the *herbes de Provence* and cloves over the onion rings. Drizzle the olive oil over all and toss to coat. Season with salt and pepper to taste, noting that the olives and tomatoes will add additional saltiness.

Place the seasoned onion rings in a nonstick baking pan, spreading them out into an even layer. Place in the preheated oven and bake, stirring frequently for about 25 minutes or until the onions are very soft, slightly caramelized and nearly dry. Remove from the oven and set aside.

Raise the oven temperature to 425°F.

Sprinkle a thin layer of cornmeal over the

> "Happy and successful cooking doesn't rely only on know-how; it comes from the heart, makes great demands on the palate and needs enthusiasm and a deep love of food to bring it to life."
>
> — CHEF GEORGES BLANC

bottom of a nonstick, 11-inch by 17-inch jelly roll pan. (You may not need all of the cornmeal.)

Line the prepared pan with the Pizza Dough, working the dough to make a smooth fit with an edge coming up the side of the pan. Using your fingertips, crimp the dough edges against the pan.

Spread an even layer of the cooked onion mixture over the dough. Sprinkle the onions with the roasted garlic and olives. Top with the anchovies or sun-dried tomatoes.

Place the pan in the preheated oven and bake for about 25 minutes or until the crust is cooked and the edges are golden. Remove from the oven and cut the entire tart into small serving pieces.

Serve warm or at room temperature.

NOTE: *Herbes de Provence*, a ready-made combination of dried herbs with a strong accent of lavender, is available from specialty food stores or by mail order or through the Internet from Penzey's Spices.

Croque Monsieur

Makes 6

This is a very special grilled cheese sandwich that is a French bistro favorite, the perfect luncheon entrée or late-evening dish to enjoy with a French literary icon. All you need is a light white wine and a little green salad, dressed with vinaigrette to complete the meal.

Twelve ½-inch thick slices peasant bread,
*   trimmed of crusts*
3 tablespoons unsalted butter plus more for
*   buttering the bread*
¾ cup honey mustard
18 slices Gruyère cheese
12 thin slices baked ham
12 thin slices tomato

Preheat the oven to 400°F.
Cover a clean, flat work surface with wax paper.
Lightly butter one side of each slice of bread.
Lay out 6 slices of the bread on the wax paper, buttered side down. Cover the top of each slice with mustard. Working with one slice at a time, lay 2 pieces of cheese on top of the mustard and coat the cheese with a light touch of mustard. Lay 2 slices of tomato on top of the cheese and then top the tomato with 2 slices of ham. Top each sandwich with a slice of bread, buttered side up. (The sandwiches may be prepared up to this point and finished just before serving.)

> **"How can you govern a country which has 246 varieties of cheese?"** — CHARLES DE GAULLE

Melt the 3 tablespoons of butter in a large nonstick frying pan over medium heat. Fry the sandwiches, turning once, for about 3 minutes or until just golden. Transfer the sandwiches to a nonstick baking sheet. Place a slice of cheese on top of each one and place in the preheated oven. Bake for about 5 minutes or until the cheese has melted and started to brown.

Remove from the oven and cut into triangles. Serve warm with more honey mustard on the side.

Frisée Salad with a Perfect French Vinaigrette

Serves 8

In France, this would be called *Frisée aux Lardons*, and it is typically found in bistros. The *lardons* or crisp bacon bits are a lovely counterpoint to the slightly bitter green. If you can't find *frisée* (or if it is, as is often true, too expensive), use any slightly bitter green that you like—even arugula will do.

½ pound slab bacon, cut into cubes
6 heads frisée, separated, washed, dried,
*   and trimmed of any brown spots*
6 tablespoons champagne vinegar or
*   white wine vinegar*
1 tablespoon minced shallots
1 tablespoon Dijon mustard
1 ½ cups peanut oil
Salt and pepper to taste
2 tablespoons minced chives

Place the bacon in a large frying pan over medium heat. Fry, stirring and turning frequently for about 7 minutes until crisp and golden brown. Use a slotted spoon to transfer the bacon to a double layer of paper towel to drain.

Lower the heat under the frying pan and add the vinegar, stirring to beat the vinegar into the fat. Add the shallots and cook, stirring, for about a minute to deglaze the pan.

Remove the pan from the heat and stir in the mustard. Using a whisk, beat in the oil. When well-emulsified, taste and, if necessary, season with salt and pepper.

Place the *frisée* in a large salad bowl. Pour the warm dressing over the top and toss to coat lightly. Garnish the top with the bacon and sprinkle with chives.

Serve immediately.

Poulet Chasseur

Serves 8 to 10

Poulet Chasseur is one of those dishes that have many cooks devising their own recipe. Traditionally, it is a rich chicken stew with mushrooms— the *"chasseur"* in the title referring to the "hunter" of wild mushrooms. It is a great dish for entertaining because, like most stews, it tastes even better when reheated, so it can be made a couple of days in advance of your guests' arrival. With a green salad (see vinaigrette dressing page 104), some crusty bread, and a lovely glass of wine, it would compose a wonderful French meal to honor the night's author.

5 tablespoons olive oil
Two 3-pound chickens, cut into serving pieces
Salt and pepper to taste
1 pound andouille *sausage, cut into bite-sized pieces* (Andouille *is a smoky, spicy French sausage. If a smoky sausage is unavailable, you may substitute any sausage you like, even a sweet Italian sausage).*
2 medium carrots, peeled, trimmed, and diced
3 cups sliced mixed wild mushrooms (If wild mushrooms are not to be found, you may substitute button mushrooms.)

1 cup chopped shallots
1 teaspoon minced garlic
1 cup dry white wine
4 cups canned plum tomatoes with juice
1 teaspoon dried thyme
½ teaspoon dried sage
1 cup heavy cream

Preheat the oven to 350°F.

Heat 3 tablespoons of the oil in a large Dutch oven over medium heat.

Season the chicken with salt and pepper to taste. Place the chicken in the hot pan, a few pieces at a time, and fry, turning occasionally, until lightly browned. Transfer to a platter as browned.

When all of the chicken has been browned, add the sausage to the pan and fry, turning occasionally, for about 3 minutes, or until just lightly colored. Add the remaining 2 tablespoons of oil and when it is hot, add the carrots, mushrooms, shallots, and garlic and continue to sauté for about 6 minutes or until softened.

Stir in the wine and bring to a simmer. Simmer for 5 minutes or until some of the alcohol has burned off.

Return the chicken to the pan. Add the tomatoes, thyme, and sage and bring to a simmer. Season with salt and pepper to taste, cover and transfer to the preheated oven.

Braise for about 1 hour or until the chicken is almost falling off the bone. Remove the pan from the oven.

Uncover and stir in the cream. Place over medium heat and bring to a simmer. Taste and, if necessary, adjust the seasoning with salt and pepper. Simmer for about 15 minutes or until the cream has thickened the sauce.

Serve hot with rice or potatoes, if desired.

"Nothing would be more tiresome than eating and drinking if God had not made them a pleasure as well as a necessity." —VOLTAIRE

PROVENÇAL PICNIC with
ANCHOIADE, ROUILLE and MARINATED CHEESE

✦ ✦ ✦

Deep into Dumas, Stendhal, Flaubert, Anatole France or Colette, readers hunger for a taste of France. Even when devouring a scene set in Paris, there is a tendency to yearn for the aromatic, savory foods of the south of France. Although you can make some of the components of the picnic spread below, others may be purchased from a gourmet grocer and bakery or picked up from supermarket salad bars, bins and shelves. You might want to complete your picnic with some cold sliced meats, such as roast beef and ham as well as some dried sausages, such as saucisson sec, or even some salamis along with grainy mustards and cornichon pickles. After the picnic elements are artfully arranged on a platter, no one will know for sure that you did not spend days in the kitchen. But I provide a few recipes to ensure the vive-la-France homemade touch.

> *Marinated Cheese (may be purchased in some locales)*
> Anchoiade
> Rouille *with Vegetables*
> *Cured Mushrooms (can be purchased)*

> "A tale without love is like beef without mustard: insipid."
> —ANATOLE FRANCE,
> La Révolte des Anges

Mixed Olives (can be purchased)
Crusty Peasant Bread (can be purchased)

Marinated Cheese

Makes 1 pound

> One-pound log fresh goat cheese
> 10 black peppercorns
> 6 cloves roasted garlic
> 4 large sage leaves
> 2 sprigs fresh rosemary
> 1 dried hot chili pepper
> 1 bay leaf
> Approximately 3 cups
>   extra virgin olive oil

Use a sharp knife to cut the cheese into 1-inch thick rounds. Place about half of the cheese into a large, nonreactive container. Add the peppercorns, garlic, sage, rosemary, chili and bay leaf, and then add the remainder of the cheese. Pour in enough olive oil to cover the cheese by about 1 inch.

Using a table knife, work around the inside edges of the container to dispel any air. Cover and refrigerate for at least 24 hours or up to 3 days to allow flavors to blend.

When ready to serve, remove from the refrigerator and bring to room temperature.

Anchoiade

Serves 12 to 16

One 24-ounce can anchovy fillets, packed
   in olive oil, drained
2 cups chopped flat leaf parsley
¼ cup roasted garlic purée
2 tablespoons minced red onion
⅔ cup red wine vinegar

Combine the anchovies, parsley, garlic purée, and onion in the bowl of a food processor fitted with the metal blade. Process, using quick on-and-off turns, just until the mixture is coarsely chopped. Add the vinegar and process to combine.

Scrape into a nonreactive container, cover, and refrigerate until ready to use, or for up to 3 weeks.

Serve with warm toast, baguette slices or crackers.

Rouille

Makes about 4 cups

2 dried red hot chilies, stemmed and seeded
2 red bell peppers, roasted, peeled, cored,
   and seeded
2 tablespoons chopped garlic
½ teaspoon saffron threads softened in
1 tablespoon hot water
½ cup fresh white breadcrumbs
2 large egg yolks, at room temperature*
2 cups extra virgin olive oil
Salt and pepper to taste
Vegetables or croutons for dipping

> "His principal vice was a mania for proposing rural parties during the summer season . . . picnics on the grass, and visits to creameries."
>
> —HONORÉ DE BALZAC, Bureaucracy

Place the dried chilies in a heatproof container with boiling water to cover by an inch. Set aside to soften for 15 minutes. Drain well.

Combine the drained chili with the roasted peppers, garlic and saffron (along with the soaking water) in the bowl of a food processor fitted with the metal blade. Process until smooth.

With the motor running, add the breadcrumbs and blend to a thick paste.

With the motor still running, add the egg yolks, one at a time, and then begin slowly adding the oil, processing until all of the oil has been added and the mixture has emulsified. Taste. If necessary, season with salt and pepper.

Scrape into a serving bowl and serve at room temperature as a dip for crisp, cooked vegetables, such as broccoli or cauliflower and/or fresh vegetables such as bell peppers, zucchini or scallions, or for croutons.

* If you are concerned with the safety of consuming raw eggs, simply microwave the finished sauce for 1 minute.

Madeleines

Makes approximately 4 dozen

I can't think of any other food that is as associated with an author as is the *madeleine* and Marcel Proust. One bite and a river of memories pour forth, memories barely contained in the quartet of novels called in English, *Remembrance of Things Past*. Madeleines are delicate little treats, more sponge cake than cookie. They are always made in special pans that contain 12 little shell-shaped molds, and are especially delicious served warm. Fortunately, these tiny genoise cakes can easily be reheated with a few seconds in a microwave—which also sends the sweet scent of lemony sugar into the air.

Serve with tea as Parisiennes do, or after dinner with espresso.

> "She sent out for one of those short, plump little cakes called petites madeleines, which look as though they had been molded in the fluted scallop of a pilgrim's shell. And soon, mechanically, weary after a dull day with the prospect of a depressing morrow, I raised to my lips a spoonful of the tea in which I had soaked a morsel of the cake. No sooner had the warm liquid, and the crumbs with it, touched my palate than a shudder ran through my whole body, and I stopped, intent upon the extraordinary changes that were taking place...at once the vicissitudes of life had become indifferent to me, its disasters innocuous, its brevity illusory."
>
> —MARCEL PROUST, *Remembrance of Things Past*, Volume I: Swann's Way

1½ cups unsalted clarified butter (See Note on page 93)
4 large eggs, at room temperature
1½ cups granulated sugar
1 teaspoon freshly grated lemon zest
1 teaspoon pure vanilla extract
2 cups all-purpose flour, sifted
Confectioners' sugar, optional

Preheat the oven to 450°F.

Generously butter the molds in *madeleine* pans. Set aside.

Place the eggs, granulated sugar, and lemon zest in the bowl of a standing electric mixer. Place the bowl in hot water and let stand, whisking occasionally, until very warm.

When warm, place the bowl in the mixer stand fitted with the paddle attachment. Beat on low for a minute or so and then raise the speed to high and beat until the mixture is light, fluffy, and tripled in volume. Add the vanilla and beat to mix.

Fold in the flour, followed by the clarified butter, taking care not to beat or the batter will fall.

Transfer the batter to a large pastry bag fitted with the large, plain round tip. Carefully pipe the batter into the prepared molds, filling about ⅔ full.

Place in the preheated oven and bake for about 10 minutes, or until the cakes are lightly colored on the top and a hint of brown is seen around the edges.

Immediately remove from the oven, turn the pans upside down, and gently tap the little cakes out onto wire racks to cool.

If necessary, again butter the molds, refill with batter, and bake and cool as above.

If desired, when the cakes are cool, lightly dust with confectioners' sugar.

"Yesterday I asked Maman if I could drink some tea. My grandmother drinks black tea at breakfast flavored with bergamot . . . At the restaurant last night Maman ordered some jasmine tea and she let me taste it. I thought it was so good that this morning I said that from now on I wanted tea at breakfast. Maman shot me a strange look (her poorly-purged sleeping tablet look) then she said yes yes sweetheart you're old enough now." —MURIEL BARBERY, The Elegance of the Hedgehog

Chapter 9

Sun-Drenched Savories and Sweets

*T*HE FOODS OF SOUTHERN EUROPE ARE AS SAVORY AS ITS LITERATURE AND, BY TURNS, salty, savage, serene. Although it is not easy to create some specialties from the countries of southern Europe, many building blocks for dishes are widely available, making it simpler for the time-pressed cook to put together an authentic meal or taste of the country on the pages of your book. Don't hesitate to purchase Spanish cheeses or hams, the elements of an Italian antipasto or Greek pastries such as baklava. Portuguese *natas* or pastries can be found in bakeries from Santa Clara to Providence, and some bakeries ship. And, of course, don't forget that marvelous Italian wines are easily found, while an advance consultation with your favorite liquor store or wine shop owner could bring forth Greek ouzo or wines from the sunny European country of your choice.

✦ ✦ ✦

Reads, Drinks & Nibbles

Sangria

Makes about 2 quarts

There are probably a million recipes for sangria. It is such a delicious and sparkling drink that every cook likes to put his or her own stamp on it. Often commercially made with cheap wine and low-grade alcohol, sangria's reputation has plummeted. But I can guarantee that this homemade version will have your club members wanting to continue reading books with an Iberian setting.

1 cup brandy
1 cup orange juice
¼ cup lemon juice
1 cup sugar
2 oranges, well-washed and cut, crosswise, into thin slices
Whatever other fruit you prefer—strawberries and peaches make excellent but optional additions.
Two 750 milliliter bottles Spanish red wine, such as Rioja
3 cups cold club soda or seltzer water

Combine the brandy, orange juice, and lemon juice in a nonreactive container. Stir in the sugar. When the sugar has dissolved, add the orange slices and, if using, whatever other fruit you desire. Set aside to marinate for at least 1 hour.

Stir in the red wine, cover, and refrigerate for at least 1 hour, but preferably up to 24 hours.

When ready to serve, transfer the wine mixture to a large pitcher. Add the club soda or seltzer. Serve over ice with an orange or lemon slice as garnish.

ANTIPASTO PLATTERS with
CAPONATA OR MARINATED MUSHROOMS

❖ ❖ ❖

In Italian, antipasto simply means "before the meal" and it can be just that—a smattering of bits and pieces of hot and cold foods to be eaten before the main meal. However, it now often refers to a large platter or buffet table laden with a marvelous assortment of meats, cheeses and vegetables, and the products can come from almost anywhere in the world. You can combine Italian products with French charcuterie, Asian pickles and American standards, salads and pickled, marinated, or cured fruits or vegetables, which are served with breads, breadsticks and crackers. A spread like this is usually much more substantial than passed hors d'oeuvre and less formal than a plated appetizer. In Greece (as well as other countries, such as Turkey), an antipasto-style platter is known as a "*meze* platter*,*" with each individual dish a *meze*. No matter where it is served, wine or an aperitif is generally offered along with it.

Despite the fact that in the United States many antipasto platters feature only Italian specialties, this does not have to be the rule. You can fashion a platter to reflect whatever country or region you wish to feature, or combinations of several countries' specialities. You can purchase all of the selections on it or create one or all of the recipes that follow. The antipasto platter is a wonderful place to bring many cultures together in harmony!

A BOUNTIFUL ANTIPASTO PLATTER SHOULD CONTAIN:

CURED MEATS such as ham: Serrano (Spain), Bayonne (France), Black Forest (Germany), Presunto (Portugal), or Parma or *prosciutto* (Italy) are some excellent choices. Among sausages or salamis, consider *Culatello*, *coppa*, *soppressata* and chorizo and blood sausage.

CHEESES such as parmesan, mozzarella, pecorino, brie, goat cheeses (fresh and cured), feta—and on and on the list goes of fine cheeses now available in the United States. Generally, sheep's and goat's milk cheeses best represent the Iberian peninsula.

VEGETABLES such as marinated bell peppers, artichoke hearts, chickpeas and mushrooms, as well as grilled vegetables, pickled hot peppers, pickles such as cornichons, and olives should be added.

PREPARED FOODS such as *caponata* (recipe follows) or tapenade are good additions. So are marinated mushrooms (recipe follows), which, like olives, are devoured throughout Mediterranean Europe.

DRIED FRUITS OR FRUIT PASTES (such as fig paste aka *mebrillo*, or guava paste) are available in fine cheese shops and specialty food stores.

Optionally, an antipasto platter can also offer some fresh fruit, such as grapes and figs to compliment the cheeses, or melon to go with the meats

On the side, breads, breadsticks and crackers should be presented along with condiments such as mustard, chutneys, extra virgin olive oil and balsamic vinegar.

Caponata

Makes about 4 cups

6 tablespoons olive oil
4 ribs celery, well-washed, trimmed and
    chopped
1 large red onion, peeled and chopped
1 tablespoon minced garlic
1 large eggplant, peeled and cubed
2½ cups chopped canned tomatoes, drained
¾ cup chopped green olives
¼ cup red wine vinegar
2 tablespoons sun-dried tomato or plain
    tomato paste
2 tablespoons capers, well-drained
½ teaspoon dried oregano
½ teaspoon dried basil
Black pepper to taste
Sugar to taste, optional
Salt to taste, optional
3 tablespoons chopped fresh flat leaf parsley
1 tablespoon chopped fresh basil

Heat 3 tablespoons of the oil in a large deep skillet over medium heat. Add the onion, celery, and garlic and cook, stirring frequently, for about 5 minutes or until the vegetables have softened and taken on some color. Using a slotted spoon, transfer the mixture to a bowl.

Add the remaining 3 tablespoons of oil in the skillet over medium heat. Add the eggplant and cook, stirring frequently, for about 8 minutes or until the eggplant has browned. Return the celery mixture to the skillet, stirring to blend.

Add the tomatoes and olives and bring to a simmer. Then stir in the vinegar, tomato paste, capers, oregano, and basil. Season to taste with pepper.

Bring the mixture to a simmer. Lower the heat and cook at a gentle simmer for about 25 minutes or until the flavors have blended and the mixture has thickened somewhat. Taste, and if any bitterness is detected, add sugar to taste. If necessary, season with salt.

Remove from the heat and stir in the parsley and fresh basil.

Serve warm or at room temperature. Store, covered and refrigerated for up to 1 week.

Marinated Mushrooms

Makes about 2 pounds

2 pounds small button mushrooms
8 cloves garlic, peeled and chopped
2 cups extra virgin olive oil
1 cup tarragon vinegar
2 tablespoons minced onion
1 teaspoon crushed red pepper flakes
Dash hot pepper sauce or to taste
Salt to taste
2 sprigs fresh basil

Combine the mushrooms with the garlic, olive oil, vinegar, onion, pepper flakes, and hot pepper sauce in a nonreactive container with a lid. Season with salt to taste. Add the basil sprigs, cover and refrigerate for at least 24 hours before using.

Store, covered and refrigerated, for up to 1 month.

Greek Salad with Red Wine Vinaigrette

Serves 8 to 10

The salad that we have come to know as a Greek salad is really a combination of two types of traditional Greek salads—a tomato-feta summer salad and a relatively plain lettuce salad. The basic mix is now romaine lettuce, tomatoes, cucumbers, feta cheese and olives, with a pungent vinegar dressing. However, you can add anchovies, other vegetables, or even chunks of canned tuna to make it your own. It is a filling salad that would make a nice luncheon or summer supper dish in homage to an author who may be Greek but is no longer foreign to you.

3 large heads romaine lettuce, well-washed,
*   dried, and cut into pieces*
6 ripe tomatoes, peeled, cored, and cut into wedges
1 large red onion, peeled and cut, crosswise, into
*   thin slices*
1 hothouse cucumber, well-washed and cut,
*   crosswise, into thin slices*
1 cup crumbled feta cheese
1 cup pitted Kalamata olives
Red Wine Vinaigrette (recipe follows)
One 2-ounce can anchovy fillets, well-drained,
*   optional*
1 bunch radishes, well-washed, trimmed, and
*   cut, crosswise, into thin slices, optional*

Line a large platter with the lettuce. Arrange the onions, tomatoes and cucumbers in an attractive pattern over the lettuce. Sprinkle with the cheese and olives. Drizzle the vinaigrette over the top. If desired, decorate with the anchovies and/or radishes.

Serve with warm pita bread.

Red Wine Vinaigrette

Makes about 1½ cups

1 cup olive oil
¼ cup red wine vinegar
1 teaspoon Dijon mustard
1 teaspoon minced garlic
1 teaspoon dried oregano
Salt and pepper to taste

Place the olive oil in a jar with a lid. Add the vinegar, mustard, garlic, and oregano, cover, and shake to emulsify. Season with salt and pepper to taste.

Use as directed in the recipe or store, covered and refrigerated, for up to 1 week. Bring to room temperature before using.

> **"The good of a book lies in its being read."**—UMBERTO ECO

Portuguese Potatoes in Almond Sauce

Serves 8 to 10

Garlic and almonds are two quintessential Portuguese flavorings. And potatoes are the constant throughout the cuisine as the base in which to infuse these flavors. This dish can be eaten either hot or at room temperature and is a wonderful addition to a platter of snacks.

½ cup olive oil
¼ cup blanched almonds
1 cup fresh French baguette cubes
1 teaspoon sliced garlic
¼ teaspoon saffron threads or to taste
1 teaspoon minced parsley
1 pound potatoes, peeled and cut into small cubes
1 cup low-sodium, nonfat chicken broth
Salt and pepper to taste

Place the oil in a very large frying pan, preferably cast iron, over medium heat. When hot, add the almonds, bread cubes and garlic, and cook, tossing and turning, for about 5 minutes or until golden brown. If the almonds and garlic brown before the bread, using a slotted spoon, remove them from the pan and set aside.

Remove the pan from the heat and drain off the oil through a fine mesh sieve, separately reserving the oil and the almond/bread mixture.

Place the almond/bread mixture in the bowl of a food processor fitted with the metal blade. Add the saffron and parsley, and process to a rough paste.

With the motor running, slowly add 1 cup cool water and blend until the sauce is smooth.

Place the potatoes in the same frying pan in which you cooked the almonds and bread cubes. Add the sauce along with the reserved cooking oil and chicken broth. Place over medium heat and season with salt and pepper to taste. Cook, stirring occasionally, for about 25 minutes or until the potatoes are tender. If the sauce gets too thick before the potatoes are tender, add water or more chicken broth, a bit at a time.

Serve hot, warm or at room temperature.

Tortilla Romesco

Serves 8 to 10

This is not the *tortilla* that we associate with Mexican food. A *tortilla* simply means "little cake," and that is exactly what this is —a savory,

"HERALD
List, ye people! As was the custom of your forebears, empty a full pitcher of wine at the call of the trumpet; he, who first sees the bottom, shall get a wine-skin as round and plump as Ctesiphon's belly.

DICAEOPOLIS
Women, children, have you not heard? Faith! do you not heed the herald? Quick! let the hares boil and roast merrily; keep them a-turning; withdraw them from the flame; prepare the chaplets; reach me the skewers that I may spit the thrushes.

CHORUS
I envy you your wisdom and even more your good cheer.

DICAEOPOLIS
What then will you say when you see the thrushes roasting? . . .

CHORUS
See, how he knows his business, what a perfect cook! How well he understands the way to prepare a good dinner!"

—ARISTOPHANES, THE ACHARNIANS

"The heat is unbearable and the spectators refresh themselves with the customary glass of lemonade, cup of water or slice of watermelon, for there is no reason why they should suffer from exhaustion just because the condemned are about to die. And should they feel in need of something more substantial, there is a wide choice of nuts and seeds, cheeses and dates. The King, with his inseparable Infantes and Infantas, will dine at the Inquisitor's Palace as soon as the auto-da-fe has ended, and once free of the wretched business, he will join the Chief Inquisitor for a sumptuous feast at tables laden with bowls of chicken broth, partridges, breasts of veal, pates and meat savories flavored with cinnamon and sugar, a stew in the Castilian manner with all the appropriate ingredients and saffron rice, blancmanges, pastries, and fruits in season. But the King is so abstinent that he refuses to drink any wine, and since the best lesson of all is a good example, everyone accepts it, the example, that is, not the abstinence."

—JOSÉ SARAMAGO, Baltasar and Blimunda

small, pan-made cake that resembles an omelet. It is also known as a *tortilla Española* or *tortilla de papas* (potatoes), and is eaten throughout Portugal and Spain as well as in many other Spanish-speaking countries. Unlike a filled French omelet, a *tortilla* is a thick, flat pancake. I love it served with the wonderfully piquant traditional Spanish *Romesco* Sauce. The *tortilla* may be served hot, warm, or at room temperature.

½ cup olive oil plus more if necessary
1 pound sweet onions, peeled and cut, crosswise, into thin slices
1 teaspoon minced garlic
Salt and pepper to taste
2 pounds new potatoes, well-washed and thinly sliced
1 dozen large eggs
Paprika to taste
Romesco *Sauce (recipe follows)*

Heat ¼ cup of the olive oil in a very large, deep skillet (preferably nonstick) over medium heat. When very hot, but not smoking, add the onions and garlic. Lower the heat and season with salt and pepper to taste. Fry, stirring frequently, for about 30 minutes or until the onions are beginning to caramelize and are golden brown. Scrape the onions into a bowl.

Return the pan to medium heat. Add the remaining ¼ cup of oil and, when hot, add the potatoes. Season with salt and pepper and fry, turning and tossing frequently, for about 25 minutes, or until the potatoes are cooked through and lightly colored. Scrape the potatoes into the onions.

Place the eggs in a mixing bowl and season with paprika, salt, and pepper to taste. Pour the eggs into the potato/onion mixture, stirring to combine.

Return the pan to medium heat and, if necessary, add enough oil to just coat the bottom of the pan. When hot, add the egg mixture, smoothing out the top with a spatula.

Lower the heat and cook, without turning, for about 10 minutes or until the bottom is golden and the omelet has begun to set. You can shake the pan to keep the omelet from sticking, but do not turn or mix it.

Using a bit of olive oil, lightly coat a plate large enough to hold the omelet. When the omelet is almost set, place the oiled plate over the pan and carefully invert the pan onto the plate. Then, maneuver the uncooked side of the omelet into the bottom of the pan. Continue to cook for an additional 5 minutes or until the omelet is thoroughly set.

Slide the omelet onto a serving plate. Cut into wedges and serve with the sauce on the side.

Romesco Sauce

Makes about 1 cup

½ pound red bell peppers, cored, seeded, and
  chopped
¼ cup chopped canned tomatoes, well-drained
⅓ cup nonfat, low-sodium chicken broth
¼ cup dry white bread crumbs
3 tablespoons chopped toasted, blanched almonds
1 teaspoon roasted garlic purée
2 teaspoons extra virgin olive oil
1 teaspoon sherry wine vinegar
Paprika to taste
Salt and pepper to taste

Combine the bell peppers and tomatoes in a small saucepan. Add the chicken broth and place over medium heat. Bring to a simmer and cook gently, stirring occasionally, for 5 minutes or until the peppers are very soft.

Remove the pan from the heat and pour the mixture into the bowl of a food processor fitted with the metal blade. Process to a smooth purée.

With the motor running, add breadcrumbs, almonds, and garlic. When well-blended, and with the motor still running, slowly add the oil and vinegar. When emulsified, add the paprika, salt, and pepper to taste.

Transfer to a small bowl and serve. (Or place in a nonreactive container, cover, and refrigerate for up to 1 week.)

"Hunger is the best sauce in the world." — MIGUEL DE CERVANTES, Don Quixote

Pasta with Pesto

Serves 8

Pesto sauce has become a year-round favorite pasta or salad sauce in many places, due to the almost continuous availability of fresh basil. However, since basil is generally very prolific, pesto can be made very cheaply during the summer months and frozen for later use. Originating in Genoa, pesto is now found throughout the world. (In France, a version known as *pistou* is often enjoyed.) The combination of basil, cheese, and nuts produces an aroma that absolutely sings of southern Europe.

4 tightly packed cups chopped fresh basil leaves
1 cup pine nuts
1 teaspoon minced garlic
1 cup freshly grated Parmesan cheese
1 teaspoon black pepper
¾ cup extra virgin olive oil
Salt to taste, optional
1 pound dried pasta of
  choice

Combine the basil with the pine nuts and garlic in the bowl of a food processor fitted with the metal blade. Process, using quick on-and-off turns, to just blend. Add the cheese and pepper and process to a coarse mix. With the motor running, slowly add the olive oil, processing to a thick paste. Taste and, if necessary, season with salt.

Scrape the mixture from the processor to a nonreactive container. (If not using immediately, cover and refrigerate until ready to use, or up to 1 day. For longer storage, cover, label and freeze.)

Cook the pasta according to package directions.

Drain well, reserving 1 cup of the cooking water.

Return the pasta to the cooking pan, adding just enough pesto to season the pasta nicely. Add the cooking water, a bit at a time, to make a creamy sauce. Return to medium heat and cook for just a minute to marry the flavors.

Serve with additional pesto and cheese on the side.

Anise Cookies

Makes about 6 dozen

These are lovely little cookies that go well with a deep, dark espresso. Nibbling these cookies makes a wonderful way to celebrate an evening immersed in Italian literature. Very good keepers, they make a nice treat for many weeks after being baked.

2 cups sifted all-purpose flour
2 teaspoons baking powder
3 large eggs, at room temperature
1 cup sugar
¼ cup melted unsalted butter
1 teaspoon anise extract
1 teaspoon anise seed
½ cup chopped almonds

Sift the flour and baking powder together. Set aside.

Combine the eggs and sugar in the bowl of a standing electric mixer fitted with the paddle. When creamy, add the butter and mix to combine. Add the flour and continue beating until well-combined and the dough is thick. Add the extract, seed, and almonds and beat to blend. If the dough seems too soft to form into rolls, add a bit more flour.

Scrape the dough from the bowl and, using your hands, form it into 4 rolls about 2 inches thick. Wrap each roll in plastic film and refrigerate for 1 hour.

Preheat the oven to 350°F.

Line 2 cookie sheets with parchment paper or spray with nonstick vegetable spray.

Remove the dough from the refrigerator. Unwrap and place the whole rolls on one of the prepared cookie sheets. Place in the preheated oven and bake for about 30 minutes or until quite firm and lightly browned. Do not turn off the oven.

Remove the rolls from the oven and, using a serrated knife, cut each roll, crosswise, into ¼ inch thick slices. Transfer the slices to both of the prepared cookie sheets and place in the hot oven.

Bake for about 5 minutes or until the cookies are lightly brown and set.

Transfer to wire racks to cool.

Store, airtight, for up to 4 weeks.

"The captain drained his jug, thinking hard. In those days, fifteen four-doubloon pieces, in gold, came to more than seven hundred reales. Enough to get him out of difficulty, buy new linens and a suit of clothes, pay off his debts . . . eat hot food without depending on the generous thighs of Caridad la Lebrijana . . .

'My future,' the captain echoed, absorbed in his thoughts."

—ARTURO PÉREZ-REVERTE,
Captain Alatriste

Baklava

Makes about 36 pieces

Although most of us think of baklava as a Greek pastry, some version of it can be found though central Asia and in many of the countries that were once part of the Ottoman Empire. It is a very rich dessert and seems difficult to make, but once all of your ingredients are in order, the process moves very quickly and easily.

4 cups shelled, toasted pistachios
2¼ cups sugar
2 teaspoons ground cinnamon
1 teaspoon ground cardamom
1¼ cups unsalted butter, melted
One 16-ounce package frozen phyllo dough, thawed and covered with a damp, clean kitchen cloth
½ cup honey
½ cup fresh orange juice, strained
2 teaspoons fresh lemon juice, strained
1 teaspoon freshly grated orange zest
1 cinnamon stick
1 cardamom pod

Preheat the oven to 350°F.

Combine the pistachios with ½ cup of the sugar, cinnamon, and ground cardamom in the bowl of a food processor fitted with the metal blade. Process, using quick on-and-off turns, just until the nuts are coarsely ground. Do not over-process or you will have nut paste, which will be unusable. Scrape the nut mixture from the processor bowl and set aside.

Using some of the melted butter and a pastry brush, generously coat the interior of a 9-inch by 13-inch glass baking dish.

Place one sheet of the phyllo dough in the bottom of the baking dish. Using the pastry brush, generously coat it with melted butter. Continue laying phyllo and brushing with butter until you have 10 layers.

Sprinkle one half of the nut mixture over the buttered phyllo dough.

Again, begin layering and brushing phyllo dough until the nut mixture is covered with 10 layers.

Sprinkle the remaining nut mixture over the top of the last layer.

Again, begin layering and brushing phyllo dough until the nut mixture is covered with 10 final layers.

Using a sharp, serrated knife, cut diagonally through the top of the dough from the top left corner to the bottom right corner. Then cut the top of the dough into rows about 1-inch wide parallel to the first diagonal cut. Then cut rows about 2-inches wide across the first cuts to form a diamond pattern through all of the layers.

Place the baklava in the preheated oven and bake for about 1 hour or until golden brown and crisp.

While the baklava is baking, make the syrup.

Combine the remaining 1¾ cups sugar with the orange juice, honey, lemon juice, and orange zest in a medium nonreactive saucepan over medium heat. Stir in ¼ water, the cinnamon stick, and the cardamom pod, and bring to a simmer. Simmer for about 15 minutes or until the syrup has thickened slightly. Remove from the heat and allow to cool slightly.

When the baklava is done, remove from the oven and immediately drizzle the top with the syrup. Then re-cut the baklava to make sure that all of the individual pieces are separate.

Again, drizzle with syrup and set on a wire rack to cool in the pan.

When cool, store, tightly covered, at room temperature for up to 2 days.

Chapter 10

Northern Literary Lights and Bites

THROUGHOUT THE NORTHERN COUNTRIES, ALTHOUGH THE CULTURES VARY, THE FOODS are quite similar. The fare is hearty with an emphasis on rich dishes, cured fish and meat, sausages, root vegetables and filling starches, such as dumplings, noodles and potatoes. Desserts, especially those of Germany or Austria, often incorporate or are

topped by whipped cream, and are a rich match for long winter nights spent with a book or in equally good book conversation. Preserves also make their bow there. The layers of a chocolate Black Forest cake from Germany are separated with a cherry filling; apricot jam coats the layers of the classic Viennese *sacher-torte;* Danish pastries are often identified by the fruit preserve they hold.

✦ ✦ ✦

Reads, Drinks & Nibbles

BEER

◆ ◆ ◆

The foods of Northern Europe absolutely call out for a stein of lager. Beer has been produced in Germany since before the Middle Ages, and the country remains the world's largest producer of beer. And its population consumes much of it! The beers range from light ones such as Berliner Weisse to Bavaria's dark, malty bock beers and many variations, in style, color, depth of flavor and alcoholic content, in between.

Since the mid-1800s, the annual days-long Oktoberfest has been held in Bavaria. The opening is announced with a 12-gun salute and the tapping of the first keg of Oktoberfest beer. Millions of celebrants indulge in the festivities, enjoying stein upon stein of local beers and dining on traditional dishes such as sausages and red cabbage. A full evening of German literature could be topped off with a dinner featuring such traditional fare.

There are also a great number of extraordinary beers produced in Belgium, Austria, the Netherlands and throughout Scandinavia. Belgium is most known for its wide variety of beers that range from very pale lagers to the cider-like lambic brew. Austria is best known for Märzen-style beer (which is similar to English lager). Of course, Americans are most familiar with Heineken and Grolsch beers produced in the Netherlands, with Heineken being the third largest producer and largest exporter of beer in the world. Scandinavia has recently seen an increase in artisanal brewing, but most beers are locally consumed and are not, as yet, imported into the United States, except in states with a large Scandinavian-American population, such as Minnesota. With the world-wide explosion of interest in brewing, many online stores and specialty food stores now feature a wide variety of beers.

And, of course, if you don't wish to serve an alcoholic beverage, you can always serve either a non-alcoholic beer or a very flavorful American artisanal root beer.

ROLLMOPS

♦ ♦ ♦

Although the name is intriguing, rollmops are nothing more than a strip of pickled herring fillet rolled around a pickle or a small pickled onion and held together with a toothpick. They are usually purchased ready-to-eat from German, Danish and other Scandinavian delicatessens, specialty food stores, or many supermarkets. The rolls are packed in a very aromatic, slightly sweet brine along with sliced onions and spices. They can be eaten as an appetizer or placed on a slice of rye or black bread to be eaten as an open-faced sandwich.

For a meal, serve the rollmops along with German or Scandinavian sausages, cheeses, pickles, cucumber salad, canned white asparagus with a sweet-pungent mustard, and dark breads and rolls. (In Germany, fresh white asparagus, called *spargel*, are celebrated when they come into season around May Day; they are steamed, then presented warm or cold, with a dollop of heavy cream.)

Star Dishes & Delicious Asides

Swedish Meatballs

Serves 6 to 8

Swedish meatballs can be served as a main course, traditionally with boiled potatoes, lingonberry jam and cucumber salad. Although called "Swedish," meatballs having this same type of flavoring can be found throughout Scandinavia and other Northern European countries. They also make terrific finger food or cocktail hors d'oeuvre served on toothpicks. They reheat very well and, in fact, the flavor is even better after an overnight rest in the fridge.

1½ pounds lean ground beef or a combination
    of ¾ pound ground beef, ½ pound ground
    veal, and ¼ pound ground pork
1 large egg
1 cup fine breadcrumbs
¼ cup minced fresh parsley
½ teaspoon freshly grated nutmeg or to taste
Pinch ground allspice
Salt and pepper to taste
1 tablespoon canola oil
1 tablespoon butter
1 cup finely chopped onion
3 tablespoons all-purpose flour
1 cup warm nonfat, low-sodium beef broth
1 cup warm nonfat, low-sodium chicken broth
1 cup warm heavy cream

Combine the ground meat with the egg, breadcrumbs, 1 tablespoon of the parsley, nutmeg, allspice, and salt and pepper in a mixing bowl. Using your hands, knead the mixture together. Then form the meat into balls about 1 inch in diameter. Set aside.

Heat the oil and butter in a large frying pan over medium heat. Add the onion and sauté for about 3 minutes or just until the onion has softened slightly. Begin adding the meatballs, a few at a time, and fry, turning frequently, until nicely browned. Transfer to paper towels to drain. Do not try to remove any onion bits that stick to the meatballs. Continue frying until all of the meatballs are cooked and drained.

Lower the heat and stir the flour into the fat remaining in the pan. (If there is none, add another tablespoon of oil and butter.) When the flour has absorbed the fat, using a whisk, beat the beef and chicken broths into the flour. When combined, return the meatballs to the pan. Stir in the cream and season the gravy with nutmeg, salt, and pepper. Cook, stirring occasionally, for about 15 minutes or until the meatballs are cooked through and the gravy is thick and well-seasoned.

Remove from the heat and stir in the remaining parsley. Serve hot with the accompaniments mentioned above or with buttered noodles or rice.

Cucumber-Dill Salad

Serves 6 to 8

Some type of cucumber salad—most often flavored with dill—can be found in all middle and northern European countries. Sometimes the salad is made with sour cream in place of the vinegar and oil, although a touch of vinegar to the sour cream creates a saucier dressing. Sugar is always added to mellow out the acid.

3 hothouse cucumbers
½ cup white vinegar
2 tablespoons canola oil
2 teaspoons sugar
Salt to taste
Dash hot pepper sauce
2 tablespoons chopped fresh dill

Wash the cucumbers well and pat dry. Using a kitchen fork, drag the fork tines down the entire outside of each cucumber, leaving indented lines. Cut the cucumbers crosswise into thin slices and place the slices in a bowl.

Combine the vinegar, oil, sugar, salt and hot pepper sauce, whisking until the sugar and salt dissolve. Pour the dressing over the cucumbers. Add the dill and toss to coat.

Refrigerate until ready to serve.

For a Moveable Feast

German Potato Salad

Serves 6 to 8

German Potato Salad is one of the two classic salads of the region. Of course it also claims

pride of place, right next to sliced cold meats, in a great many informal lunches from coast to coast in North America. And, in fact, it was through German immigrants to America that the salad came to be called "German." In Germany and in many central and eastern European countries it is simply a dish of warm potatoes flavored with vinegar, meat fat, and fresh herbs. The version I offer here is a combination of many flavors that evoke traditional central European cooking.

This salad can be made early in the day for later service.

2 pounds waxy potatoes such as new red,
    well-washed and cut in half
6 slices lean bacon
¾ cup finely diced onion
¼ cup apple cider vinegar
1 teaspoon sugar
1 teaspoon Dijon mustard
½ teaspoon celery seed
½ cup sour cream
1 large dill pickle, chopped, optional
Salt and pepper to taste
2 tablespoons chopped fresh flat-leaf parsley

Place the potatoes in cold, salted water to cover by at least 1 inch. Place over high heat and bring to a boil. Lower the heat and simmer for about 20 minutes or until tender.

While the potatoes are cooking, fry the bacon.

Place the bacon in a skillet over low heat. Fry, turning occasionally, for about 10 minutes or until all of the fat has rendered out and the bacon is crisp. Transfer the bacon to a double layer of paper towels to drain.

Drain off all but about 2 tablespoons of the bacon fat. Place the skillet over medium heat and add the onions. Fry for about 8 minutes or until the onion is very soft. Stir in the vinegar, sugar, mustard, and celery seed and remove from the heat.

Drain the potatoes and cut them into bite-sized pieces. Crumble the bacon into the potatoes, tossing to blend.

Whisk the sour cream into the onion mixture and then pour the warm dressing over the hot potatoes. If using, add the dill pickle. Season with salt and pepper and toss to coat well.

Scrape the mixture into a serving bowl and serve warm or at room temperature.

Literary Tea or Sweet Ending

Sachertorte

Makes one 8-inch cake

This cake is the signature dessert of the world famous Hotel Sacher in Vienna. There is, however, another version made at the famous Demel pastry shop in Vienna that differs slightly from what is considered the original. There has never been an official release of the recipe, and many pastry chefs have had a hand in trying to duplicate it. This is my version. It does take some doing to create it, but it is an unforgettable treat so is well worth the time and effort. It is traditionally served with a dollop of whipped cream and a cup of strong coffee.

6 ounces bittersweet chocolate, chopped
¾ cup unsalted butter, at room temperature
⅔ cup plus 2 tablespoons sugar
5 large eggs, separated, at room temperature
2 teaspoons pure vanilla extract
¾ cup all-purpose flour,
    sifted twice
¾ cup fine quality
    apricot jam
Glaze (recipe
    follows)

Glaze

6 ounces bittersweet chocolate, chopped
1 tablespoon unsalted butter, at room
  temperature
¼ cup water
3 tablespoons confectioners' sugar

Lightly butter the interior of an 8-inch springform and then line the bottom with a piece of parchment paper cut to fit.

Preheat the oven to 350°F.

Place the chocolate in the top half of a double boiler over simmering water. Heat, stirring just until the chocolate has melted completely. Remove from the heat.

Combine the butter with the 2/3 cup of sugar in the bowl of a standing electric mixer fitted with the paddle. Beat on medium until very light and fluffy.

Lower the speed and, with the motor running, add the egg yolks, one at a time, beating to incorporate. Add the melted chocolate along with the vanilla and beat to blend.

With the motor running, slowly add the flour, beating just until the flour is incorporated into the batter. Remove the bowl from the mixer and set aside.

Place the egg whites in a mixing bowl and, using a hand-held electric mixer, beat the egg whites until frothy. Add the remaining 2 tablespoons sugar and beat on high until stiff and shiny.

Using a spatula, gently fold about one-third of the egg whites into the reserved chocolate batter. When completely blended, begin folding in the remaining egg whites in small batches.

Pour the batter into the prepared pan. Place in the preheated oven and bake for about 45 minutes or until a cake tester inserted in the center comes out clean. Remove from the oven and place on a wire rack to cool for 15 minutes.

Remove the ring from the pan. Then invert the cake onto the wire rack and carefully remove the bottom plate. Let cool completely.

While the cake is cooling, make the glaze.

Combine the chocolate and butter in a heatproof bowl.

Combine the water and sugar in a small saucepan over medium heat. Bring to a boil. Immediately remove from the heat and beat the sugar water into the chocolate, beating until the mixture is shiny and smooth and the chocolate is melted. Keep warm while finishing the cake.

When the cake has cooled completely, using a serrated knife, cut the cake, crosswise, into two equal halves. Leaving the bottom half on the wire rack, generously coat the cut side with half of the apricot preserves. Cover the jam-covered half with the top half. Set aside.

Place the remaining apricot preserves in a small saucepan over medium heat. When hot, remove from the heat and press the jam through a fine mesh sieve into a small bowl, discarding the solids.

Using a pastry brush, lightly coat the entire exterior of the cake with the warm jam.

Pour the warm glaze over the top of the cake and, using a metal (offset) pastry spatula, smooth the glaze over the top and sides of the cake, allowing any excess to drip off.

Using a spatula, carefully transfer the cake to a cake plate. Let rest for at least 1 hour before cutting.

> **"Chocolate is a perfect food, as wholesome as it is delicious, a beneficent restorer of exhausted power. It is the best friend of those engaged in literary pursuits."**
>
> **— BARON JUSTUS VON LIEBIG**

Chapter 11

Food for Thought in Eastern Europe

Eastern Europe—by which I mean Slovenia, the Czech Republic, Slovakia, Hungary, Romania, Bulgaria, Poland, Estonia, Lithuania, Latvia and the Ukraine—is as much a checkerboard of nationalities and connected tastes as central/northern Europe, but more complicated. A history of shifting political domination and oppression has been accompanied by shifts of tastes and food availability, punctuated by rebellious and creative outbursts. Who more truly represents Prague—Franz Kafka, the freethinking German Jew whose very name came to define unfathomable bureaucracy and bizarre transformation, or Vaclav Havel, the Czech literary intellectual who led his country out of Communism? The answer is obvious: They both do.

READS, DRINKS & NIBBLES

Mushroom-Onion Dumplings

STAR DISHES & DELICIOUS ASIDES

Cherry Soup
Chicken Paprika

FOR A MOVEABLE FEAST

Noodle Pudding

LITERARY TEA OR SWEET ENDING

Hungarian Tea Cake
Pancakes with Jam

Now that foods move easily over national borders, the table of each country is influenced by its neighbors. For instance, in small Slovenia, people enjoy the cream-sauce traditions of Austria to the north and the pizza of a western neighbor, Italy, while sprinkling that pizza with relatively inexpensive truffles from Croatia, to the south.

Through decades of tumult in Eastern Europe, dumplings have remained—known as *pierogi* in Poland, Slovakia and the Ukraine, or *pirogen* in Yiddish. A bread or potato dumpling called *knedliky* in the Czech Republic is served with meat, or as an entrée accompanied by sauerkraut.

Reads, Drinks & Nibbles

Mushroom-Onion Dumplings

Makes about 4 dozen

Throughout Eastern Europe you will find some type of dumpling, either meat, cheese, or vegetable-filled. Dumplings are very much at home served from a street cart or at an elegant table. This is a simple vegetarian dumpling, but you should feel free to make it with any filling you like; farmer cheese or cottage cheese or any chopped, cooked meat flavored with onions and herbs make an equally appealing dumpling.

> **"We don't want any dumplings, honey-cakes, poppy-cakes, or any other such messes: give us a whole sheep, a goat, mead forty years old, and as much corn-brandy as possible, not with raisins and all sorts of stuff, but plain scorching corn-brandy, which foams and hisses like mad."** —NIKOLAI GOGOL, *Taras Bulba*

1 envelope active dry yeast

¼ cup cool water

1 cup whole milk

½ cup unsalted butter, cut into pieces, at room temperature

Approximately 5 cups all-purpose flour, sifted

1 tablespoon sugar

1½ teaspoons salt plus more to taste

¼ cup olive oil

1 cup finely chopped red onion

1 tablespoon minced garlic

2 pounds finely chopped mushrooms (button or a mixture of button and shiitake, cremini, portobello or any wild mushroom)

1 teaspoon lemon juice

Ground pepper to taste

¼ cup heavy cream

1 teaspoon fresh thyme

1 tablespoon chopped fresh flat-leaf parsley

1 tablespoon chopped fresh dill

1 large egg, at room temperature

Place the yeast and water in the bowl of a standing electric mixer fitted with the dough hook. Stir and let stand for about 2 minutes or until the yeast has dissolved.

Add the milk and butter to the yeast mixture. Then, add 4 cups of the flour along with the sugar and salt and begin mixing on low. When the mixture is blended, raise the speed to high and beat for about 10 minutes or until the dough begins to pull away from the edges of the bowl, adding flour as needed to make a fairly stiff dough.

Lightly coat the interior of a large mixing bowl with vegetable oil. Scrape the dough into the bowl. Cover with a clean kitchen towel and set aside in a warm spot for about 1 hour or until doubled in volume.

While the dough is rising, make the filling.

Heat the olive oil in a large skillet over medium heat. Add the onion and garlic and cook, stirring, for about 2 minutes or just until softened. Add the mushrooms, stirring to combine. Add the lemon juice and season with salt and pepper to taste. Cook, stirring frequently, for about 10 minutes or until the mixture is almost dry.

Stir in the cream and thyme and continue to cook for another minute.

Remove from the heat. Taste and, if necessary, season with additional salt and pepper. Stir in the parsley and dill. Set aside.

Lightly oil two large baking sheets or cover with nonstick silicon liners. Set aside.

Lightly flour a clean, flat work surface.

Remove the dough from the bowl and divide it into 48 balls of equal size.

Working with one ball at a time, roll the dough out on the floured surface into small circles about 3½ inches in diameter.

Spoon a heaping tablespoon of the filling into the center of each circle. Using your fingertips, lightly dampen the edges of the circle. Fold one half of the dough over the filling and onto the other side. Tightly pinch the edges together or gently fold the edge up and over itself to make a raised edge.

As the dumplings are made, place them on the prepared baking sheets.

When all of the dumplings have been formed, cover with a clean kitchen towel and set aside in a warm spot for 30 minutes or until they have risen slightly.

Preheat the oven to 350°F.

Place the egg in a small bowl, whisking until frothy.

Uncover the dumplings and, using a pastry brush, lightly coat the top of each one with the beaten egg.

Place in the preheated oven and bake for about 20 minutes or until puffed and golden brown.

Remove from the oven and serve warm or at room temperature.

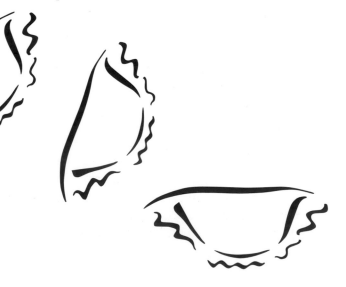

Cherry Soup

Serves 6 to 8

Throughout Eastern Europe, summertime signals cherry time. This soup is generally made with fresh Bing cherries, but you can easily substitute frozen or canned. It is a refreshing beginning—or even end—to the rich dishes that are the mainstay of these countries.

3 pounds Bing cherries, well-washed
*   and pitted*
4 cups cold water
1 cup sweet white wine
2 tablespoons sugar
¾ cup fresh orange juice
1 tablespoon fresh lemon juice
2 teaspoons freshly grated orange zest
1 teaspoon freshly grated lemon zest
Sour cream for garnish

Place the cherries in a large nonreactive saucepan. Add the water, wine, sugar, orange juice, and lemon juice along with the orange and lemon zest. Place over medium heat and bring to a simmer. Lower the heat and cook at a bare simmer, stirring occasionally with a wooden spoon, for about 12 minutes or just until the cherries have softened.

Remove from the heat and set aside to cool.

When cool, strain the liquid through a fine mesh sieve, separately reserving both the liquid and the cherries.

Place the cherries along with about ½ cup of the liquid in a blender jar. Process on high until very smooth.

Combine the cherry purée with the cooking liquid. Place in a nonreactive container, cover, and refrigerate for at least 6 hours or overnight.

Serve chilled with a dollop of sour cream in the center.

Chicken Paprika

Serves 8 to 10

Chicken Paprika (*Csirke Paprikas* in Hungarian) is probably the most well-known of the many, many Eastern European stews. It is quite

> "Whenever his sister came into his room he had to content himself with hearing her utter only a sigh now and then and an occasional appeal to the saints. Later on, when she had gotten a little used to the situation—of course she could never get completely used to it—Gregor would occasionally catch a remark which was kindly meant or could be so interpreted. 'Well, he liked his dinner today,' she would say when Gregor had gobbled down all of his food; and when he had not eaten, which gradually happened more and more often, she would say almost sadly: 'Everything's been left untouched again.'"
>
> —FRANZ KAFKA, The Metamorphosis.

simple to make, but it does require a healthy dose of fine-quality Hungarian paprika, both for its distinct flavor and beautiful color. It keeps and travels well, so it is a great dish to prepare in advance when guests are expected or a potluck supper is at hand.

2 tablespoons butter
2 tablespoons canola oil
Two 2½- to 3-pound chickens, cut into
*   serving pieces and rinsed well*
Salt and pepper to taste
3 cups chopped sweet onions
1 cup diced red bell pepper
¼ cup sweet Hungarian paprika
1 tablespoon all-purpose flour
1 cup nonfat, low-sodium chicken broth
1 bay leaf
1½ cups sour cream, at room temperature
Buttered noodles for serving, optional

Preheat the oven to 375°F.

Combine the butter and oil in a Dutch oven over medium heat. Season the chicken pieces with salt and pepper to taste and begin searing the chicken in the hot fat, adding just enough pieces so as not to crowd the pan. Sear, turning frequently, for about 5 minutes or until golden. Transfer the seared chicken to a platter while you continue to sear the remaining chicken.

When all of the chicken has been seared, you should still have a nice layer of fat in the pan. If not, add an equal combination of butter and oil to generously coat the bottom of the pan.

Place the pan over medium heat. When very hot, add the onions and bell peppers, and cook, stirring frequently, for about 12 minutes or until the onions are just soft with a tinge of color. Sprinkle the paprika and flour over the onions and continue to cook, stirring, for about 1 minute or until well blended.

Add the chicken broth and bay leaf, and bring the mixture to a simmer. Return the chicken pieces along with any accumulated juices to the pan, and return to a simmer. Taste and, if necessary, season with salt and pepper.

Cover the pan and place it in the preheated oven. Braise, turning the chicken from time to time, for about 30 minutes or until the chicken is very tender.

Remove the pan from the oven. Uncover and, using a slotted spoon, transfer the chicken pieces to a warm platter. Tent lightly with aluminum foil to keep warm. Remove and discard the bay leaf.

Let the sauce cool just enough to allow the fat to rise to the top. Carefully skim off and discard the excess fat.

Return the pan to high heat and bring to a boil, boiling just until the sauce gets quite thick. Immediately remove from the heat and stir in the sour cream. When blended, return the chicken pieces to the pan. Taste and, if necessary, season with salt and pepper. Place over medium heat and cook, spooning the sauce over the chicken, for about 5 minutes or until hot and thick.

Remove from the heat and serve with hot buttered noodles, if desired.

For a Moveable Feast

Noodle Pudding

Makes one 13-inch by 9-inch pan

There are many, many versions of noodle pudding (*kugel* in Yiddish) throughout the world. In America, the best known are those associated with the Jewish holiday season, when both savory and sweet noodle puddings often are served. However, in the Midwest, those with Czech or Hungarian ancestry also make their version of this rich side dish or dessert. Traditionally, a rich noodle pudding signified prosperity and a sweet life, so it was served as a main part of the holiday or Sabbath meal, rather than as dessert. This sweet pudding can be served warm or chilled or at room temperature.

1 pound dried egg noodles
3 large eggs, at room temperature
1 pound creamy cottage cheese
1 pound cream cheese
2 cups sour cream
½ cup milk
½ cup sugar
1 tablespoon pure vanilla extract
1 teaspoon ground cinnamon
1½ cups golden raisins, optional
1 cup chopped walnuts, optional
¼ cup melted butter

Preheat the oven to 350°F.

Lightly coat the interior of a 13-inch by 9-inch baking pan with nonstick vegetable spray. Set aside.

Place the noodles in boiling, salted water and cook according to the package directions. Drain well.

While the noodles are cooking, combine the eggs with the cottage cheese, cream cheese, sour cream, milk, sugar, vanilla and cinnamon in a large mixing bowl, beating to blend well.

Place the drained noodles in the egg mixture, tossing to coat well. Add the raisins and walnuts, tossing to distribute evenly.

Scrape the mixture into the prepared pan, spreading it out evenly with a spatula. Drizzle the melted butter over the top and place in the preheated oven.

Bake for about 45 minutes or until the top is golden brown and the edges are beginning to crisp.

Remove from the oven and let rest for about 15 minutes before cutting into squares and serving.

NOTE: A savory pudding can be made by eliminating the sugar, vanilla, cinnamon, raisins and walnuts. They should be replaced with 2 cups cooked chopped mushrooms and 1 cup cooked chopped onion.

Literary Tea or Sweet Ending

Hungarian Tea Cake

Makes one 9-inch cake

This is a traditional Hungarian "grandma" cake—one that was always available, is made with fresh cherries in the summer and with canned cherries all winter long. It is the perfect accompaniment to a wonderfully aromatic cup of tea or a strong cup of coffee flavored with cherry brandy.

1½ cups canned pitted Bing cherries
½ cup unsalted butter, at room temperature
½ cup plus 2 tablespoons sugar
3 large eggs, separated
2 tablespoons fresh lemon juice, strained
1 teaspoon pure vanilla extract
½ cup all-purpose flour, sifted
Zest of 1 lemon
2 tablespoons confectioners' sugar for dusting

Preheat the oven to 350°F.

Lightly coat the interior of a 9-inch springform pan with butter. Then, line the bottom of the pan with a piece of parchment paper cut to fit it. Set aside.

Remove the outside ring from the pan. Return the cake to the wire rack and let it cool completely.

When cool, carefully remove the bottom plate of the pan and transfer the cake onto a cake plate. Place the confectioners' sugar in a sieve and place the sieve over the cake. Carefully tap on the sides of the sieve to lightly dust the top of the cake with sugar.

Serve with whipped cream on the side, if desired.

Pancakes with Jam

Serves 8

This very simple dessert appears on celebratory tables across the northern arc of Eastern Europe, from Lithuania to Finland. In Hungary, where it is a coffee-house favorite, this dessert is known as *palacsinta*, while in the Czech Republic and Slovakia it is called *palatschinke*. It can be as easy as a stack of jam-coated pancakes or one pancake filled with jam and rolled. This recipe is a bit more elaborate, but if you don't have the time to make it, take the easy road and stack the jam-coated pancakes into a cake, sprinkle with confectioners' sugar, and cut into wedges.

⅓ cup unsalted butter, at room temperature
¼ cup granulated sugar
Pinch salt
6 large eggs, separated, at room temperature
¾ cup all-purpose flour, sifted
½ cup milk
1 teaspoon pure vanilla extract
Approximately ½ cup raspberry eau de vie
1½ cups raspberry jam
¾ cup chopped toasted walnuts
Confectioners' sugar for dusting

Place the cherries in a fine mesh sieve and allow all of the liquid to drain off while you prepare the cake batter.

Combine the butter and ½ cup of the sugar in the bowl of a standing electric mixer fitted with the paddle. Beat on low to blend, and then raise the speed and beat on medium until light and fluffy. With the motor running, add the yolks, one at a time, beating to incorporate. Add the lemon juice and vanilla. When blended, slowly add the flour.

Remove the bowl from the mixer and stir in the zest. Set aside.

Place the egg whites in a mixing bowl and, using a hand-held mixer, beat them until light, firm peaks form. Using a spatula, carefully fold about one-third of the egg whites into the batter, folding just until the batter has stiffened slightly. Then, fold in the remaining egg whites, folding until blended.

Scrape the batter into the prepared pan, smoothing down the top with a spatula. Carefully place the well-drained cherries over the top of the cake. Sprinkle the remaining sugar over the cherries.

Place the pan in the preheated oven and bake for about 30 minutes or until a cake tester inserted into the center comes out clean.

Remove from the oven and set on a wire rack to cool for 12 minutes.

Combine the butter and sugar in the bowl of a standing electric mixer fitted with the paddle. Beat on medium speed until light and fluffy. Beat in the salt. Add the egg yolks, one at a time, beating well after each addition. Alternately add the flour and milk. When well incorporated, beat in the vanilla. Remove the bowl from the mixer stand and set the batter aside.

Place the egg whites in a mixing bowl and, using a hand-held electric mixer, beat on high until soft peaks form.

Fold the egg whites into the batter, folding just until a few specks of white are visible.

Heat a nonstick griddle over medium heat. When very hot, reduce the heat to medium-low. Making one pancake at a time, spread just enough batter out on the hot griddle to make a circle about 4-inches in diameter. Cook for about 2 minutes or until bubbles form on the top and the bottom is golden brown. Using a spatula, turn and cook until the other side is golden brown and the pancake is cooked through. You should have enough batter to make at least 16 pancakes.

When all of the pancakes are made, put the cakes together.

Preheat the oven to 300°F.

Lay 4 pancakes out on a nonstick baking sheet.

Drizzle the top of each pancake with a very light sprinkle of eau de vie. Using an offset spatula, cover the top of each pancake with an even layer of the jam. Sprinkle with the walnuts and then top with another pancake. Again, drizzle and coat with the jam and walnuts. Repeat with another pancake and then top with a final pancake. Drizzle the top with eau de vie.

Place the cakes in the oven and bake for about 12 minutes or until heated through.

Remove from the oven and dust lightly with confectioners' sugar. Cut each cake into 4 equal wedges and serve warm or at room temperature.

Chapter 12

Russian Reveries and Repasts

$\mathcal{U}$NTIL THE END OF THE 20TH CENTURY, THE CUISINE OF MOST RUSSIANS—PEASANT stews—was notably sturdy and bore minimal influence from the rest of the world. The punitive weather and political climate kept the bulk of the population dependent on those foods that were readily available—grains, wild plants and fruits, root vegetables, and local fish and game—products that were either seasonally available or easily pickled or otherwise preserved.

Of course, the Tsarist aristocracy enjoyed an extended menu, most particularly including entries from France. The French or French-trained cooks of the elite also brought imported cooking techniques to Russia. Thus an expanded Russian culinary repertoire produced such rich dishes as Chicken Kiev and the various stroganoffs.

Still, by the end of the 19th century, one could say that the originality of the literature of Russia surpassed its culinary development. And very rarely did the 20th-century Soviet kitchen produce results to compare either with the literary achievements of Fyodor Dostoevsky, Leo Tolstoy or Alexander Pushkin, or with writers such as Mikhail Bulgakov or Aleksandr Solzhenitsyn, who challenged Soviet norms.

The new wealthy of Russia, like its princes of yore, import chefs, and the newly rich can patronize exceptionally expensive if not always exceptional restaurants in Moscow and St. Petersburg. Yet the bulk of the population feels lucky to visit a McDonald's. Ironically, while middle- and working-class city dwellers have more extensive market choices available for their home tables, not all are affordable, and access to the fruits and fish of the near countryside may be limited. On the other hand, Russians may now read the works of all their own best writers, and those from elsewhere, without fear of government retaliation. Even Disney now serves classic elements of Russian literature, making Russian-language films of beloved folk-literature stories.

You might begin or end a celebration of a Russian literary hero or heroine just as prosperous Russians would: with a toast of icy vodka and a display of caviar.

◆ ◆ ◆

READS, DRINKS & NIBBLES
■ ■ ■

Kvas
Vodka neat
Caviar plate

STAR DISHES & DELICIOUS ASIDES
■ ■ ■

Chakhokbili (Chicken Stew)
Borscht

FOR A MOVEABLE FEAST
■ ■ ■

Russian Salad with Smoked Sturgeon

LITERARY TEA OR SWEET ENDING
■ ■ ■

Russian Teatime

Reads, Drinks & Nibbles

Kvas

Makes about 2 quarts

*K*vas is found throughout Russia as well as in most other Eastern and Central European countries, now usually purchased from street vendors or commercially bottled. But it would be fun to make this to share with readers of Russian or regional plays, poetry or novels. The brew is only slightly alcoholic and can be made more flavorful with the addition of smashed berries. You do need to start with excellent, dark rye bread to achieve the full measure of the traditional drink. And it will certainly add some interest to your after-reading conversation!

¼ *pound deep, dark rye bread*
2 quarts boiling water
6 tablespoons sugar
1 teaspoon active dry yeast
¼ *cup raisins*
Mint sprigs for garnish

"The station-master coming up asked her whether she was going by train. A boy selling kvas never took his eyes off her. 'My God! where am I to go?' she thought."

—LEO TOLSTOY, Anna Karenina

Preheat the oven to 250°F.

Place the rye bread on a nonstick baking sheet in the preheated oven. Bake for about 12 minutes or until very dry but with no added color. Remove from the oven and smash the dried bread into crumbs.

Place the breadcrumbs in a heatproof, nonreactive container. Add 2 quarts of boiling water, cover, and set aside in a dark, warm place for 2 hours, stirring from time to time.

Strain the liquid through a fine mesh sieve, discarding the solids. Place the liquid in a clean, nonreactive container.

Combine the yeast and sugar in a small bowl. Add about a tablespoon of cold water and stir to dissolve slightly. Stir the mixture into the strained liquid, stirring to blend. Set aside to ferment for 12 hours, checking occasionally.

When the mixture begins to vigorously foam, strain it through a fine mesh sieve lined with cheesecloth into a clean nonreactive container (a glass bottle is terrific). Add a handful of raisins to the liquid, cover, and set aside for 2 hours.

Place the container in the refrigerator and let rest for 3 days.

Serve chilled with a mint sprig.

NOTE: If you desire a fruitier flavor, add a cup of smashed fresh berries to the final refrigerated storage. Then, again strain the liquid before serving.

Star Dishes & Delicious Asides

Chakhokbili (Chicken Stew)

Serves 8 to 10

This is a very zesty stew, made with a good amount of garlic, lemon and dill, which add freshness to the final flavor. The stew can be served alone but goes very well with buttered noodles or a bowl of nutty kasha, the grain of choice in Eastern Europe and Russia.

2 tablespoons butter
2 tablespoons canola oil
Two 2½- to 3-pound chickens, well-washed and cut into serving pieces
Salt and pepper to taste
3 large onions, peeled and cut, crosswise, into thin slices
¼ cup minced garlic
One 28-ounce can chopped tomatoes, drained
⅔ cup nonfat, low-sodium chicken broth
½ cup fresh lemon juice
¾ cup chopped fresh dill
1 teaspoon sweet paprika

Combine the butter and oil in a Dutch oven over medium heat. Season the chicken pieces with salt and pepper to taste and begin searing the chicken in the hot fat, adding just enough pieces so as not to crowd the pan. Sear, turning frequently for about 5 minutes or until golden. Transfer the seared chicken to a platter while you continue to sear the remaining chicken.

When all of the chicken has been seared, you should still have a nice layer of fat in the pan. If not, add an equal combination of butter and oil to generously coat the bottom of the pan.

Place the pan over medium heat. When very hot, add the onions and 2 tablespoons of the garlic and cook, stirring frequently for about 12 minutes or until the onions are just soft with a tinge of color.

Return the chicken pieces to the pan. Add the tomatoes, chicken broth, lemon juice, ¼ cup of the dill, and paprika. Season with salt and pepper to taste. Bring to a simmer; lower the heat, cover, and cook at a gentle simmer for about 30 minutes or just until the chicken is tender and the sauce has thickened slightly. Remove from the heat and stir in the remaining garlic and dill. Serve hot with noodles, boiled potatoes or kasha.

Borscht

Serves 8

This is another recipe that has about a million variations, ranging from a soup made from just beets and water to luxe versions brimming with meat, and vegetables beyond beets and herbs. This is my version of the more traditional make-a-meal-of soup. It is so filling that all you need is some Russian black bread and sweet butter to complete your tribute to Dostoevsky or another Russian author. However, if you would like to make the Mushroom-Onion Dumplings on page 127, they can be floated in this soup for an extra delight.

2 pounds beets, well-washed
2½ pounds beef short ribs or pork spareribs, cut into 2-inch pieces
Wondra flour for dusting
Salt and pepper to taste
¼ cup canola oil
2 ribs celery, well-washed and cut into pieces
2 cloves garlic, peeled and chopped
1 large onion, well-washed, peel on, stuck with 3 whole cloves
1 large carrot, peeled, trimmed and cut into pieces
4 cups nonfat, low-sodium beef broth
4 cups water
One 28-ounce can chopped tomatoes, drained
2 tablespoons chopped fresh dill plus more for garnish
1 tablespoon tomato paste
3 cups shredded red cabbage
2 tablespoons red wine vinegar
2 teaspoons lemon juice
2 teaspoons light brown sugar
½ teaspoon caraway seed
Sour cream for garnish

Preheat the oven to 375°F.
Wrap the beets in aluminum foil, taking care that they are completely enclosed. Place on a baking pan in

the preheated oven and bake for about 1 hour or until the point of a small, sharp knife can be easily inserted into the thickest beet.

Remove from the oven and set aside to cool.

When cool, using your fingertips, push the skin and stem end off of each beet. Using a sharp knife or a box grater, cut the beets into thin strips. Set aside.

While the beets are roasting, begin the soup.

Lightly dust the meat with the flour and season with salt and pepper to taste.

Heat the oil in a large soup pot over medium heat. Add the meat, in batches if necessary, and sear, turning frequently until nicely browned.

Return all of the meat to the pot and add the celery, garlic, onion, and carrot along with the broth and water, stirring to blend. Raise the heat to high and add the tomatoes along with the dill and tomato paste. Season with salt and pepper to taste, and bring to a boil. Then lower the heat and simmer for about 45 minutes or until the meat is almost tender.

Add the cabbage and continue to simmer for 15 minutes.

Add the beets, vinegar, lemon juice, sugar, and caraway seed and return to the simmer. Taste and, if necessary, season with additional salt and pepper. Simmer for an additional 15 minutes or until the soup is well-seasoned and slightly thick.

Remove from the heat and ladle into soup bowls. Top with a dollop of sour cream and a sprinkling of chopped fresh dill.

Russian Salad with Smoked Sturgeon

Serves 8

In classic French cooking, there is a preparation called *à la Russe*, meaning "in the Russian style," in which delicately diced potatoes and carrots and other tiny vegetables are served in a rich mayonnaise dressing. This is a version of that preparation, which I serve with smoked sturgeon (a Russian staple) and black bread. You can, of course, use any smoked fish you like; a smoked trout would be particularly nice.

2 pounds Yukon gold potatoes, peeled and diced

2 large carrots, peeled, trimmed and diced

One 15-ounce can whole beets, well-drained and diced

1 cup frozen petit peas, thawed and well-drained

1 cup mayonnaise

3 tablespoons white wine vinegar

1½ tablespoons Dijon mustard

1 tablespoon orange juice concentrate

1 tablespoon chopped fresh dill

Salt and pepper to taste

2 pounds smoked sturgeon, picked clean of any bones, and sliced

1 tablespoon chopped fresh flat-leaf parsley

Combine the potatoes and carrots in a saucepan with cold, salted water to cover by at least 1 inch. Place over high heat and bring to a boil. Lower the heat and simmer for about 12 minutes or just until barely tender. Remove from the heat and drain well.

Set aside to cool.

When the potatoes and carrots are cool, combine them with the beets and peas in a mixing bowl.

Combine the mayonnaise, vinegar, mustard, orange juice concentrate, and dill in a small mixing bowl, whisking to blend well. Season with salt and pepper to taste.

Pour about half of the dressing over the vegetables, tossing to coat well.

Mound the salad in the center of a serving platter. Place the slices of sturgeon around the vegetables and garnish the platter with chopped parsley and a drizzle of the dressing. Pass the remaining dressing on the side and serve with buttered black bread.

> " 'Stay, listen; tell them to put in cheese, Strasburg pies, smoked fish, ham, caviar and everything, everything they've got, up to a hundred rubles, or a hundred and twenty . . . But wait: don't let them forget dessert, sweets, pears, watermelons, two or three or four—no, one melon's enough, and chocolate, candy, toffee, fondants; in fact, everything . . .' "
>
> —FYODOR DOSTOEVSKY,
> The Brothers Karamazov

Literary Tea or Sweet Ending

RUSSIAN TEATIME

◆ ◆ ◆

Russian tea is quite a bit different than a classic English tea or the American tea bag in a cup. A mixture, pronounced "zavarka," is brewed in a small pot using a large amount of black tea leaves—a smoky Chinese tea such as Keemun or a dark Indian blend called Russian Caravan—often combined with herbal or fruit-flavored tea. The resulting brew is exceedingly strong, which allows a small amount of it to be poured into a cup at any point during the day and then reheated with an infusion of hot water. If you used standard English or American tea leaves for this procedure, the brew would turn bitter as it sat.

At the end of a meal or during the afternoon, the zavarka becomes the base for dessert. A teaspoon of jam, usually cherry or strawberry, is placed in the bottom of a heat-proof glass. The brewed mixture is then poured over the jam to fill the glass about one-quarter full. Boiling water is then poured in and the jam is stirred in to sweeten the tea. A small amount of dark chocolate might also accompany the tea.

"A spoon cannot taste of the food it carries. Likewise, a foolish man cannot understand the wise man's wisdom even if he associates with a sage." —LIN YUTANG

Bound Books, BOUNDLESS SATISFACTIONS

Chapter 13

Into the Near East and Out of Africa

𝒯HIS IMMENSE REGION TRAVELS EAST FROM TURKEY THROUGH THE MIDDLE EAST AND encompasses all of Africa. Vast as it is, there are some surprising culinary similarities in places far apart, possibly due to shared religious influences, arid climate and/or centuries-old overland and sea trading routes.

When we look to the Near East, we are teased with the evidence that this is where civilization started, as there's much evidence that both agriculture and inscription began in Mesopotamia.

Many, of course, reside near one of the region's long coastlines. This promises not only access to fish

(shellfish is not eaten by observant Moslems or, for that matter, Jews) but other shared food preferences. For example, grapevines and olive trees grace both the northern and southern shores of the Mediterranean—that is, both the European and North African landscapes.

The Greek love of yogurt is shared by Turks, Iranians and Afghanis. These cuisines also often feature flatbreads as well as the basmati rice of the Subcontinent.

Many Africans live on grain-based diets, with protein likely to come from legumes. Meat and poultry are consumed sparingly, although lamb may be as frequently roasted for special occasions as it was in Biblical times. Few Near or Middle Easterners or Africans eat pork, forbidden by the Old Testament and Koran alike. Oasis fruits such as dates and figs are loved even beyond the desert.

The literary output of this enormous area is also tasty, ranging from the oldest market accounts and descriptive annotations to oral stories and provocative fables first rendered in writing in the 19th- or 20th-centuries. Thousands of years ago, the library in Alexandria, Egypt, was the biggest repository of manuscripts in the world. After it burned, the lights of learning stayed on in North Africa when reading and writing became lost skills for most of the lay population of Medieval Europe. Meanwhile, Persian poets jotted down love verse that is still cherished today. Broadly speaking, the contemporary literature of the area includes commentaries on religious precepts, age-old tales made new in illustrated books, as well as the stories and novels of recent Nobel laureates and other writers grappling with both colonial legacies and the human condition.

The cuisine of the region may be as intricate as its storytelling, and some recipes that yield subtly splendid combinations of flavor are time-consuming to make from scratch. Even basic subsistence foodstuff takes village women a long time to prepare. The staple of life, variously known as *fufu* (Nigeria) or *pap* (Namibia and South Africa) or by a half-dozen other names depending on locale, is a porridge made from ground starchy roots or grains. It's flavored with

> ## "The hand that dips into the bottom of the pot will eat the biggest snail."
> **—WOLE SOYINKA**

READS, DRINKS & NIBBLES
■ ■ ■

Bisteeya
Marinated Olives

STAR DISHES & DELICIOUS ASIDES
■ ■ ■

Chicken *Berbère*
Herbed Laban Salad
Bobotie
Oven-Baked Lamb Chops
Nigerian *Jollof* Rice

FOR A MOVEABLE FEAST
■ ■ ■

Pita and Middle Eastern Spreads
Hummus
Baba Ghanoush

LITERARY TEA OR SWEET ENDING
■ ■ ■

Mint and Fruit Teas
Turkish Coffee
Liberian Coconut Bread
Ma'amoul

whatever is locally available, such as palm oil or peanuts or bits of dried fish, or sometimes it's served with stew. A version made of maize is not unlike the grits of the American South.

If the recipes seem too difficult to attempt, you can always put together a wonderful array of fresh and dried fruits, a bit of plain cake, and an assortment of herbal and fruit teas. Distinctive flatbreads (sometimes used as plates) may be available in specialty food stores, ethnic markets or large supermarkets. Particular teas, dried fruits, breads or cake would be an appropriate salute to almost any country in this region.

✦ ✦ ✦

DRINKS

✦ ✦ ✦

National and tribal groups throughout Central and Southern Africa ferment grains for ceremonial occasions, or just as a party drink. Potent local brews can be found at small bars in many African towns, but are not exported.

Devout Moslems are expected to abstain from alcohol, so bottling spirits is not a major industry in North Africa and the Mideast. However, wine grapes from North Africa are sent to Europe, and both Lebanon and Morocco have vineyards that bottle. Morocco's leading wine, Meknes, is legally sold in the country only to non-Moslem tourists. South Africa exports wines.

That said, if your reading buddies like to imbibe, a California or Southern European wine can complement African meals. More authentically, you might offer room-temperature tea or devise a non-alcoholic punch that includes pomegranate juice.

Bisteeya

Serves 8-10

A *bisteeya* is a traditional North African meat pie that is both savory and sweet. It is, classically, made with pigeon meat, but chicken is an excellent substitute. It's generally served as a main course in Morocco, but I've made these small pies to serve with cocktails or as a snack. Whatever the size, the flavors will transport your readers to this colorful and enticing land. You might serve these with wine or with mint tea (see page 150).

¼ cup butter
2 tablespoons olive oil
1 cup minced red onion
1 tablespoon minced garlic
Salt and pepper to taste
2 teaspoons ground cinnamon, divided
1 teaspoon ground coriander
½ teaspoon ground ginger
Pinch saffron threads
Pinch cayenne pepper or to taste
2 tablespoons all-purpose flour
1½ cups nonfat, low-sodium chicken broth
3 tablespoons fresh lemon juice
3 large eggs, beaten
4 cups minced cooked chicken meat
½ cup toasted slivered almonds
1 tablespoon finely chopped preserved lemons
   (see Note)
6 tablespoons confectioners' sugar
1 pound box frozen phyllo dough, thawed
   according to manufacturer's directions
1 cup melted unsalted butter

Preheat the oven to 375°F.

Heat the butter and oil in a large frying pan over medium heat. Add the onion and garlic, season with salt and pepper to taste, and fry, stirring frequently, for about 5 minutes or until the onions have begun to color. Add 1 teaspoon cinnamon, the coriander, ginger, saffron and cayenne, stirring to blend. Beat in the flour and, when blended, add the broth and lemon juice and bring to a simmer. Whisk in the eggs and simmer for about 10 minutes or just until the mixture is almost dry and the eggs curdle somewhat.

Remove from the heat and stir in the chicken, almonds, preserved lemon and 2 tablespoons of the confectioners' sugar. Set aside to cool.

When ready to prepare, preheat the oven to 350°F.

Line a baking sheet with parchment paper. Set aside.

Combine the remaining 4 tablespoons of confectioners' sugar with the remaining 1 teaspoon cinnamon. Place in a fine mesh sieve and set aside on a plate.

Working quickly so that the dough does not dry out, cut the phyllo dough into 6-inch squares, keeping the dough covered with a damp towel once cut.

Make one *bisteeya* at a time so that the dough stays damp and pliable.

Place one phyllo square on a clean, flat work surface. Using a pastry brush, lightly coat with the melted butter. Repeat using 5 additional phyllo squares, piling one on top of the other to make a stack of 6 buttered phyllo squares. Place about ¼ cup of the chicken mixture in the center of the stacked squares, leaving about an inch around the edges. Using the pastry brush, lightly coat the edges with melted butter. Fold the phyllo up and over to enclose the filling.

Turn the packet upside down so that the seam-side is on the bottom and place, seam-side down on the prepared baking sheet. Lightly coat the top with melted butter and sprinkle with the reserved cinnamon-sugar mixture. Continue making *bisteeyas* until all of the filling has been used.

Place in the preheated oven and bake for about 20 minutes or until golden and crisp.

Remove from the oven and serve hot, warm, or at room temperature.

NOTE: Preserved lemons are available from Middle Eastern markets, specialty food stores, some supermarkets, and some Internet markets.

Marinated Olives

Makes about 2 cups

2 cups mixed black and green olives
2 cloves garlic, peeled and sliced
1 dried hot red chili pepper, split
¼ teaspoon cracked black pepper
Olive oil
Red wine vinegar

Place the olives in a 2-cup container with a lid. Add the garlic and chili, tossing to distribute evenly. Add the black pepper and then fill the container about two-thirds full of olive oil. Then, fill to the top with vinegar. Cover and shake vigorously to blend.

Transfer to the refrigerator to marinate for at least 2 days or up to 1 month before using.

Star Dishes & Delicious Asides

Chicken *Berbère*

Serves 6 to 8

*B*erbère is a spice mix used in many, many Ethiopian and Eritrean dishes. It usually contains a mix of spices such as coriander, clove, allspice, and ginger, as well as chili peppers and herbs native to those countries. In this recipe, I bring all of the spices together, but you can also find the pre-made variety in African markets or through the Internet. It is intensely hot, but you can cut the amount of chili and cayenne if you don't fancy burning your tongue!

2 pieces dried orange peel
1 dried hot red chili
One 2-inch cinnamon stick
½ cup paprika
1 tablespoon cayenne pepper
1 tablespoon ground turmeric
1 tablespoon mustard seeds
2 teaspoons coriander seeds
1 teaspoon cardamom seeds
1 teaspoon fenugreek seeds
1 teaspoon ground nutmeg
1 teaspoon ground allspice
1 teaspoon cracked black pepper
Salt to taste
½ cup dry white wine
¼ cup fresh orange juice
¼ cup corn oil
1 tablespoon minced fresh ginger
4 pounds skin-on chicken pieces
3 limes, cut into wedges

Combine the orange peel, dried chili, cinnamon stick, paprika, cayenne, turmeric, mustard, coriander, cardamom, and fenugreek seeds, nutmeg, allspice, cracked pepper and salt to taste in a heavy frying pan over medium heat. Cook, stirring frequently, for about 5 minutes or until lightly colored and very fragrant.

Remove from the heat and cool slightly. Then transfer to a spice grinder and grind to a very fine powder.

Return the frying pan to low heat. Add the wine, orange juice, oil, and ginger along with the finely ground spices. Bring to a simmer and cook, stirring constantly, for 5 minutes.

Remove from the heat and set aside to cool.

Rinse the chicken and pat dry. Using your hands, generously coat all sides of the chicken with the spice rub. Place the chicken on a baking tray as coated. Cover with plastic film and refrigerate for at least 4 hours or up to 24 hours.

Preheat and oil a grill.

Remove the chicken from the refrigerator. Place on the preheated grill and grill, turning frequently, for about 25 minutes or until the chicken is cooked through and the skin is crisp.

Serve hot or at room temperature with lime wedges to cut the heat.

Herbed Laban Salad

Makes about 3 cups

1 large hothouse cucumber, well-washed and cut, crosswise, into thin slices
2 cups Greek-style yogurt
1 tablespoon dried mint
Salt and pepper to taste

Combine the cucumber with the yogurt and mint, tossing to coat well. Season with salt and pepper to taste.

If not serving immediately, cover and refrigerate until ready to serve.

Bobotie

Serves 6 to 8

*B*obotie is a South African recipe that has made its way to Botswana and other African countries. *Bobotie* is a very flavorful dish, fusing sweet and hot to create a wonderfully complex taste. Although there are many variations, almost all of them include dried fruits, curry and eggs. There is no greater dish to celebrate the cooking of Southern Africa.

3 tablespoons canola oil
1 cup chopped onion
1 tablespoon minced garlic
1 tablespoon minced hot red chili or to taste
2 pounds very lean ground lamb
½ cup diced dried apricots
¼ cup golden raisins
½ cup fresh lemon juice
½ cup canned diced tomatoes, well-drained
¼ cup fresh orange juice
2 tablespoons apricot preserves
2 tablespoons curry powder
½ teaspoon ground cumin
2¾ cups heavy cream, at room temperature
¾ cup slivered almonds
4 large eggs, at room temperature

Heat the oil in a large heavy frying pan over medium heat. Add the onion, garlic and chili and fry, stirring frequently, for about 4 minutes or until slightly softened.

Stir in the lamb and continue to fry, stirring frequently, for about 8 minutes or until the lamb is quite brown. Stir in the apricots and raisins, mixing to blend well.

Add the lemon juice, tomatoes, orange juice, preserves, curry powder, and cumin and cook, stirring frequently, for about 12 minutes or until flavors are well-blended and the pan is almost dry. Stir in ¾ cup of the cream along with the almonds. Remove from the heat and set aside to cool.

When ready to bake, preheat the oven to 375°F.

Lightly coat the interior of a 2-quart casserole with nonstick vegetable spray.

Whisk the eggs, remaining 2 cups of heavy cream, and nutmeg together in a mixing bowl.

Scrape the lamb mixture into the casserole and pour the egg mixture over the meat. Place in the preheated oven and bake for about 1 hour, or until the custard has set. The dish may be made ahead and reheated just before serving.

Remove from the oven and serve with rice, if desired.

Oven-Baked Lamb Chops

Serves 6 to 8

Although Middle Eastern in origin, this dish tastes almost Provençal. You will find a version of this dish throughout the Mediterranean—some are highly seasoned with cumin and sweet spices and some with chili; some contain more vegetables than meat. This version is definitely Israeli. It can be served hot or at room temperature, and goes very nicely with a rice salad.

½ cup plus 3 tablespoons olive oil
2 teaspoons paprika
Salt to taste
12 baby lamb chops, trimmed of excess fat
¾ cup Wondra flour
Pepper to taste
1 cup dry red wine
2 cups nonfat, low-sodium beef broth
10 cloves garlic, peeled
3 onions, peeled and quartered
3 large beefsteak tomatoes, cored, seeded, and
    quartered

Preheat the oven to 400°F.

Combine ½ cup of the olive oil with the paprika and salt to taste in a small bowl.

Using a pastry brush, lightly coat each lamb chop with the olive oil mixture, reserving any of the mixture that remains.

Lightly dust both sides of each chop with Wondra flour and season with pepper to taste.

Heat the remaining 3 tablespoons of oil in a large frying pan over medium-high heat. When very hot but not smoking, add the seasoned chops, in batches if necessary, and sear, turning once, until both sides are nicely colored.

Place the seared chops in a shallow baking dish large enough to hold them in a single layer. Set aside.

Return the frying pan to high heat. Add the wine and bring to a boil, scraping up the bottom of the pan with a wooden spoon to release any browned bits. Add the broth and again bring to a boil.

Remove from the heat and pour the hot liquid over the chops. Add any of the remaining seasoned oil to the pan. Nestle the garlic, onions, and tomatoes around the chops. Cover tightly with aluminum foil and transfer to the preheated oven.

Bake for 20 minutes; then lower the oven temperature to 300°F and continue to bake for about 40 minutes, or until the meat is almost falling off the bone and the liquid has become sauce-like.

Remove from the oven, unwrap, and transfer to a serving platter. Serve hot or at room temperature.

"Mama dashed out to the market and bought three chicken necks and two wings, and fried them in a little palm oil. 'Especially for Nnamdi,' she said gaily. Mama, who used to make Coq Au Vin without a cookbook.

"We toasted Nnamdi with palm wine. 'To our Future Son-In-Law,' Papa said, raising his mug."

—CHIMAMANDA ADICHIE, *Half a Yellow Sun*

Nigerian *Jollof* Rice

Serves 8 to 12

This is a classic Nigerian side dish that is almost always used as an accompaniment to meat dishes or with dodo, another traditional dish made with fried green plantains. However, it would make a wonderful, aromatic side dish to serve with roasted meats or stews.

2 large ripe tomatoes, peeled, cored, seeded, and
   cut into pieces
1 large red onion, peeled and chopped
1 large red bell pepper, cored, seeded, and chopped
4 cups long grain white rice
Salt to taste
Cayenne pepper to taste
¼ cup vegetable broth

Preheat the oven to 350°F.

Combine the tomatoes, onion, and pepper in the bowl of a food processor fitted with the metal blade. Process to a smooth puree and set aside.

Combine the rice with 6 cups of cold water in a Dutch oven over medium-high heat. Bring to a boil and reduce the heat to a gentle simmer. Simmer for 15 minutes and then add the reserved tomato mixture, stirring to blend well. Season with salt and cayenne pepper to taste.

Return the mixture to a simmer and stir in the vegetable broth.

Cover and transfer to the preheated oven and bake for about 30 minutes or until the rice is very dry. Check from time to time to make sure that the liquid has not evaporated too quickly, as you don't want the rice to burn before it is cooked, but you also do not want the rice to be soupy.

Remove from the oven and serve hot.

PITA and MIDDLE EASTERN SPREADS

Serves 10 to 12

❖ ❖ ❖

Throughout the Mediterranean and Middle East, almost every country has its own take on these recipes, adding spices and herbs that are local favorites. Chickpea and eggplant spreads are very tempting, particularly when served with chunks of feta cheese, warm pita and/or seasoned flat breads and plenty of extra virgin olive oil. Plus, if you don't feel like cooking, pre-made hummus, tabbouleh (a wonderful bulghur wheat salad), and baba ghanoush, along with pita and other flat breads or crackers, are available from many supermarkets, and are easy to pack for a picnic or potluck at someone else's place.

Hummus

Makes about 2 cups

One 19-ounce can chickpeas
¼ cup tahini *(see Note)*
3 cloves garlic, peeled and chopped
⅓ cup fresh lemon juice
¼ cup olive oil
Hot pepper sauce to taste
Salt to taste
Extra virgin olive oil for drizzling
Toasted sesame seeds for sprinkling

Drain the chickpeas through a fine mesh sieve, separately reserving the liquid.

Combine the chickpeas with the *tahini* and garlic in the bowl of a food processor fitted with the metal blade. Process to blend well. Add the lemon juice, olive oil, hot pepper sauce, and salt to taste and process until very smooth. Add a bit of the reserved chickpea liquid if the mixture seems too thick.

Scrape into a bowl and, if not serving immediately, cover and refrigerate for up to 3 days.

When ready to serve, drizzle the top with extra virgin olive oil and sprinkle with toasted sesame seeds.

Baba Ghanoush

Makes about 2 cups

2 large eggplants
2 tablespoons tahini *(see Note)*
2 tablespoons fresh lemon juice
2 cloves garlic, peeled and chopped
Salt to taste
Ground cumin to taste
Extra virgin olive oil for drizzling
2 teaspoons roughly chopped fresh
    flat-leaf parsley

Preheat the oven to 375°F.

Place the eggplants in a baking pan in the preheated oven. Bake for about 1 hour or until the skin is charred and the flesh is very soft.

Remove from the oven and set aside until cool enough to handle.

When cool, cut the eggplants open with a sharp knife and, using a tablespoon, scrape the flesh out into a fine mesh sieve. Discard the skin.

Using the back of a spoon, lightly press on the eggplant flesh to eliminate excess liquid. Transfer the flesh to the bowl of a food processor fitted with the metal blade. Add the tahini, lemon juice, and garlic and process until smooth.

Scrape into a bowl and season with salt and cumin to taste. If not serving immediately, cover and refrigerate for up to 3 days.

When ready to serve, drizzle the top with extra virgin olive oil and sprinkle with chopped parsley.

If not serving immediately, cover and refrigerate until ready to serve.

NOTE: *Tahini* is sesame seed paste. It is available from Middle Eastern markets, specialty food stores, most supermarkets, and through the Internet.

MINT and FRUIT TEAS

✦ ✦ ✦

Perhaps the best known African tea is *rooiboos*, a slightly sweet herbal tea that comes from a plant of the legume family informally called redbush. It is a favorite drink in South Africa, but has made its way all around the world. I have even seen it in coffee bars in the United States. Throughout Africa, fruit-flavored and herbal teas are served and many of them are now available in tea bags in American markets; passion fruit, citrus, hibiscus, orange blossom, and rosehip are just of the few that would offer a flavor of the African continent.

Mint Tea

Makes 4 cups

10 sprigs fresh mint
1 piece orange peel, no pith attached
2 tablespoons sugar or to taste
4 cups boiling water
4 fresh mint leaves

Place the mint and orange peel in a tea pot and, using the end of a wooden spoon, smash the leaves and peel to release their oils. Cover with sugar, then pour the boiling water into the pot. Cover and let steep for 4 minutes.

Serve with a mint leaf floating in each cup.

Liberian Coconut Bread

Makes one 13-inch by 9-inch bread

This is a very typical coconut-flavored bread from Liberia. It is quite sweet, so it is best served as a rich breakfast treat or as a dessert. It would be perfect with a spiced tea or strong coffee.

4½ cups all-purpose flour, sifted
½ cup sugar
1 tablespoon baking powder
¼ teaspoon salt
1¼ cups unsalted butter, at room temperature
1 cups milk
Coconut Filling (recipe follows)

Preheat the oven to 350°F.

Lightly coat the interior of a 13-inch by 9-inch baking pan with nonstick vegetable spray or Baker's Joy. Set aside.

TURKISH COFFEE

✦ ✦ ✦

Coffee beans are grown in Kenya and elsewhere in East Africa, most for export.

The style of coffee favored in North Africa is Turkish coffee, which can be brewed from various types of beans. A version of this thick, often very sweet brew is found throughout the Middle East as well as in the Balkans and the Caucasus.

To make an authentic cup, you need the proper pot, called a *"kanaka"* (among many other names), or just a Turkish coffee pot as well as very finely ground coffee beans. The pot is copper (usually), and ranges in volume from 1 cup to many. It has a long handle, often wood, and a pour spout. These pots can be found in many kitchen supply stores or Middle Eastern markets.

The coffee is best prepared from freshly roasted beans that are ground to the finest possible powder. Although traditionally done in a mortar and pestle, it can also be done in an electric coffee grinder, but you must insure that the grind is almost like face powder.

For each cup of coffee, 1 to 2 heaping teaspoons of coffee is placed in the bottom of the pot. The desired amount of sugar then covers the coffee powder. Sweetness is measured by the following: *çok ekerli* (extremely sweet, 1½ to 2 teaspoons sugar), *orta ekerli* (medium sweet, about 1 teaspoon sugar), *az ekerli* (little sweetness, about ½ teaspoon sugar), and *sade* (no sugar). Cold water is added; the amount desired is measured by the volume of the pot being used. The mixture is then stirred until the sugar has dissolved and all of the coffee powder has fallen to the bottom of the pot.

The pot is then placed over moderate heat and, without stirring, brought to just a boil. The pot is immediately removed from the heat and allowed to rest for a minute or two. It is then returned to moderate heat and, without stirring, brought to a boil at least one more time or up to three additional times. The desired result is a rich mix with a thick layer of foam on top. The foam can be increased by holding the pot high above the cup into which you are going to pour the coffee and letting the liquid slowly pour into the cup. An honored cup of Turkish coffee is thick and homogenous, with no visible coffee particles and a very thick layer of foam on top.

In every country where this style of coffee is served, there is a unique native method for making it, with spices and dried or fresh citrus peel often added to the mix. You might want to devise your own way.

Combine 4 cups of the flour with the sugar, baking powder, and salt in the bowl of a food processor fitted with the metal blade. Process, using quick on-and-off turns to just blend. Add the butter and process just until crumbly. With the motor running, add the milk and process just until the dough comes together. If it is too sticky to handle, add the remaining ¼ cup of flour.

Scrape the dough from the processor and divide it into two equal pieces.

Lightly flour a clean, flat work surface. Working with one piece at a time and using a rolling pin, roll each piece of dough out to a rectangle about 14 inches by 10 inches. Carefully fit one piece into the bottom of the prepared pan. Then use a spatula to spread an even layer of the filling over the dough. Top with the remaining dough rectangle, pushing the edges together to seal.

Place in the preheated oven and bake for about 40 minutes or until the bread is golden brown and cooked through.

Remove from the oven and let rest at least 30 minutes before cutting into squares and serving.

Coconut Filling

1 pound flaked unsweetened coconut
One 5-ounce can evaporated milk
2 cups coconut water (see Note)
cup sugar
2 tablespoons unsalted butter
2 teaspoons pure vanilla extract

Combine the coconut with the evaporated milk, coconut water, sugar, butter, and vanilla in a medium heavy-bottomed saucepan over medium heat. Bring to a boil. Then lower the heat and cook, stirring frequently, for about 12 minutes or until the coconut is very moist and most of the liquid has evaporated.

Remove from the heat and set aside to cool until ready to use.

NOTE: Coconut water is available from Asian or African markets, some specialty food stores, or through the Internet.

> "I climbed a tree and ate these green, sour apples. My stomach swelled and became hard like a drum, it hurt a lot. Mother said that if I'd just waited for the apples to ripen, I wouldn't have become sick. So now, whenever I really want something, I try to remember what she said about the apples."
>
> **—KHALED HOSSEINI, The Kite Runner**

Ma'amoul

Makes about 3½ dozen

Some version of these cookies can be found throughout Mediterranean Africa and in central Africa as well as the Middle East, where dried fruits are often the sweet of choice. You can use dried apricots or peaches in place of the dates. These cookies are usually made in a press called a *ma'amoul* mold, but I just use my fingers to make the final molded cookie.

2 ½ cups all-purpose flour
½ cup semolina flour (see Note)
1 cup cold unsalted butter, cut into cubes
2 teaspoons lite olive oil
¼ to ½ cup water
1 cup chopped walnuts
½ cup chopped dates
¼ cup granulated sugar
¼ cup packed light brown sugar
1 teaspoon ground cinnamon
Approximately 1 cup confectioners' sugar

Combine the all-purpose and semolina flours in the bowl of a standing electric mixer fitted with the dough hook. Add the butter and oil and mix on low speed until a crumbly dough forms.

Begin adding water, a bit at a time, adding and mixing until a smooth dough forms. You may need more or less water than called for, but do not over-mix or the dough will become pasty.

Transfer the dough to a clean, flat work surface and, using your hands, knead it into a ball. Tightly wrap in plastic film and refrigerate for 20 minutes.

Combine the walnuts, dates, granulated and brown sugars, and cinnamon in a small mixing bowl. Using your fingers, mash the mixture together until almost paste-like. Set aside.

Preheat the oven to 350°F.

Line two cookie sheets with parchment paper. Set aside.

Remove the dough from the refrigerator and unwrap.

Form the dough into walnut-size pieces. Working with one piece at a time, hold a piece of dough in the palm of your hand and, using the other hand, make a little hollow in the center of the dough to receive the filling. Place the filling in the hollow and then close the dough up and around the filling.

As each cookie is filled, place it, seam side down, on a prepared cookie sheet.

When all of the cookies have been formed, gently press on the top of each one with the tines of a dinner fork to make a neat line design.

Place in the preheated oven and bake for about 30 minutes or until just set. The cookies should not color—they should remain almost white.

Place the confectioners' sugar in a large shallow container.

Remove the cookies from the oven and, while still hot, roll each one in the confectioners' sugar to coat heavily.

Transfer to wire racks to cool.

Store in single layers, airtight, for up to 1 week.

NOTE: Semolina flour (coarsely ground durum wheat flour) is available at Middle Eastern and Italian food markets and some supermarkets.

"As a child sitting at the Ramadan Iftar [breaking of the fast] table, my problem was fuul [fava beans]. I didn't want to eat anything else; so much so that my father decreed that fuul should be the last dish to come to the table. He wouldn't let me eat fuul until I had eaten from all the other dishes. So I would only take a small bite from each of the plates, and leave enough room for my favorite dish, the plate of fuul that I was eying all the time. My family made an art of fuul cooking. They would prepare it with olive oil, lemon and parsley, or with tomato sauce, or with coriander and garlic."
—NAGUIB MAHFOUZ

Chapter 14

Pleasures of the Subcontinent

*N*O LAND OR REGION IS ENTIRELY DIFFERENT FROM ALL OTHERS IN ITS CULINARY preferences. Cooking styles, foods or seeds long have been frequent travelers. Still, the cooking of the Indian Subcontinent—India, Pakistan, Bangladesh, Nepal and Sri Lanka—is exceptionally distinctive, very different from Europe, the Americas and Africa, if less so from neighbors such as Afghanistan or Tibet.

DARIO DIAMENT

The Anglo-American and European palates are likely to find the food of this area deliciously spicy. Its base spice mixes—curry or *garam masala*—are complex, multi-note combinations that many accomplished chefs of the region, including housewives, themselves cultivate or select, pound and combine. Fragrant spices, such as saffron or cardamom, are more frequently used in savory appetizers or entrees than they are in the West. Yogurt is used in many sauces or gravies, served hot or at room temperature. The *tandoor* oven, which can be used for meats, fish, vegetables and breads, is special because its intense smoky heat cooks quickly, resulting in a crisp exterior and moist, succulent interior.

A large array of handcrafted flatbreads includes versions with significant quantities of a vegetable or herb baked into them. The most basic food of the Subcontinent, however, is long-grained rice, preferably basmati.

There are a few important differences among peoples of the Subcontinent in their eating choices. Pakistan and Bangladesh are Moslem countries, where most observe religious dictates of not eating dairy products and meat together, not eating pork or shelled seafood, not drinking alcohol. These rules are also followed by the Moslem majority in Kashmir, and Moslem minorities in other Indian states and nearby areas. The majority of Indians are Hindus, and observant Hindus regard the cow as sacred and so eat no beef. Many people in South India are vegetarians. One pocket of culinary difference is in the Indian state of Kerala, where most dishes are recognizably Indian, but a few bear the stamp of the Portuguese who once lived there.

It's my impression that food is rather often mentioned in works set on the Subcontinent, and in novels and essays written in English by writers with roots in the Subcontinent who now are settled elsewhere. British chroniclers of the *Raj* couldn't help but notice the spicy dishes preferred by the Indians. Immigrants or the offspring of immigrants sometimes express feelings of distance or homesickness with loving descriptions of the preparation and aromas of favorite dishes.

Some Westerners like to accompany spicy Indo-Pakistani foods with wine, while others prefer cold beer to tamp down its heat. The Indian Kingfisher beer is a good choice. Traditionally, Indians have enjoyed a yogurt drink called *lassi*, or excellent tea.

◆ ◆ ◆

READS, DRINKS & NIBBLES
■ ■ ■
Lassi
Vegetable *Samosas* with Cilantro Dipping Sauce
Breads

STAR DISHES & DELICIOUS ASIDES
■ ■ ■
Tandoori Chicken

FOR A MOVEABLE FEAST
■ ■ ■
Dal Pancakes

LITERARY TEA OR SWEET ENDING
■ ■ ■
Fragrant Teas of India
Chai
Cardamom-Spiced *Crème Brûlée*

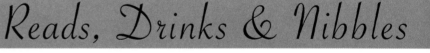

Reads, Drinks & Nibbles

Lassi

Serves 6

This is the most traditional of all hot Indian summer thirst quenchers. It can be drunk on its own or as an accompaniment to a spicy Indian meal.

2 cups lemon-flavored or plain yogurt
1 cup ice cold water
3 tablespoons sugar
2 teaspoons fresh lemon or lime juice
6 ice cubes
6 sprigs fresh mint

Combine the yogurt with the water, sugar, and citrus juice in a blender jar. Add the ice cubes and process until the ice is crushed and the mixture is whipped and frothy. Pour into chilled glasses and garnish each with a mint sprig.

Vegetable *Samosas* with Cilantro Dipping Sauce

Makes about 18

Samosas are a much-loved traditional Indian snack. They may be made with a filling of meat, vegetables, or legumes. Like most foods of India and Pakistan or Sri Lanka, they do take some amount of intense preparation. However, if you live in a major city, you can also purchase them along with many other snack-type foods at Indian or Pakistani markets, or from a modestly priced restaurant—or, of course, via the internet.

2 cups sifted all-purpose flour
½ cup vegetable oil
Salt to taste
Approximately ¼ cup warm water
1 teaspoon garam masala (See Note)
1 teaspoon ground cumin
1 teaspoon ground coriander
½ teaspoon ground turmeric
½ cup chopped red onion
½ teaspoon minced garlic
1 fresh hot green chili, stemmed and seeded,
*   or to taste*
2 teaspoons minced fresh ginger
3 tablespoons fresh orange juice
1 cup chopped cooked potatoes
½ cup frozen petit peas, thawed and
*   patted dry*
½ cup chopped cooked parsnips or carrots
½ cup chopped cooked spinach
Cayenne pepper to taste
Approximately 2 cups peanut oil for frying

Combine the flour and ¼ cup of the vegetable oil with salt to taste in the bowl of a food processor fitted with the metal blade. Process until coarse crumbs form. With the motor running, slowly add the warm water until a stiff dough forms.

Scrape the dough from the processor and, using your hands, form it into a ball. Again, using your hands and using about 1 tablespoon of the remaining oil, generously coat the dough. Wrap in plastic film and set aside for at least 30 minutes.

Combine the *garam masala*, cumin, coriander, and turmeric in a small, nonstick frying pan over medium heat. Cook, stirring constantly, for about 3 minutes or until the spices begin to brown and are very fragrant. Immediately remove from the heat and set aside.

Heat 3 tablespoons of the remaining oil in a medium frying pan over medium-high heat. When hot but not smoking, add the onion and garlic and fry, stirring constantly, for about 5 minutes or until nicely colored but not burned. Stir in the chili and ginger, followed by the orange juice. Lower the heat, cover and cook for 3 minutes.

Uncover and stir in the potatoes, peas, parsnips (or carrots), and spinach. When well-blended, stir in the reserved toasted spice mixture along with the cayenne and salt to taste. Recover and cook for 5 minutes. If the mixture seems dry, add water, about 1 tablespoon at a time.

Remove from the heat and set aside to cool thoroughly.

Lightly flour a clean, flat work surface.

Divide the reserved dough into 9 equal pieces. Wrap each piece in plastic film to keep it from drying out.

Working with one piece at a time, roll the dough out into a circle about 6 inches in diameter.

Cut each circle in half, then fold the edges in toward

[A poor Indian with] "no more elephants than one, none sometimes," and, "only a little food" would "have it arranged nicely" and "never cease to show hospitality."

—E.M. FORSTER, A Passage to India

> **"On a sticky August evening two weeks before her due date, Ashima Ganguli stands in the kitchen of a Central Square apartment, combining Rice Krispies and Planters peanuts and chopped red onion in a bowl. She adds salt, lemon juice, thin slices of green chili pepper, wishing there were mustard oil to pour into the mix. Ashima has been consuming this concoction throughout her pregnancy, a humble approximation of the snack sold for pennies on Calcutta sidewalks and on railway platforms throughout India."**
>
> —JHUMPA LAHIRI, The Namesake

each other to form a cone shape (similar to a coffee filter), allowing the edges to overlap slightly. Place a bit of cold water along the cut edge and press to seal.

Place about 2 tablespoons of the cooled vegetable mixture into the pocket that has been formed. Then, seal the rounded edges together with a bit of cool water. Use your thumb and forefinger to flute the edges. Continue making *samosas* until all of the dough has been used.

Place the peanut oil in a deep frying pan over medium heat. When just hot, add the *samosas*, a few at a time, and fry, turning frequently, until golden brown on all sides.

BREADS

✦ ✦ ✦

There are any number of flatbreads served with a meal from this region, with each area of the Subcontinent having favorites. Among the breads available commercially in the United States are *roti, chapati, paratha, naan* and *uttapam*. Some of them are available in the freezer section of supermarkets (particularly in areas with large Indian or Pakistani populations), and many are available from specialty food stores or through the internet.

Using a slotted spoon, transfer the cooked *samosas* to a double layer of paper towel to drain.

Serve hot or at room temperature with Cilantro Dipping Sauce.

Cilantro Dipping Sauce

1 small hot green chili, stemmed and seeded, or to taste
2 cups fresh cilantro leaves
2 tablespoons fresh mint leaves
1 tablespoon orange juice concentrate
1 teaspoon fresh lime juice
Salt to taste

Combine the chili with the cilantro, mint, orange juice concentrate, and lime juice in a blender jar. Process until smooth.

Pour into a nonreactive container and season with salt to taste. Cover and refrigerate until ready to serve.

NOTE: *Garam masala* is a mixture of ground spices ("*garam*" meaning "hot" or "warm", and "*masala*" meaning mix) that is common in Indian cooking and quite individual in the mix. It might contain cinnamon, coriander, cumin, cardamom, black pepper, cloves and nutmeg among other spices, as well as dried hot chilies. In India, it is usually made at home to the cook's specifications. Ready-made, it can be found in many supermarket spice sections, specialty food stores, or in East Indian or Pakistani markets.

Tandoori Chicken

Serves 6 to 8

Classic *tandoori* meat or seafood dishes are baked in a *"tandoor,"* the traditional clay oven of India. I think that this recipe is a great approximation of the real thing. I don't use the food coloring frequently employed to give tandoori entrees their bright orange color. However, if you like, you can brush the chicken with orange food coloring before marinating it.

Although I use chicken pieces, you can use whole chickens or a combination of any pieces you desire.

4 chicken breasts, cut in half
4 chicken thighs
4 chicken legs
¼ cup fresh lemon juice
Salt to taste
2½ cups plain yogurt
½ fresh hot red chili, seeded and chopped
¾ cup chopped onion
2 tablespoons fresh lime juice
1 tablespoon minced fresh ginger
1 tablespoon paprika
2 teaspoons garam masala
   (see Note on page 157)
1 teaspoon ground
   turmeric
1 teaspoon minced garlic

Using a small, sharp knife, carefully make slits, about 1½ inches long and through to the bone, on the skin side of the breasts and on all sides of the thighs and legs. Rub the chicken pieces on all sides with the lemon juice and sprinkle with salt. Place in a nonreactive container or re-sealable plastic bag and set aside.

Combine the yogurt with the chili, onion, lime juice, ginger, paprika, *garam masala,* turmeric, and garlic in a blender jar. Process until smooth.

Pour the yogurt mixture over the chicken, tossing to coat well. Cover or reseal and refrigerate for at least 8 hours or up to 24 hours.

When ready to cook, preheat the oven to 500°F and remove the chicken from the refrigerator to allow it to come to room temperature.

Place wire racks on baking pans with sides. Place the chicken pieces on the wire racks, at least 1 inch apart.

Transfer to the preheated oven and bake for 25 minutes or until a deep golden brown (or orange-brown if food coloring was used) and the chicken is cooked through.

Remove from the oven and serve hot or at room temperature.

MYMENSINGH DISTRICT EAST PAKISTAN, 1967

"An hour and forty-five minutes before Nazneen's life began…her mother, Rupban, felt an iron fist squeeze her belly. Rupban squatted on a low three-legged stool outside the kitchen hut. She was plucking a chicken because Hamid's cousins had arrived from Jessore and there would be a feast. 'Cheepy-cheepy, you are old and stringy,' she said, calling the bird by name as she always did, 'but I would like to eat you, indigestion or no indigestion. And tomorrow I will have only boiled rice, no parathas.' "

—MONICA ALI, Brick Lane

Dal Pancakes

Serves 6 to 8

In Indian cooking, *dal* refers to all manner of lentils and other legumes. No meal is complete without some version of *dal*, and sometimes a *dal* dish is the only dish of a simple meal or snack. These pancakes are easy to make, with flavors that absolutely mark them as from the Subcontinent. They can be used as a side dish or a snack.

1 cup pale yellow lentils or yellow split peas
½ cup vegetable broth
½ cup finely chopped onion
1 tablespoon minced garlic
1 tablespoon minced fresh ginger
1 teaspoon minced fresh green chili
¼ teaspoon ground cumin
¼ teaspoon ground turmeric
Pinch ground cinnamon
Salt to taste
½ cup thick plain yogurt, such as Greek yogurt
2 tablespoons minced fresh cilantro
1 tablespoon minced fresh flat-leaf parsley
1 tablespoon minced scallions
¼ cup clarified butter (see Note on page 94)
  or vegetable oil*

Place the lentils in warm water to cover by at least 2 inches, and set aside to soak for 2 hours. Drain well.

Combine the drained lentils with the vegetable broth, onion, garlic, ginger, chili, cumin, turmeric, cinnamon, and salt in the bowl of a food processor fitted with the metal blade. Process until well-combined and frothy, and then pour into a mixing bowl.

Stir in ¼ cup of the yogurt along with the cilantro, parsley, and scallions. Pour the batter into a large glass measuring cup with a pour spout (or any other container with a pour spout)—this is just to facilitate the pouring.

Heat a nonstick griddle over high heat. Lightly coat the griddle with clarified butter. When very hot, lower the heat and pour in just enough batter to make a 5-inch round pancake.

Cook the pancake for about 2 minutes or until the underside is beginning to brown. Using a spatula, turn and cook the remaining side for about 2 minutes or until set and lightly browned. Transfer to a warm plate and tent lightly with aluminum foil to keep warm. Continue making pancakes until all of the batter has been used.

The pancakes can be made ahead of time and re-heated in a warm oven for about 5 minutes.

Serve warm with a dollop of yogurt on top.

*Although you can use vegetable oil to fry the pancakes, they will have a much richer flavor when fried in clarified butter.

LONDON, 1985

"Nazneen could say two things in English: sorry and thank you. She could spend another day alone. It was only another day. She should be getting on with the evening meal. The lamb curry was prepared. She had made it last night with tomatoes and new potatoes. There was chicken saved in the freezer from the last time Dr. Azad had been invited but had canceled at the last minute. There was still the dal to make, and the vegetable dishes, the spices to grind, the rice to wash, and the sauce to prepare . . . What if it went wrong? The rice might stick. She might oversalt the dal."

—MONICA ALI, Brick Lane

Fragrant Teas of India

Not only does India produce some of the finest black teas in the world, it produces most of the tea that is consumed throughout the world. Since it is such a large country, with so many varying climates, Indian teas can be quite different in flavor. Sri Lanka is also a tea producer—its tea is often called "Ceylonese" tea.

The three main types of teas grown in India are Assam, Darjeeling and *Nilgiri*. Assam is a very full-bodied tea grown in the north-eastern part of the country. Darjeeling tea, considered by many to be the finest in the world, comes from a very wet, cool area in the foothills of the Himalaya Mountains. There are three harvests (called a "flush"), each of which produces a tea with an identifiable, unique flavor. The first is a very light, ambrosial tea, the second a tea with the same notes but deeper flavor, and the third a tea of lower quality, still drinkable but not as aromatic and delicate. The subtle *Nilgiri* tea comes from the mountainous region of southern India, and it is often blended with darker, heartier teas to soften their flavor.

Nowadays, one of the most famous teas associated with India is *chai*. It is not a type of tea, but a style of making tea, and can often be found in coffee bars and tea houses throughout the world. Every cook and every shop has their own way of preparing *chai*. The following mix is very flavorful and keeps well, so it can always be on hand to make a warming pot of tea while you're engrossed in a book

written by one of the contemporary brilliant female writers of the Indian Subcontinent or of the diaspora.

Chai

Makes about 3½ cups

¾ *cup toasted cardamom seeds*
¼ *cup whole cloves*
¼ *cup dried orange peel*
2 teaspoons toasted fennel seeds
4 cups powdered whole milk
1 cup light brown sugar or to taste
1 tablespoon ground ginger

Combine the cardamom, cloves, orange peel, and fennel seeds in a spice grinder and process to a coarse grind. You may have to do this in batches.

Combine the ground spice mix with the powdered milk, sugar, and ginger in a mixing bowl, stirring to blend well.

Pack into an airtight container and store in a cool, dry spot for up to 6 months.

To serve, add 2 tablespoons *chai* mix to each cup of hot water when brewing a pot of tea. Serve hot or iced.

Cardamom-Spiced *Crème Brûlée*

Makes 6 or 8

Just a few short years ago, few outside France knew what a *crème brûlée* was, but now you can find that lovely caramelized custard in restaurants and some bakeries in much of the world, including India. This version of the French dessert classic is flavored with a favorite Indian spice, cardamom. You could also use cinnamon, ginger, *garam masala* or even a bit of clove. It is a dessert that travels well, and so could also be a great addition to a potluck book club tea or other meal where one of the many exceptional 20th-century or contemporary novels set on the Subcontinent is being chewed over.

8 large egg yolks, at room temperature
¾ cup superfine sugar
2 cups heavy cream
1 teaspoon pure vanilla extract
1 teaspoon ground cardamom
¼ cup light brown sugar, sifted

Combine the egg yolks and sugar in a heatproof mixing bowl, whisking vigorously to blend and help the sugar dissolve into the yolks.

Place the cream in a small saucepan over medium heat. Heat just until tiny bubbles form around the edge of the pan. Immediately remove from the heat and, whisking constantly, beat about ¼ cup of the hot cream into the egg yolk mixture to temper. Continuing to whisk, beat in the remaining cream along with the vanilla and cardamom.

Pour the mixture through a fine mesh sieve into either eight 4-ounce or six 6-ounce custard or *crème brûlée* dishes.

Place a baking dish large enough to hold the custard dishes in the oven. Carefully transfer the filled dishes to the baking dish. Add enough cold water to come at least 1 inch up the sides of the custard dishes.

Heat the oven to 300°F. Bake for about 1 hour, or just until the custards have begun to set but are still a bit loose in the center when the dish is moved.

Remove the pan from the oven and transfer the dishes to wire racks. Let cool to room temperature.

When cool, cover each dish with plastic film and transfer to the refrigerator. Refrigerate for at least 8 hours or up to 2 days.

When ready to serve, preheat the broiler.

Remove the custards from the refrigerator. Uncover and, using a paper towel, remove any moisture that is sitting on top of the set custard. Place the dishes on a baking sheet of a size that will fit under the broiler.

Place the brown sugar in a fine mesh sieve and lightly coat the top of each custard with the sugar.

Place the dishes under the preheated broiler and broil for about 1 minute, or just until the sugar has melted and bubbled. It will harden as it cools.

Serve while the custards are still cold with a crackling caramel top.

Chapter 15

Scrolling through Asia

As we scroll through Asia, you will find that the recipes are as diverse as the literature connected to Japan, Korea, China and the countries of Southeast Asia. Some interesting works are by Western authors inspired by an "exotic" setting; others are by writers who share a cultural heritage with the land in which their story is placed. Either circumstance may lead to a story of personal conflict and estrangement.

Not known to many is the fact that what is likely the world's first novel—or, at the least, extant novel—is the 11th century, six-volume *Tale of Genji*, written by Murasaki Shikibu, a Buddhist lady in the imperial court of Kyoto. Japanese writers have been at their fiction a long time. The Chinese also boast centuries-old novels.

Contemporary literature has brought us many best-selling American authors of Asian heritage such as Amy Tan, Bette Bao Lord, and Gish Jen, as well as

up-and-coming writers like the Korean-American author, Min Jin Lee.

Another wonderful modern development is that many Asian ingredients, and some prepared foods, may now be purchased in American markets. Sushi, relatively rare just a couple of decades ago, is now available in many places. *Kimchi*, Korea's national dish, which is eaten with every meal as a side dish or incorporated into main dishes, can now be purchased either in the produce section or jarred in those same sophisticated markets. Almost every town has a Chinese restaurant that will deliver, or where you can pick up, a delicious hot meal almost as quickly as you can make a telephone call. In some places, this is also true for Thai and Vietnamese restaurants.

READS, DRINKS & NIBBLES
■ ■ ■
Cocktails
Steamed Shrimp Dumplings with Ginger Dipping Sauce
Yakitori

STAR DISHES & DELICIOUS ASIDES
■ ■ ■
Hacked Chicken
Singapore Mai Fun with Yellow Curry Sauce
Gado Gado with Peanut Sauce
Laab

FOR A MOVEABLE FEAST
■ ■ ■
Sesame-Soy Tofu Squares

LITERARY TEA OR SWEET ENDING
■ ■ ■
Flower and other Exceptional Teas
Puffed Rice Cookies
Fragrant Fruit Salad

Reads, Drinks & Nibbles

Steamed Shrimp Dumplings with Ginger Dipping Sauce

Serves 6 to 8

These easy-to-make dumplings will certainly transport you to a table in Shanghai (or elsewhere in China). The dumplings and dipping sauce can be made in advance and the dumplings steamed just before serving. Following this same recipe, you can make pork or chicken dumplings and then serve a variety—all with the same dipping sauce.

Using *gyoza* wrappers (which are thinner than wonton skins), this same filling, with the addition of 1 teaspoon of minced garlic, could be used to make Japanese dumplings called *gyoza*.

RICE WINES, BEERS and COCKTAILS

✦ ✦ ✦

There are two Asian rice beverages often served in the United States: The Japanese sake and the Chinese Shaoxing wine. Sake is actually beer. It is served warm in small porcelain cups made especially for this purpose, although it is now sometimes offered chilled in the United States. Sake is not aged and is to be drunk within a year of its bottling.

In China, Shaoxing wine is used as much in cooking as it is drunk. When used as a beverage, it is served exactly as is sake. It can also be salted. In this case, it is only used for cooking. Shaoxing is similar in flavor to sherry wine, which can be used as a substitute in recipes calling for the Chinese wine.

The Japanese also make *mirin*, a sweet rice cooking wine, used to give a distinct, sweet flavor to sauces, dips, glazes and braises. *Aji mirin* is salted.

Several Asian beers are imported, including Tsingtao (from China), Kirin and Sapporo (from Japan), and Singha (from Thailand). Needless to say, they are good accompaniments to spicy or salty dishes of their homelands.

Since the early 1900s, bartenders have been creating cocktails that reflect the flavors and climate of Asian countries. Among the more famous is the Singapore Sling and the Lichitini—which is a Western notion of what a Chinese martini-style drink might be: Flavored with lichico liqueur, a French-made vodka/brandy-based beverage that is infused with lychee, guava and peach.

SHRIMP DUMPLINGS

½ pound shrimp, peeled, deveined, and finely minced
½ cup minced water chestnuts
1 tablespoon sesame seeds
1 tablespoon chopped fresh cilantro
2 teaspoons minced shallots
1 teaspoon minced fresh flat-leaf parsley
½ teaspoon minced fresh ginger
1 large egg white
1 teaspoon sherry wine
1 teaspoon sesame oil
1 teaspoon lite soy sauce
30 wonton wrappers (or gyoza wrappers)
8 large lettuce leaves

Combine the shrimp with the water chestnuts, sesame seeds, cilantro, shallots, parsley and ginger in a mixing bowl.

Combine the egg white with the sherry, sesame oil, and soy sauce in a mixing bowl, whisking until frothy. Add to the shrimp mixture and stir to blend well.

Bring a small amount of water to the boil. Lower the heat to a bare simmer and then place a spoonful of the shrimp mixture into the water. Poach for just a minute, or just until cooked through. This is simply a taste test—taste and, if necessary, adjust the seasoning.

Using a biscuit cutter, cut the wonton wrappers into 3-inch circles. As they are cut, cover them with a damp kitchen towel to keep them from drying out.

Working with one at a time, hold a wonton wrapper in the middle of your palm. Spoon about 2 teaspoons of the shrimp filling into the center. With the other hand, use your fingers to gently pleat the wonton wrapper around the filling. Place the dumpling on a dry, flat surface and flatten the bottom by gently tapping it down.

Line a bamboo steamer or steamer basket with lettuce leaves. Place the dumplings on top of the lettuce and then place the basket over boiling water. Cover and steam for about 10 minutes or until the filling is cooked. This may have to be done in batches.

Remove from the heat and serve with the Ginger Dipping Sauce.

Ginger Dipping Sauce

1 cup white vinegar
2 tablespoons lite soy sauce
¼ loosely packed cup light brown sugar
1 hot green chili pepper, stemmed and seeded or to taste
¼ cup finely diced seedless cucumber
1 tablespoon chopped fresh mint
1 teaspoon grated fresh ginger
1 teaspoon fresh lime juice

Combine the vinegar, soy sauce, and sugar in a small mixing bowl. When well-blended, stir in the chili, cucumber, mint, ginger and lime juice. Cover and refrigerate until ready to serve.

> **In this plate of food, I see the entire universe supporting my existence.**
>
> **—ZEN BLESSING**

Yakitori

Serves 6 to 8

In Japan, Yakitori is traditionally made from either pieces of chicken meat or skin, chicken wings, chicken tails, or bits of chicken offal, such as the gizzard or heart. The meat is skewered and grilled. In the United States, many Japanese restaurants also offer yakitori made from beef, and serve chicken or beef yakitori with a slightly sweet sauce. Yakitori can be eaten hot or at room temperature, which makes it an easy snack for guests. You will, however, need to purchase disposable bamboo skewers.

Throughout Southeast Asia, most countries have some version of skewered meats, poultry, or fish, known as *satay* or *satti*. These skewers of sizzling meat are often found on street carts in Singapore, Thailand, Malaysia and the Philippines.

1 pound boneless, skinless chicken breast or very lean beef, such as tenderloin
1 cup soy sauce (many people use the "lite" variety)
½ cup light brown sugar
½ cup mirin (see Note)
¼ cup water
1 tablespoon sesame oil

With a very sharp knife, cut the meat into long thin strips. Place the chicken (or beef) strips in a re-sealable plastic bag.

Combine the soy sauce, brown sugar, *mirin,* water and sesame oil in a mixing bowl, stirring until the sugar has dissolved. Pour the marinade over the chicken (or beef). Seal and toss to coat. Set aside for 30 minutes.

Place small bamboo skewers in cold water to cover. You will need as many skewers as you have meat strips. Let soak for at least 30 minutes.

Remove the skewers from the water.

Remove the meat from the refrigerator and thread one strip on each skewer.

Preheat and oil a grill or place a nonstick stove-top grill pan on high heat.

When hot, begin placing the skewers on the grill or in the pan. Grill, turning frequently, for about 5 minutes or just until the meat is glazed and cooked through.

Remove from the grill or the pan and serve hot or at room temperature.

Dipping Sauce

¾ cup sake
1 cup soy sauce
¼ cup mirin (see Note)
¼ cup light brown sugar
1 teaspoon minced fresh
*   ginger*

Combine the sake, soy sauce, *mirin*, and brown sugar in a small, nonreactive saucepan over medium heat. Bring to a boil and boil for 1 minute.

Remove from the heat and stir in the ginger. Set aside to cool.

NOTE: *Mirin* is a Japanese sweetened rice wine that is used to flavor savory dishes, sauces, and glazes. It is available from most supermarkets and specialty food stores, as well as from Asian markets.

Star Dishes & Delicious Asides

Hacked Chicken

Serves 6 to 8

Based on a traditional Chinese recipe, this is a terrific make-ahead dish. All of the components can be prepared early in the day and put together just before serving.

You can then use the broth in which the chicken was cooked to make a quick soup opener or accompaniment for your meal. Just add some tiny slices of fresh ginger and perhaps a bit of diced tofu, reheat and you have a soup course!

Add a bowl of white rice and a pot of tea to your hacked-chicken meal and you'll transport your book group to the Far East.

3 whole boneless, skinless chicken breasts
4 cups nonfat, low-sodium chicken broth
1 small onion, skin on, stuck with 2 cloves
1 rib celery, well-washed and cut into pieces
1 carrot, peeled, trimmed, and cut into
*   pieces*
½ ancho chili pepper (see Note)
½ cup sesame paste (see Note)
¼ cup soy sauce
⅓ cup chopped scallion, including some
*   of the green part*
3 tablespoons rice wine vinegar
3 tablespoons sesame oil
2 tablespoons smooth peanut butter
2 tablespoons chili paste (See Note)
1 tablespoon minced fresh ginger
2 teaspoons light brown sugar
1 teaspoon minced garlic
1 tablespoon peanut oil
1½ pounds fresh spinach, washed, dried,
*   and trimmed of any tough stems*
¼ cup toasted sesame seeds

"Midori's cooking was far better than I had expected: an amazing assortment of fried, pickled, boiled and roasted dishes using eggs, mackerel, fresh greens, aubergine, mushrooms, radishes, and sesame seeds, all cooked in the delicate Kyoto style.

'This is great,' I said with my mouth full."

—HARUKI MURUKAMI, Norwegian Wood

Place the chicken breasts in a medium saucepan. Add the chicken broth along with the onion, celery, carrot and chili. Place over high heat and bring to a boil. Lower the heat and simmer for about 15 minutes or just until the chicken is barely cooked.

Remove from the heat and allow the chicken to cool in the cooking broth. When cool, drain well, reserving the broth for another use. Using your fingers, pull the meat off in long, thin strips. Set aside.

Combine the sesame paste, soy sauce, scallion, rice wine vinegar, 2 tablespoons sesame oil, peanut butter, chili paste, ginger, brown sugar, and garlic in a small nonreactive bowl, stirring to blend well. If the dressing is too thick, add a bit of the chicken cooking broth. Set aside.

Heat the remaining 1 tablespoon of sesame oil with the peanut oil in a wok. When very hot but not smoking, add the spinach and quickly stir-fry just to wilt the leaves slightly. Place the spinach on a platter. Place the chicken over the top of the spinach and pour the dressing over all, and then sprinkle the top with toasted sesame seeds.

NOTE: *Ancho* chilies are dried *poblano* chilies that are dark brown in color and add a complex sweetness without heat to many dishes. They are available from supermarkets and specialty food stores or Asian or Latin markets.

Sesame paste and chili paste are available from Asian food stores and markets, and are stocked by some supermarkets as well being obtainable through the Internet.

Singapore Mai Fun with Yellow Curry Sauce

Serves 6 to 8

Although a Singapore street food, *mai fun* or curry noodles are sometimes served in Chinese restaurants in America. A zesty dish that tastes as good cold as it does warm, it is filled with the flavors and aromas of Asia. And it is as pretty to look at as it is delicious to eat.

Mai Fun

1 pound rice noodles or rice sticks (see Note)
4 large eggs
2 tablespoons sesame oil
Salt to taste
2 tablespoons peanut oil
1 hot green chili, stemmed, seeded, and minced
1 shallot, peeled and minced
1 clove garlic, peeled and minced
½ cup bean sprouts
¼ cup julienned carrot
¼ cup julienned yellow squash
¼ cup julienned zucchini
¼ cup julienned onion
¼ cup julienned red bell pepper
Black pepper to taste
¼ cup chopped scallion
½ cup chopped fresh cilantro leaves

Place the rice noodles in a bowl with warm water to cover by at least 2 inches. Soak for 20 minutes. Drain well and set aside.

Combine the eggs with 2 teaspoons of the sesame oil in a small bowl. Season with salt to your taste, and whisk to blend well. Set aside.

Place a nonstick frying pan over medium-high heat. Lightly coat pan with nonstick vegetable spray. Add just enough of the egg mixture to coat the bottom of the pan, swirling the pan to make an even layer. Cook for about 1 minute or until completely set. Flip the egg pancake from the pan. Continue spraying and cooking until you have used all of the egg mixture.

When all of the egg "pancakes" have been made, roll each one up, cigar-fashion, and cut crosswise into thin strips. Open the strips and shake them loose. Set them aside.

Prepare the Yellow Curry Sauce and set aside.

Place a wok over high heat. Add the remaining 4 teaspoons of sesame oil along with the peanut oil.

When the oil is hot, but not smoking, add the chili, shallot and garlic, and sauté for about 30 seconds or just until fragrant. Stir in the bean sprouts, carrot, yellow squash, zucchini, onion and bell pepper, tossing for about 1 minute or just until the vegetables have begun to wilt. Add the curry sauce and the reserved noodles, tossing and turning constantly to blend all of the components together. Cook for about 4 minutes or until heated through. Season with salt and pepper to taste.

Remove from the heat and transfer to a large platter. Sprinkle the reserved egg strips, scallion and cilantro over the top. and serve.

Yellow Curry Sauce

2 tablespoons peanut oil
1 shallot, peeled and minced
1 tablespoon minced fresh ginger
1 tablespoon minced fresh garlic
2 tablespoons Thai yellow curry paste (see Note)
¼ cup rice wine (see Note)
1 cup nonfat, low-sodium chicken broth
2 cups unsweetened coconut milk
2 tablespoons lite soy sauce
Salt and pepper to taste

Place the oil in a heavy-bottomed saucepan over medium heat. Add the shallot, ginger, and garlic and sauté for 1 minute. Lower the heat and stir in the curry paste. Cook, stirring constantly, for about 4 minutes or until the vegetables are quite soft.

Raise the heat and add the rice wine. Bring to a boil and immediately lower the heat and simmer for 1 minute. Add the broth and return to the boil. Lower the heat and simmer for 6 minutes or until the liquid is reduced by half.

Add the coconut milk, raise the heat, and return to the boil. Immediately lower the heat and simmer for about 8 minutes or until again reduced by half. Stir in the soy sauce and season with salt and pepper to taste.

Remove from the heat and strain through a fine mesh sieve. Use immediately or cool and store, covered and refrigerated, for up to 3 days.

NOTE: Rice noodles, Thai yellow curry paste, and rice wine are available from Asian markets, specialty food stores, and many supermarkets or, of course, through the Internet.

Gado Gado with Peanut Sauce

Serves 8 to 10

This is the star of Indonesian cooking. It is always beautiful—a large glass bowl filled to the brim with fresh and tasty ingredients is so inviting. You may use any vegetable that is in season when putting together this dish. It certainly will engage diners in lively conversation.

1½ pounds firm tofu, well-drained and cut into
*   ½-inch cubes*
Wondra flour for dusting
2 tablespoons peanut oil
½ pound green string beans, French cut
*   (see Note)*
1 cup shredded carrot
1 cup shredded spinach leaves
1 cup shredded green cabbage
1 cup shredded red cabbage
1 cup shredded cooked potatoes
1 cup matchstick hothouse cucumber
1 cup bean sprouts
3 large hard-boiled eggs, peeled and cut, cross-
*   wise, into thin slices or cut into quarters*
2 ripe tomatoes, well-washed, cored, and cut,
*   crosswise, into thin slices or cut into quarters*

Place the tofu on a plate and sprinkle with Wondra flour to just lightly coat.

Heat the oil in a large frying pan over medium heat. Add the tofu cubes and fry, turning frequently, for about 10 minutes or until the tofu is golden brown. Using a slotted spatula, transfer the tofu to a double layer of paper towels to drain.

Place the string beans in rapidly boiling salted water. Blanch for about 1 minute or just until crisp-tender. Immediately remove from the heat and drain well. Rinse under cold, running water. Pat dry. Repeat same step with the carrots.

Toss the spinach and green and red cabbage together in the bottom of a large glass bowl. Then begin making layers, starting with the carrots, followed by the string beans, potatoes, cucumber and bean sprouts. Decorate the top with alternating slices of egg and tomato.

Pour the peanut sauce over the top and serve.

Peanut Sauce

1 cup unsweetened coconut milk
¾ cup smooth peanut butter
1 fresh hot red chili, stemmed and seeded
  or to taste
One 2-inch piece lemon rind
2 tablespoons fresh lemon or lime juice
1 tablespoon soy sauce
1 tablespoon light brown sugar
1 teaspoon minced garlic
1 teaspoon shrimp paste (see Note)
1 teaspoon tamarind paste dissolved in
  1 tablespoon hot water

Combine the coconut milk, peanut butter, chili, lemon rind, juice, soy sauce, brown sugar, garlic, shrimp paste and tamarind in a medium heavy-bottomed saucepan over medium heat. Bring to a boil. Lower the heat and simmer, stirring frequently, for about 5 minutes, or until slightly thick. If mixture seems too thick, add water, a tablespoon at a time.

Remove from the heat. Remove and discard the lemon rind. Pour the mixture into a blender jar and process until very smooth.

Pour into a nonreactive container and, if using immediately, keep warm. Otherwise, cover and refrigerate until ready to use, or up to 1 week. Reheat before serving.

NOTE: To French cut string beans, simply cut them, on the diagonal, into long, thin strips.

Shrimp paste and tamarind paste are available from Asian markets, specialty food stores, and many supermarkets. Shrimp paste is known under many names, including *terasi* and *belacan*, depending upon which Asian country has made it.

> "Her mother was singing a hymn in her remarkable voice while she ladled scallion sauce over the roasted porgy. Leah's voice trilled at the close of the verse, 'Waking or sleeping, thy presence my light.' . . . She'd left the store early that morning to shop and to cook her daughters' favorite dishes."
>
> —MIN JIN LEE, Free Food for Millionaires

Laab

Serves 6 to 8

This is a typical Thai street food or snack, which can be served just warm or at room temperature. Light and refreshing, *laab* could also be made with ground poultry. However, if the meat is very lean, you might have to use a bit of peanut oil to fry it.

1 pound lean ground beef
2 tablespoons minced garlic
2 tablespoons minced shallot
3 tablespoons fresh lime juice
3 tablespoons minced red onion
3 tablespoons chopped fresh mint
2 tablespoons minced scallions, including
   some green part
2 tablespoons chopped fresh cilantro
2 tablespoons minced fresh hot red or
   green chili or to taste
2 tablespoons Thai fish sauce
   (nam pla) (see Note)
Salt to taste
24 small Bibb lettuce leaves,
   washed and dried
24 whole mint leaves

Place the beef in a large nonstick skillet over medium-high heat. Add the garlic and shallots and fry, stirring frequently to break up the meat, for about 8 minutes or until nicely browned. Remove from the heat and scrape into a mixing bowl.

Add the lime juice, onion, chopped mint, scallions, cilantro, chili and fish sauce, stirring to blend well. Taste and, if necessary, add salt to taste.

When ready to serve, spoon an equal portion of the meat mixture into a small lettuce leaf. Top with a mint leaf and then wrap the lettuce around the filling. Serve immediately.

NOTE: Thai fish sauce, known as *nam pla*, is available at Asian markets, specialty food stores, and many supermarkets. It can be replaced with any of the Asian fish sauces, such as *nuoc nam* (Vietnamese*)*, *patis* (Philippine) or *shottsuru* (Japanese).

For a Moveable Feast

Sesame-Soy Tofu Squares

Serves 6 to 8

These delightful and tasty squares are often part of a Japanese *bento*, a homemade or prepared takeout meal carried in a box. The box may be a beautiful lacquer-ware creation or a utilitarian and disposable container. If you're arty, you might wish to create *bento* boxes for your bookish guests to take home as favors.

The meal usually consists of a serving of fish, meat, or tofu, rice and pickled vegetables. I will guarantee that even those who say they don't like tofu will enjoy these squares. And they can be prepared up to 3 days in advance and stored, covered and refrigerated, and then brought to room temperature before serving.

¾ cup pineapple juice
½ cup lite soy sauce
¼ cup Worcestershire sauce
¼ cup packed light brown sugar
2 tablespoons sesame oil
2 tablespoons fresh ginger julienne
1 pound grilled tofu, cut into 1-inch cubes (see Note)
2 tablespoons sesame seeds

Combine the pineapple juice, soy sauce, Worcestershire sauce, brown sugar, and sesame oil in a mixing bowl. When blended, stir in the ginger.

Add the tofu and toss to coat. Cover and refrigerate for at least 2 hours or up to 4 hours.

When ready to cook, preheat the oven to 375°F.

Lightly coat a nonstick baking sheet with nonstick vegetable spray.

Remove the tofu from the refrigerator and place the cubes on the prepared baking sheet, leaving about an inch between each cube.

Place in the preheated oven and bake for about 15 minutes or until nicely colored.

Remove from the oven and sprinkle with the sesame seeds. Immediately return the pan to the oven and bake for an additional 5 minutes or until the tofu begins to crisp.

Remove from the oven and serve hot, warm, or at room temperature.

NOTE: Grilled tofu is available at Asian markets, health food stores, and many supermarkets—just in case you're better at crafting boxes than cooking.

FLOWER and OTHER EXCEPTIONAL TEAS

◆ ◆ ◆

Green tea, now tea-bagged on supermarket shelves, is one of the oldest teas in the world. In Japan, green tea is so much the preferred drink that it is simply called "tea," while in other countries it is often called "Japanese tea." It is made from a single type of tea leaf that is minimally processed, resulting in a light flavor and fragrant aroma. Recent medical studies are indicating that the regular consumption of green tea may play a fairly significant role in lowering heart disease.

Oolong tea, a Chinese favorite, is a blend of tea that, in flavor, is somewhere between green and black tea. It has a light bitterness that leaves a slightly sweet but acrid taste on the tongue. It is often the tea served in Chinese restaurants in America.

There is also a group of flower teas such as hibiscus, chrysanthemum, rose, and chamomile where the unprocessed dried flower is rehydrated in hot water, brewing a light, fragrant tea and a lovely opening bloom in the bottom of the cup or glass. Jasmine flower tea is made from a combination of the buds of *jasminum sambac* and oolong or green tea. These teas are served mainly in Japan and China.

Puffed Rice Cookies

Makes about 2 dozen

This cookie recipe was given to me by a Korean cook. It has delicate Asian flavor with the sesame seeds and oil, so

I like to think that it is baked by many Korean grandmothers.

1 tablespoon sesame oil
½ cup sugar
½ cup light corn syrup
1 teaspoon water
1 cup puffed rice cereal
½ cup toasted sesame seeds
2 tablespoons pine nuts
2 tablespoons currants

Line a baking pan with parchment paper. Lightly coat the parchment paper with sesame oil. Set aside.

Combine the sugar, corn syrup and water in a medium heavy-bottomed saucepan over high heat. Bring to a boil. Lower the heat and simmer for about 5 minutes or until the mixture has caramelized. Stir in the puffed rice, sesame seeds, pine nuts and currants, stirring to combine well.

Pour the mixture into the prepared pan, spreading it out in an even layer with a rubber spatula. Work quickly, as it hardens very fast.

Using a small, sharp knife, cut the hardened mixture into bars about 4 inches long and 1 inch wide.

Store airtight for up to one week.

Fragrant Fruit Salad

Serves 8 to 10

Asian cuisines are not big on dessert, and some of their relatively few sweets do not appease the Western sweet tooth. But I usually serve a fragrant fruit salad at the end of a Northern or Southeast Asian meal. Asians like fruit as much or more than other people do; they just don't think of separating courses in the European or American manner.

I happen to think that a fruit salad, particularly one that contains bits of such Asian fruits as lychee, dragon fruit, mangosteen, rambutan or papaya is the perfect way to celebrate their subtle flavors, and to relax your palate after the spicy foods that came first.

If you have any fruit syrup left, use it to flavor drinks, such as iced tea, seltzer, white wine or champagne. It is so delicious!

3 ½ cups water
2 cups sugar
6 star anise
6 cloves
3 cinnamon sticks
2 sticks lemon grass, smashed
1 vanilla bean
Peel (without any pith) of 1 orange
Peel (without any pith) of 1 lemon
*10 to 12 cups fresh fruit, such as pineapple,
    star fruit, papaya, mango, lychee, oranges,
    pomegranate seeds or whatever is fresh
    and perfect (see Note)*
½ cup shredded coconut
2 tablespoons shredded fresh mint leaves

Combine the water and sugar in a medium saucepan over medium heat. Add the star anise, cloves, cinnamon sticks, lemon grass, vanilla bean and citrus peels, stirring to blend. Bring to a simmer and simmer for 3 minutes.

Remove from the heat and allow to cool. Cover and refrigerate for at least 1 hour or up to 3 months.

About 3 hours before you are ready to serve, strain the syrup through a fine mesh sieve. Arrange the fruit on a platter and drizzle with the syrup. Sprinkle with the coconut and mint and serve.

NOTE: Cut the fruit into attractive pieces so that they may be nicely arranged on a platter. The star fruit is a particularly important addition as, when cut crosswise, it offers its own decorative pattern.

Chapter 16

Literature Afloat

THESE RECIPES HAIL SEAGOING stories and poems and island literary settings. This chapter is for the fans of literature's heroic sailors and memorable characters who live or work at the water's edge. This is a salute to writers inspired by the sea. Fishy recipes for fishy tales! And island dreams.

✦ ✦ ✦

READS, DRINKS & NIBBLES
■ ■ ■

Salty Dogs
Sex on the Beach
Clams on the Grill with Herbed-Citrus Sauce
Oysters on the Half Shell with a Crisp White Wine

STAR DISHES & DELICIOUS ASIDES
■ ■ ■

Fish Chowder

FOR A MOVEABLE FEAST
■ ■ ■

Coconut Shrimp with South Seas Sauce

LITERARY TEA OR SWEET ENDING
■ ■ ■

Îles Flottantes/Floating Islands
Island Baked Bananas

Salty Dogs and Sex on the Beach

Although a very refreshing drink, a Salty Dog is also the slang expression used to describe a savvy sailor. And Sex on the Beach, although a very potent cocktail, is something that experienced sailors (and some wild and crazy writers) have been known to have. You can mix and match as you salute the sea.

FOR EACH SALTY DOG:
Salt
¼ cup gin or vodka
½ cup fresh grapefruit juice

Place the salt on a flat surface or plate. Slightly dampen the rim of each highball glass and dip it into the salt.

Fill the glass with ice and then add the gin or vodka and grapefruit juice, stirring to blend.

Serve immediately.

FOR EACH SEX ON THE BEACH:
¼ cup vodka
¼ cup fresh orange juice
¼ cup cranberry juice
1 tablespoon peach schnapps

Combine the vodka with the orange and cranberry juices and schnapps, stirring to blend. Pour over ice in a highball glass. Serve immediately.

Clams on the Grill
with Herbed-Citrus Sauce

Serves 6 to 8

This is a perfect appetizer, cocktail tidbit or snack. Grilling clams is quick to do while chatting with guests. Served topped with a light, refreshing herb sauce, there is nothing more elegant or easy to do. These clams would be a wonderful way to end an afternoon's reading of one of the books of the sea, or a grand cap to a good beach read. If clams are not available, mussels would work just fine. This is a light repast to tide one over till dinner, or to begin one.

3 to 4 dozen clams, well scrubbed

Preheat the grill on high.

Place the clams on the grill with the flatter side up. This will help hold the juices in the rounder shell side as the clams open from the heat. Grill for about 4 minutes or until the clams open.

As they open, remove the clams from the grill, dollop with a bit of the sauce, and eat them hot, straight from the shell.

Herbed-Citrus Sauce

2 cups chopped flat-leaf parsley
½ cup chopped scallions with some green part
¼ cup chopped cilantro
2 tablespoons chopped fresh oregano
1 tablespoon chopped garlic
Juice and zest of 1 lemon
1 teaspoon orange zest
1 cups extra virgin olive oil
¼ cup champagne vinegar
Coarse salt to taste

Combine the parsley, scallions, cilantro, oregano, garlic, lemon juice and zest, and orange zest in the bowl of a food processor fitted with the metal blade, pulsing until just minced. Scrape the mixture into a nonreactive container. Stir in the oil and vinegar. Season with salt, cover, and refrigerate until ready to use.

OYSTERS on the HALF SHELL with a CRISP WHITE WINE

Six oysters per person

✦ ✦ ✦

Oysters and a beautifully chilled white wine make a stellar culinary treat and a superb way to salute those writers who sing of the sea. Oysters derive their particular flavor and texture from their environment, from the salinity of the water in which they have grown, the tidal forces, and the nutrients upon which they feed.

"As I ate the oysters with their strong taste of the sea and their faint metallic taste that the cold white wine washed away, leaving only the sea taste and the succulent texture, and as I drank their cold liquid from each shell and washed it down with the crisp taste of the wine, I lost the empty feeling and began to be happy and to make plans."

—ERNEST HEMINGWAY, *A Moveable Feast*

Oysters from icy waters tend to be sweeter, plumper, and more delicately flavored; saltier water produces oysters with a sharp, briny taste. Whatever style you have, oysters are meant to be served with a chilled white wine or champagne. Of the French white wines, Sancerre, Chablis, Pouilly-Fuisse or Pouilly-Fume are superb. Of the California, an oaky Chardonnay would do equally well. And, of course, a lovely champagne will add a sparkling note to your festivities.

Fresh oysters are relatively easy to open once you get the knack of it.

Make sure the shells are scrubbed clean, even if this means a good scrub with a wire brush.

After scrubbing, refrigerate to allow the oysters time to relax before opening.

Wearing an oyster glove (see Note), place the oyster, flatter side up, in your non-writing hand (for most of us, the left hand). Firmly holding the oyster knife in your other hand, place the tip of the knife into the hinged end of the oyster, slightly wiggling the knife as you prod and push.

As quickly as possible, jab the knife point into the oyster and give it a fast half turn to snap the shell open and break the tight seal. Then move the blade around the edge of the shell to break the two halves apart.

Slightly turn the knife to an upward angle and slice across the interior of the top shell to separate the muscle from the shell, taking care that you do not spill out the liquid (known as oyster liquor). Discard the top shell.

Holding the bottom shell in the palm of your hand to keep the juices from leaking out, carefully pry the oyster meat loose from the shell.

Place the shucked oysters in their bottom shells on a bed of ice on a platter, and refrigerate as you continue to open oysters.

NOTE: Oyster gloves are available at specialty stores, or through the internet.

Fish Chowder

Serves 8 to 10

This is a very simple and not too caloric chowder. I have eliminated the usual pork fat that enriches a classic chowder and given you the option of cream. Chowders were usually the meal of rugged fishermen who threw the leftover catch of the day into the pot and then added whatever they had on hand to fill the pot. You can actually do the same—there are no rules in chowder making. Whatever you do, use firm- fleshed fish or shellfish to bring your guests right to the seaside.

2 tablespoons canola oil
¾ cup finely diced shallots
¼ cup finely diced celery
1 teaspoon minced garlic
2½ cups diced potatoes
2 cups diced carrots
1 cup diced red bell pepper
4 cups clam broth
4 cups nonfat, low-sodium chicken broth
1 tablespoon minced fresh flat-leaf parsley
1 teaspoon minced fresh thyme
Salt and pepper to taste
2 cups canned diced tomatoes
3 pounds firm white fish, such as cod, tilapia
*   or halibut, cut into pieces*
1 cup heavy cream, optional

> "That evening he had a can of minestrone with crackers, cleaned the galley and settled down to listen to the marine forecast."
>
> —ROBERT STONE, Outerbridge Reach

> "Fish is the only food that is considered spoiled once it smells like what it is." — P. J. O'ROURKE

Heat the oil in a large heavy-bottomed saucepan over medium heat. Add the shallots, celery, and garlic and sauté for about 3 minutes, or just until vegetables have softened. Stir in the potatoes, carrots, and bell pepper and sauté for another minute or so. Add the clam and chicken broths, parsley and thyme, and season with salt and pepper to taste.

Bring to a boil and stir in the tomatoes. Again bring to a boil; then lower the heat and simmer for 20 minutes, or until vegetables are tender and the broth is well-flavored.

Add the fish and simmer for about 7 minutes or just until the fish is cooked through. Taste and, if necessary, adjust the seasoning with salt and pepper.

If using, stir in the cream and cook for 1 minute.

Remove from the heat and serve. Or allow to cool, then store covered and refrigerated, for up to 2 days. Reheat before serving.

> "How inappropriate to call this planet Earth when it is clearly Ocean." —ARTHUR C. CLARKE

Coconut Shrimp with South Seas Sauce

Serves 6 to 8

Here not only do we taste the sea in the shrimp, we get a bit of island pleasure with the coconut coating. These shrimp are a marvelous cocktail tidbit or snack, and perfect for entertaining, as they can be coated early in the day and cooked just before serving or served at room temperature.

2 pounds large shrimp, peeled and deveined,
*   tails intact*
3 large eggs
2 tablespoons water
2 tablespoons fresh lime juice
1 tablespoon hot pepper sauce or to taste
Salt to taste
3 cups panko breadcrumbs (see Note)
2 cups unsweetened coconut flakes
1 cup Wondra flour
1 teaspoon cayenne pepper or to taste
Approximately 6 cups vegetable oil for frying

Line a baking pan with wax or parchment paper. Set aside.

Rinse the shrimp and then pat dry. Set aside.

Whisk together the eggs, water, lime juice, and hot pepper sauce. Season with salt to taste. Set aside.

Combine the panko, coconut, flour, and cayenne in a large, shallow dish.

Working with one piece at a time, dip the dry shrimp into the egg mixture and then roll in the panko mixture to completely cover. Place the coated shrimp on the prepared baking pan as finished.

When all of the shrimp have been coated, cover lightly with plastic film and refrigerate for 1 hour to set the coating.

When ready to cook, remove the shrimp from the refrigerator. Heat the oil in a deep-fryer over medium-high heat. When the temperature reaches 365°F on a candy thermometer, place the shrimp in the fry basket, a few pieces at a time, and fry for about 3 minutes or until golden.

Transfer the cooked shrimp to a double layer of paper towels to drain. Serve hot or at room temperature with the South Seas Sauce below, or any other sauce you desire.

South Seas Sauce

1 cup lite soy sauce
½ cup orange marmalade
½ cup rice wine vinegar (see Note)
3 tablespoons minced fresh ginger

Combine the soy sauce, marmalade, vinegar, and ginger in a small, nonreactive saucepan over medium heat. Bring to a simmer, stirring constantly. Immediately remove from the heat and allow to cool for 30 minutes.

Strain through a fine mesh sieve and serve at room temperature.

NOTE: Panko breadcrumbs, a Japanese-style breadcrumb that creates a crisp coating when fried, are available from Asian markets, specialty food stores, and most supermarkets— as is rice wine vinegar.

Îles Flottantes/ Floating Islands

Serves 6

This is a classic French dessert, a puffy island of meringue floating in a sea of custard; despite its name, it is more at home in a fancy restaurant in Biarritz or on the *Île de Paris* than a far-off shore. Nonetheless, it has traveled the world and might be particularly enjoyable at a dressy dinner honoring the Jules Verne classic, *Twenty Thousand Leagues under the Sea*, or saluting a French-flavored island such as Tahiti or Martinique. The look of this dessert also makes it an amiable choice for snowy terrain circled by a cold sea.

2 cups whole milk
½ cup plus 3 tablespoons sugar
2 strips orange peel without any pith
½ vanilla bean, split in half, lengthwise
5 large eggs, at room temperature, separated
1 tablespoon pure vanilla extract
Fresh raspberries, blueberries, or strawberries
  for garnish, optional

Combine the milk with 3 tablespoons of the sugar, the orange peel, and the vanilla bean in a medium saucepan over medium-low heat. Bring to just a simmer. Immediately remove from the heat and set aside to cool completely.

Combine the egg yolks with 3 tablespoons of the remaining sugar in a medium mixing bowl, whisking to blend completely.

Return the milk to low heat. When just warm, whisk about ½ cup into the egg yolks, whisking to temper. Add the remaining egg yolk mixture to the warm milk, whisking constantly. Continue to cook, stirring constantly with a wooden spoon, for about 7 minutes, or until the custard coats the back of a metal spoon when lifted from the pan. Do not simmer or boil or the custard will curdle.

As soon as the custard has thickened, immediately remove it from the heat and pour through a fine mesh sieve into a clean container, discarding the orange peel and vanilla bean. (You can scrape the seeds from the vanilla bean into the custard.) Cover lightly with plastic film and refrigerate until well-chilled.

Preheat the oven to 275°F.

Lightly coat the interior of six 2-inch round ramekins with butter. Using about 1 tablespoon of the remaining sugar, generously coat the interior of each ramekin. Set aside.

Place the egg whites in the bowl of a standing electric mixer fitted with the whisk and beat on low until frothy. Raise the speed and beat until soft peaks form. With the motor running, slowly add the remaining ¼ cup sugar

> "There was a sort of side-cloth in one corner, upon which, in bright, buff jackets, lay the fattest of bananas; "avees" red-ripe: guavas with the shadows of their crimson pulp flushing through a transparent skin, and almost coming and going there like blushes; oranges, tinged, here and there, berry-brown; and great, jolly melons, which rolled about in very portliness. Such a heap!"
> —HERMAN MELVILLE, Omoo

along with the vanilla extract and beat until stiff peaks form. Do not over-beat or the meringue will be dry.

Spoon an equal portion of the meringue into each of the prepared ramekins.

Place a baking pan large enough to comfortably hold the ramekins into the oven. Place the ramekins into the pan, leaving a couple of inches between each one. Add cold water to come halfway up the sides of the ramekins. Bake for about 20 minutes, or just until the meringues have set.

Remove from the oven and remove the ramekins from the water bath. Immediately transfer to the refrigerator to cool quickly. (The meringues may be made up to 12 hours before serving.)

When ready to serve, spoon an equal portion of the chilled custard onto each of 6 shallow soup bowls. Working with one at a time, loosen the meringues by gently tapping the bottom of each one and quickly inverting it over the soup plate so that the meringue falls into the center of the custard. If desired, scatter some berries around the custard and serve.

Island Baked Bananas

Serves 8

This is an easy and quick dessert. It's quite simple, but it can reach elegant heights when each serving is garnished with a scoop of banana or coconut ice cream and a sprig of mint.

8 ripe but firm bananas
Juice of 3 limes
1 teaspoon orange juice concentrate
¼ cup light brown sugar
3 tablespoons unsalted butter, cut into pieces

Preheat the oven to 375°F.

Lightly butter the interior of a large baking dish. Set aside.

Peel the bananas and, using a sharp knife, cut them in half, lengthwise. Lay them, cut side down, in the prepared baking dish.

Combine the lime juice and orange juice concentrate and drizzle the mixture over the bananas. Sprinkle with the brown sugar, making sure that each banana has been covered. Dot with the butter.

Transfer to the preheated oven and bake, basting with the liquid from time to time, for about 30 minutes or until the bananas are caramelized.

Remove from the oven and serve hot, spooning the caramelized sauce over the top. Or let cool to room temperature and serve with a dollop of banana or coconut ice cream drizzled with the caramelized sauce.

Chapter 17

The Best and Worst of Places

*U*TOPIAS, OF COURSE, SHOULD HAVE THE MOST DELICIOUS OF MEALS—HOW COULD they be ideal if they offered anything less? But if you or your book club has just finished reading a novel of dystopia, no matter how artfully portrayed, you're bound to be a bit depressed and in need of a Utopian meal to recover. Here, then, are a few ambrosial recipes that I hope will maintain the moods of those who have experienced a bit of literary paradise, or lift the spirits of readers reeling from a visit to a land of horrors or from intimate acquaintance with a completely disoriented protagonist.

These recipes are frankly intended to promote happiness.

◆ ◆ ◆

READS, DRINKS & NIBBLES

■ ■ ■

Ambrosia Cocktail
Sweet and Salty Almonds

STAR DISHES & DELICIOUS ASIDES

■ ■ ■

Beef Tenderloin with Horseradish Sauce
Asparagus with Lemon Butter and Truffles

FOR A MOVEABLE FEAST

■ ■ ■

Basket of Perfect Fresh Fruits

LITERARY TEA OR SWEET ENDING

■ ■ ■

Chocolate Tart with Chocolate Ganache,
Whipped Cream and Raspberry Sauce

Sailing to Byzantium

That is no country for old men. The young
In one another's arms, birds in the trees
—Those dying generations—at their song,
The salmon-falls, the mackerel-crowded seas,
Fish, flesh, or fowl, commend all summer long
Whatever is begotten, born, and dies.
Caught in that sensual music all neglect
Monuments of unageing intellect.
An aged man is but a paltry thing,
A tattered coat upon a stick, unless
Soul clap its hands and sing, and louder sing
For every tatter in its mortal dress,
Nor is there singing school but studying
Monuments of its own magnificence;
And therefore I have sailed the seas and come
To the holy city of Byzantium.

O sages standing in God's holy fire
As in the gold mosaic of a wall,
Come from the holy fire, perne in a gyre,
And be the singing-masters of my soul.
Consume my heart away; sick with desire
And fastened to a dying animal
It knows not what it is; and gather me
Into the artifice of eternity.
Once out of nature I shall never take
My bodily form from any natural thing,
But such a form as Grecian goldsmiths make
Of hammered gold and gold enameling
To keep a drowsy Emperor awake;
Or set upon a golden bough to sing
To lords and ladies of Byzantium
Of what is past, or passing, or to come.

—WILLIAM BUTLER YEATS

Ambrosia Cocktail

This is an extremely powerful blend; it is best consumed at home after you've shuttered your book, or with a designated driver on hand.

FOR EACH COCKTAIL:
3 tablespoons applejack brandy
3 tablespoons brandy
2 teaspoons triple sec
2 teaspoons fresh lemon juice
Champagne to fill

Combine the brandies with the triple sec and lemon juice in a champagne flute, stirring to blend. Add chilled champagne to fill the flute and serve.

Sweet and Salty Almonds

Makes about 2¼ cups

A little sweet and a little salty, these nuts are a perfect snack. They are easy to make and the recipe can be doubled or tripled, so you might want to make a batch to keep on hand for last-minute cocktail celebrations.

2¼ cups whole shelled almonds with inner
*   skin on*
1½ cups sugar
½ cup coarse salt or sea salt

Line a baking sheet with parchment or waxed paper. Set aside.

Combine the almonds with sugar in a heavy-bottomed (preferably nonstick) saucepan over medium heat. Cook, stirring constantly, until the sugar has dissolved. Continue to cook, stirring constantly, for about 15 minutes or until the sugar is deeply caramelized and slightly thick.

Immediately remove the pan from the heat and quickly dip it into a bowl of ice to stop the cooking. As soon as the cooking stops, remove the pan from the ice or the syrup will begin to harden.

Using a large soup spoon and working quickly, drop the nuts onto the prepared baking sheet. Use a knife or the tips of your fingers (if you can stand the heat) to make sure that the almonds do not stick together.

Put aside to set for about 15 minutes. Then sprinkle with the salt, letting the grains fall randomly. You do not want to coat the entire nut, just a few grains on both sides of each one. Let stand for about another hour or until very cool and dry, with the salt sticking to the caramel.

Store airtight in a single layer separated by parchment or waxed paper. If the nuts absorb moisture they will be sticky and soft.

> "One of the nicest things about eating is the sensation you get when you first put something like salted nut-meats or caramels in your mouth. There is that sudden taste and the shape of the food—the sharp edges on caramels that were formed by the waxed paper wrappings. The first sensations are the best. They're so full of promise." —JOHN UPDIKE

Beef Tenderloin
with Horseradish Sauce

Serves 10 to 12

Although a filet of beef can be expensive, I think it's worth the price, as there is absolutely no waste and it is a rare person who doesn't enjoy its tender goodness. Fanned out on a platter with a sprinkling of herbs and Horseradish Sauce as garnish, it is a perfect buffet dish. Tenderloin can be served hot or at room temperature, which makes it a wonderful entrée to serve when you want to spend time with your guests, engaged in talk about great ideas.

One 5-pound filet of beef, trimmed of all fat
*   and silverskin*
3 tablespoons olive oil
Coarse salt and freshly ground pepper to taste

Preheat the oven to 450°F.

Fold the thinner tail end of the filet up and under the thicker tail end to make the entire filet of an equal size. Using kitchen twine, tie the entire piece of meat, placing each piece of twine about 1½ inches apart. This not only holds the folded piece together, but helps the roast keep its shape as it cooks. Using your hands, generously coat the meat with the oil and then generously season with salt and pepper to taste.

Place the roast on a rack in a roasting pan. Roast for about 12 minutes for rare (120°F), then turn and roast for another 12 minutes, increasing the roasting time for each side by about 5 to 7 minutes for each incremental rise in desired final temperature. You should not cook the meat beyond medium, as it is so delicately tender that over-cooking will render it tasteless. It is best to use an instant-read thermometer to gauge doneness, remembering that the internal temperature will continue to rise 5°F to 10°F as the meat rests before cutting.

Remove from the oven and let rest for about 10 minutes.

Untie the strings and, using a sharp knife, cut the meat, crosswise, into ½-inch thick slices. Fan the slices out on a serving platter and serve with Horseradish Sauce on the side.

Horseradish Sauce

½ cup heavy cream
¼ cup crème fraîche or sour cream
1 tablespoon lemon juice
Hot sauce to taste
3 tablespoons well-drained prepared white
*   horseradish*
Salt to taste
2 tablespoons minced fresh chives
*   (or flat-leaf parsley)*

Place the heavy cream in a mixing bowl and beat, using an electric mixer, until stiff peaks form. Beat in the *crème fraîche* (or sour cream), lemon juice, and hot sauce. When blended, fold in the horseradish and season with salt to taste. Transfer to the refrigerator and let the flavors blend for about 30 minutes, but not more than 1 hour.

When ready to serve, fold in the chives.

Asparagus with Lemon
Butter and Truffles

Serves 10 to 12

Because of its short growing season and wonderful sweet-nutty flavor, the first green asparagus of the spring often comes with a high price tag and an even higher demand. Its crisp texture, beautiful green color, and complex flavor need little more than a touch of acid and a hint of saltiness as an accent. In addition, the trimmed stalks make a very inviting presentation at the table. Add a shaving of black truffle and you will take the dish to sybaritic heights.

3 pounds jumbo green asparagus
½ cup (1 stick) unsalted butter
Juice and zest of 1 lemon
Salt and white pepper to taste
1 black truffle, optional

Using a swivel vegetable peeler and starting just below the tip, carefully peel the thin outer skin from each asparagus stalk. From the middle to the end, peel a little deeper to remove any toughness. There should be no remaining outer skin evident.

Using a small, sharp knife, cut off about 1 inch of the tough bottom end (or more, if it is particularly fibrous) of each stalk. Work slowly and carefully, as you don't want to waste any of the edible stalk.

As they are peeled, rinse each stalk under cold, running water and place on a double layer of paper towels to drain.

Place enough cold, salted water to cover the asparagus by at least 1 inch in a pan large enough to hold all of the asparagus, preferably in a single layer. Place over high heat and bring to a boil.

Carefully add the asparagus, making sure that all stalks are covered with water. Return to a simmer; then lower the heat and simmer for about 10 minutes, or until the asparagus is crisp-tender.

While the asparagus is cooking, prepare the lemon butter.

Place the butter in a small pan over medium-low heat. Bring to a simmer and cook just until the butter begins to brown slightly and have a lovely nutty aroma. Remove from the heat and stir in the lemon juice and zest. Season with salt and white pepper. Set aside, but keep warm.

Remove the asparagus from the heat and, using tongs, carefully transfer the asparagus to a double layer of paper towels to drain. When drained, transfer to a platter.

Drizzle the warm lemon-butter over the asparagus and, if using, shave the truffle over all.

Serve immediately.

For a Moveable Feast

BASKET of PERFECT FRESH FRUITS

✦ ✦ ✦

Philosophers and poets alike agree that nothing is as Utopian as a perfect fruit, and nothing better characterizes a dystopia than destruction of what is ripe and sweet.

For many of us, a first bite into a perfect new fruit is the stuff of happy memory. Although we hear much talk about local, seasonal cooking, we remain easily lured by that beautiful purple plum or luscious-looking peach invitingly displayed in the middle of winter.

I have learned that there is absolutely no sure-fire indication that the beauty of a piece of fruit is an augury of its ripeness, texture, juiciness or flavor. In fact, it is often the ugly one that delivers the most pleasure! However, since a lovely basket or hamper piled high with luxurious fruits is as dramatic a presentation as you could possibly want, here is a bit of advice on putting one together.

Always start with a wonderful basket. This will probably be your least expensive purchase—plain, woven baskets or hampers are the perfect background for the colorful fruit.

Try to use only seasonal fruits. Even in winter, different types of seasonal citrus fruits will fill a basket with color and aroma, promising a welcome snack or end to a meal.

If you happen on a batch of really ripe, alluringly fragrant fruit, purchase one piece and taste it on the spot. If it turns out to be as epicurean as it looks, buy as much as you need to fill a basket and find a reason to use your moveable feast.

If your market (and many supermarkets do) features an array of exotic fruits (such as *carambola* (starfruit), passion fruit, cactus pears, dragon fruit, lychees), create a presentation of the exotica with some tropical fruits (such as pineapple, papaya or mango), along with a bit of lore and instructions on how to eat each one. (As long as you know the name, this information can be found on the Internet).

Don't forget that berries are fruit, and that they can often be sweet, juicy orbs even in the dead of winter. If you carefully pile ripe berries in a small basket and place a pitcher of cream and a bowl of sugar right next to them, dessert is ready to go.

Nestle some lemon or magnolia leaves or greens (easily purchased from a local florist) in among the fruit to add some greenery to the presentation.

For real luxury, add some cheeses and nuts, creating a moveable feast that will be a very hedonistic end to an extravagant meal.

"... the perfect June days and nights, (leaning toward crisp and cool,) ... the air, the fruit (especially my favorite dish, currants and raspberries, mixed, sugar'd, fresh and ripe from the bushes—I pick 'em myself) ..."
— WALT WHITMAN

"There are only ten minutes in the life of a pear when it is perfect to eat."
— RALPH WALDO EMERSON

"This Is Just To Say that I have eaten the plums that were in the icebox and which you were probably saving for breakfast. Forgive me they were delicious so sweet and so cold."
— WILLIAM CARLOS WILLIAMS

Chocolate Tart with Chocolate *Ganache*, Whipped Cream and Raspberry Sauce

Makes one 10-inch tart

For centuries, chocolate has been used to lift the spirits. Although there are now many medical indications of its benefit to humans, it is the simple pleasure of its sweet, dark, and delicious flavor that entices us. Of course, the ancient belief that it can also be an aphrodisiac makes it even more delightful. This is a very dense, rich tart—so cut very thin wedges, as a little goes a very long way to delight!

> "Five hours New York jet lag and Cayce Pollard wakes in Camden Town to the dire and ever-circling wolves of disrupted circadian rhythm. It is that flat and spectral non-hour, awash in limbic tides, brainstem stirring fitfully, flashing inappropriate reptilian demands for sex, food, sedation, all of the above, and none really an option now."
>
> —WILLIAM GIBSON, Pattern Recognition

I have, in a nod to the raspberry pill in Aldous Huxley's *Brave New World*, added a raspberry sauce that, if you wish to make a fancier dessert, can coat the bottom of each plate. Or, if you like, you may just add a few raspberries to the plate.

¼ pound fine quality bittersweet chocolate, cut into pieces
½ cup unsalted butter, at room temperature
½ cup plus 2½ tablespoons sugar
¼ cup cake flour, sifted
3 large eggs, at room temperature
Chocolate Ganache *(recipe follows)*
Raspberry Sauce, optional (recipe follows)
Unsweetened whipped cream or vanilla ice cream for serving, optional

Preheat the oven to 375°F.

Lightly butter the interior of a 10-inch round springform pan. Cut a piece of parchment paper into a 10-inch circle and fit it into the bottom of the pan. Set aside.

Combine the chocolate and butter in the top half of a double boiler over simmering water. Heat, stirring constantly, for about 4 minutes or until completely melted and blended.

Combine the sugar and flour in the bowl of a standing electric mixer fitted with the whisk. With the motor running on low, add the eggs, one at a time.

When all of the eggs have been incorporated, with the motor running, add just a bit of the warm chocolate to the mixture to temper it. Then slowly add the remaining chocolate. Beat on low for about 8 minutes, or until the mixture is very thick and smooth.

Scrape the batter into the prepared pan, smoothing the top with a spatula. The batter should be no more than 1 inch high in the pan, or the finished cake will not hold together.

Place in the preheated oven and bake for about 30 minutes or until a cake tester inserted into the center comes out clean. Remove from the oven and place on a wire rack to cool for 15 minutes.

Open and remove the springform and invert the cake onto the wire rack. Set aside to cool completely then remove the bottom of the pan.

When cool, leaving the cake on the wire rack, pour the *ganache* over the top and, using a spatula, carefully spread the ganache over the entire cake, allowing the excess to drip off. Allow the *ganache* to set for at least 15 minutes.

Transfer the cake to a serving plate. Cut into small wedges and serve.

Alternately, if desired, coat the bottom of individual dessert plates with Raspberry Sauce. Place a small wedge of the cake in the center of each plate and garnish with a dollop of unsweetened whipped cream or vanilla ice cream.

Chocolate *Ganache*

3 ounces fine quality semi-sweet chocolate, cut into pieces
1 teaspoon unsalted butter, at room temperature
6 tablespoons heavy cream

Combine the chocolate and butter in the top half of a double boiler over simmering water. Heat, stirring constantly, for about 3 minutes or until completely melted and blended. Remove from the heat.

While the chocolate is heating, place the cream in a small saucepan over medium heat. Bring to just a bare simmer and immediately remove from the heat.

Whisk the hot cream into the chocolate, beating with a wooden spoon until smooth and shiny.

Set aside to cool slightly before using. Do not let harden.

> "If more of us valued food and cheer and song above hoarded gold, it would be a merrier world."
> —J. R. R. TOLKIEN

> "He remained obstinately gloomy the whole afternoon; wouldn't talk to Lenina's friends (of whom they met dozens in the ice-cream soma bar between the wrestling bouts); and in spite of his misery absolutely refused to take the half-gramme raspberry sundae which she pressed upon him."—ALDOUS HUXLEY, Brave New World

Raspberry Sauce
(optional)

1 pint fresh raspberries
2 tablespoons Simple Syrup (see page 63)
1 teaspoon fresh lemon juice

Combine the raspberries, syrup, and lemon juice in a blender jar. Process until smooth.

Pour through a fine mesh sieve, pressing on the solids with a rubber spatula, into a clean container.

Serve immediately or store, covered and refrigerated, for up to 3 days.

"The greatest gift is the passion for reading. It is cheap, it consoles, it distracts, it excites, it gives you knowledge of the world and experience of a wide kind."

—ELIZABETH HARDWICK